GOLDEN

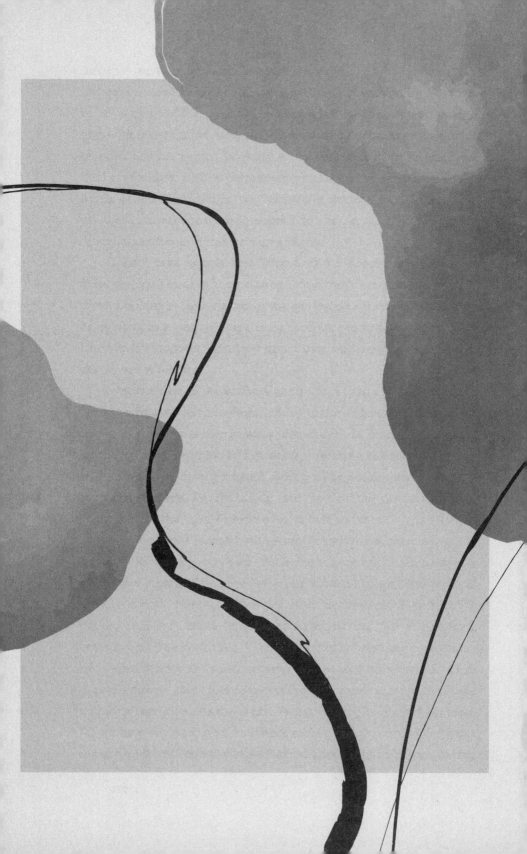

GOLDEN

THE POWER OF SILENCE IN A WORLD
OF NOISE

JUSTIN ZORN AND
LEIGH MARZ

HARPER WAVE

An Imprint of HarperCollins*Publishers*

HarperCollins books may be purchased for educational, business, or sales promotional use. For information, please email the Special Markets Department at SPsales@harpercollins.com.

Excerpt from "Keeping Quiet" from *Extravagaria* by Pablo Neruda, translated by Alastair Reid. Translation copyright © 1974 by Alastair Reid. Used by permission of Farrar, Straus and Giroux. All Rights Reserved.

FIRST EDITION

Designed by Elina Cohen
Title page art courtesy of Shutterstock / Stacey_M
Part title art courtesy of Leigh Marz and Bob von Elgg at Bigfish Smallpond Design

Library of Congress Cataloging-in-Publication Data
Names: Zorn, Justin, author. | Marz, Leigh, author.
Title: Golden : the power of silence in a world of noise / Justin Zorn and Leigh Marz.
Description: New York, NY : Harper Wave, [2022] | Includes bibliographical references and index.
Identifiers: LCCN 2021062983 | ISBN 9780063027602 (hardcover) | ISBN 9780063027626 (ebook)
Subjects: LCSH: Silence. | Noise. | Quietude.
Classification: LCC BJ1499.S5 Z67 2022 | DDC 128--dc23/eng/20220118
LC record available at https://lccn.loc.gov/2021062983 ISBN 978-0-06-302760-2

22 23 24 25 26   LSC   10 9 8 7 6 5 4 3 2 1

FOR MEREDY AND MICHAEL

AND IN MEMORY OF ROB ERIOV AND RALPH METZNER

CONTENTS

GOLDEN

PART I

A SHARED YEARNING

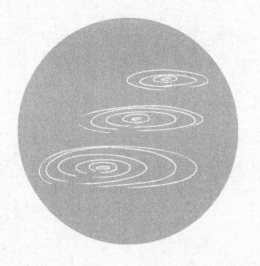

AN INVITATION

What's the deepest silence you've ever known?

You can trust the first memory that comes to you.

No need to overthink it.

As you remember the experience, see if you can settle into it. Recall where you are, what's happening around you, and who, if anyone, is present. See if you can summon the atmosphere—the quality of light, the mood in the air, the feeling in your body.

Is it quiet to the ears?

Or is it the kind of silence that comes when no person or thing is laying claim to your attention?

Is it quiet in your nerves?

Or is it the kind of silence that lives deeper still—like when the turbulent waters of internal chatter suddenly part, revealing a clear path forward?

Take a moment to consider what might sound like a strange question: *Is the silence simply the absence of noise—or is it also a* presence *unto itself?*

O

Over the past several years, we've been exploring these questions with an unusual mix of people: neuroscientists, activists, poets, corporate executives, national politicians, teaching physicians, environmental advocates, a whirling dervish, a White House staffer, Buddhist teachers, Christian preachers, a Grammy-winning opera singer, a man incarcerated on death row, a Hollywood sound engineer, a heavy metal front man, a cowboy-lumberjack, and an air force lieutenant colonel. We've been exploring these questions for ourselves, too. The explorations, both personal and shared, have taken us to many places, including:

The balmy air at sunrise over a vast ocean.

The stillness amidst untrampled high mountain snow.

The questions have also taken us to places that aren't auditorily quiet: Births. Deaths. Moments of awe. Moments of dramatic and unexpected change when we're left grasping for familiar explanations until we finally have to surrender to the fact that there's nothing left to say.

For us and for others, moments of profound silence have sometimes come through surprisingly high-decibel settings:

Running the perfect line through roaring rapids.

Dusk in the thick woods amidst an electric orchestra of cicadas.

Yielding all self-referential thought to the *whomp-whomp* beat of a crowded dance floor.

If there's one common denominator to all these improbably diverse varieties of deep silence, we believe it's through the answer to the last of the questions that we posed to you. The deepest silence isn't just an absence; it's also a *presence*. It's a presence that can center us, heal us, and teach us.

In his 1836 novel, *Sartor Resartus*, the Scottish philosopher and mathematician Thomas Carlyle writes of a Swiss inscription: "*Sprechen ist silbern, Schweigen ist golden* (Speech is silvern, Silence is golden)."

"Or," Carlyle writes, "as I might rather express it: 'Speech is of Time, Silence is of Eternity.'"

This is the first known instance in English of the aphorism that inspired the title of this book. However, variants stretch back millennia in Latin, Arabic, Hebrew, and Aramaic. An early Islamic *isnad*—a lineage of transmitters of a sacred teaching across generations—holds that the origin of the proverb "If speech is of silver, then silence is of gold" comes from Solomon, the great king of wisdom. To this day, the words are shorthand for the wisdom of knowing when to speak and when to abide.

In our exploration of the meaning of the proverb "Silence is golden," we come back again and again to the notion that true silence, profound silence, is more than the absence of noise. It's this presence, too.

In early 2017, we were pretty despondent about the state of the world. You probably know the feeling. It was well before COVID-19 and the most recent and dire reports about climate change. It was before the latest economic upheavals and the murders of Breonna Taylor and George Floyd. But, even then, we just couldn't see a way forward through the deadlock. We couldn't quite imagine a plausible vision for repairing politics, building a humane economy, or restoring our relationship with nature. It felt as if there was something blocking the capacity for deep conversation about difficult topics and, ultimately, blocking our ability to find creative solutions. Personally, as activists and advocates and parents of young kids, we were at a loss for what to do.

Around that time, we both started feeling a strange intuition. We got the same intimation of where to look for an answer: *in silence.*

At that particular moment, you could have called both of us "lapsed meditators." But what we both felt, independently, wasn't exactly the same thing as a calling to get back on the cushion or escape to a long retreat. It wasn't an impulse to run away. Rather, it was a simple sense that the most intractable problems won't be solved with more thinking or talking. With due respect to the voice and the intellect and the buzzing machinery of material progress, we started feeling that the solutions to the most serious personal, communal, and even global challenges could be found somewhere else: *in the open space between the mental stuff.*

As we looked more at our intuition, we realized we were feeling something about the *quality* of the change necessary in the world. In the dialectical dance of human life—affirming/denying, progress/resistance, boom/bust—are we all just doomed to endure, as Winston Churchill supposedly put it, "one damn thing after another"? Or is there the possibility of something more spacious—an opening, maybe even the grace of reconciliation? We weren't sure. But we had a hunch about what might be the first step toward exploring the luminous possibility of transcending tired old opposites. Get beyond the noise.

We suspected this intuition might seem a little bit New Agey. So, we decided to try to write an article about it for the least New Agey publication that we could think of—*Harvard Business Review*. We were surprised when they accepted our proposal and more surprised when the eventual article turned out to be one of the most shared and viewed on their website in recent years. Our piece, "The Busier You Are, the More You Need Quiet Time," was about silence as a path to greater creativity, clarity, and connection. We wanted to be careful not to just write another article advertising "how you can get more productive through mindfulness." So we wrote about silence as the experience of "resting the mental reflexes that habitually protect a reputation or promote a point of view." We called on readers to take "a temporary break from one of life's most basic responsibilities: Having to think of what to say." We did our best to offer a simple proposition that you don't often see in business or political publications: that silence isn't just the absence of something. It's a presence. It can bring genuine insight, healing, even social transformation.

A few days after the piece came out, Justin went to an economic policy conference in Pittsburgh and split a taxi back to the airport with a new acquaintance named Jeff—a manufacturing executive, a practicing Catholic, and a close friend to conservative politicians. With his dark suit, his managerial demeanor, and his decidedly red-meat lifestyle, Jeff might have been the last person you'd imagine sauntering into a yoga studio or contemplating a Buddhist philosophy text. As they sat in rush-hour traffic, Justin mentioned the piece, and Jeff went on to read it. Jeff reached out to Justin a little while later to say that it reminded him why he liked to go hunting in the misty, early-morning hours and why he so loved attending Jesuit youth retreats as a kid. It was a reminder that he needed to seek silence in his life.

Justin's exchange with Jeff was simple and casual. But we found something important in it. Jeff was on the other side of many of those divisions about which we had been despondent. He and Justin were at the conference to present conflicting views. And here Jeff was, expressing the same deep yearning. While we were under no illusions that encountering silence would be any kind of automatic panacea for overcoming the very real divisions in the world, the exchange with Jeff brought us back to the intuition that we had initially felt. In the space of silence, we can find a prerequisite to deeper understanding and maybe even to progress beyond the tedious push-pull of a point-and-counterpoint culture.

It's hard to find open space in a world of noise. There are mighty forces today devoted to hijacking attention and keeping things loud. The most powerful institutions in business and government and education tell us that our responsibility is to get more prolific and efficient at the production of mental stuff. The clamor of advertising and expectations of busyness are subtle instruments of social control.

Yet here's the thing about silence: *it's always available.*

It's in the breath. It's in the gaps between breaths, between thoughts, between words exchanged among friends in conversation. It's in the cozy moment in the blankets just before the alarm clock rings. It's in the three-minute getaway from the cubicle, sitting on the bench outside connecting to the rays of the sun. It's in the simple moments of stopping and remembering to *listen*—to the birds, to the rain, or to nothing in particular, just tuning in to the simple essence of what is. We can start to encounter this open space by noticing where there's noise and turning down the volume, day by day.

When we seek the very deepest silence, we'll find that it doesn't really depend on the auditory or informational conditions of our lives. It's an unalterable presence that's always here and now, deep inside. It's the pulse of life.

This is a book about why and how to tune in to it.

NAVIGATING NOISE

Over the past fifty years, mindfulness meditation has taken a remarkable journey from the remote monasteries of Burma and Thailand to the pinnacles of mainstream power—places like Apple, Google, GE, and the Pentagon. While some of this rise is attributable to an increasing openness to new mindsets and worldviews since the revolutions of the 1960s, we believe the biggest reason for its newfound popularity is straightforward: there is a deep yearning for silence in a world of more and more noise. Whether we consciously realize it or not, we sense that pristine attention is increasingly scarce. We need ways to cope.

It's good news that mindfulness is now mainstream. While we haven't always kept up a rigorous practice, it's helped both of us manage the noise at important moments in our lives, and we know meditation and mindfulness have profoundly helped millions of others. In fact, we've played our own very small roles in their spread. Leigh has integrated meditation into her leadership and organizational development work with nonprofits, major universities, and U.S. federal agencies. And during Justin's years as a policy adviser and strategist in the U.S. Congress, he helped launch a mindfulness program and led meditation sessions for policy makers on both sides of the aisle.

But "going mainstream" implies successful adaptation, not necessarily measurable results. In 1992, the Jungian psychologist James Hillman and the cultural critic Michael Ventura published a book called *We've Had a Hundred Years of Psychotherapy—and the World's Getting Worse.* You could say something similar today. *We've had forty years of mindfulness, and the world is more distracted than ever.* Even as advocates and practitioners of formal sitting meditation, we're not convinced that it's a cure-all. It's extremely valuable. But it's just not for everybody.

Joshua Smyth, a professor at Pennsylvania State University and a leading researcher in the field of biobehavioral health and medicine, explains, "A lot of the claims about the benefits of mindfulness pertain to individuals who are serious practitioners." Smyth sees great value in these studies but warns against extrapolating the findings too broadly. "When you randomly assign people [to mindfulness studies], 70 percent do not adhere to the recommended levels," he tells us. In other words, they don't follow the protocol. He adds, "As many as a third to a half completely stop doing their practice even within the context of a trial—let alone persisting after they've been paid to be in a research study." These percentages are as bad as or worse than weight-loss studies. Smyth sums up the challenge: "If you don't take the medicine, the treatment won't work."

This isn't a judgment about mindfulness or of the people who don't maintain the practice. It's just evidence that any one-size-fits-all approach is unlikely to be an enduring solution to the complex challenge of staying centered amidst the destabilizing winds of modern mental hyperstimulation.

As people, we all have different styles, different preferences, different ways of learning, and different ways we make meaning as we go. We have varying degrees of command and autonomy over how we organize our days, weeks, months, and years, and those realities change over time. What's more, there can be cultural, religious, psychological, or physical barriers to what's typically called mindfulness meditation—the mostly Buddhist-derived practice of alert sitting or walking and observing the breath and the thoughts for a sustained period.

So, how, then, do we respond to the onslaught of noise? If meditation isn't for everyone, then how do we bring remedies to the scale that's necessary in today's world?

In this book, we propose an answer:

Notice noise. Tune in to silence.

There are three basic steps to the process:

1. Pay attention to the diverse forms of auditory, informational, and internal interference that arise in your life. Study how to navigate them.

2. Perceive the small pockets of peace that live amidst all the sounds and stimuli. Seek these spaces. Savor them. Go as

deeply into the silence as you possibly can, even when it's only present for a few seconds.

3. Cultivate spaces of profound silence—even rapturous silence—from time to time.

When it comes to the work of finding equilibration and clarity amidst the noise, we can look beyond the formal rules and tools of what's typically called meditation these days. We can forget about questions like "Am I doing it right?" Each one of us—in our own way—knows what silence feels like. It's something inherent to being human. It's a gift of renewal that's available to us, always, even if it's sometimes hidden.

In the chapters ahead, we'll explore how to understand and manage the noise so that we can more consciously *tune in* to nature, to one another, and to the sonic essence of life itself.

In part 1, we'll come to understand the *meaning of noise*—as unwanted distraction at the auditory, informational, and internal levels of perception. Then we'll contemplate the *meaning of silence* as both the absence of noise and this presence unto itself. We'll next consider why silence matters, not only for our own personal calmness and clarity, but also for the shared work of healing our world: building a better social, economic, political, and ecological future. In part 2—"The Science of Silence"—we'll look at the importance of transcending auditory, informational, and internal noise for our physical health, cognition, and emotional well-being. We'll investigate the meaning of "silence in the mind," looking to the frontiers of contemporary neuroscience. In part 3—"The Spirit of Silence"—we'll explore the promise of silence as a pathway to awareness, empathy, creativity, and ethics. We'll then look at why virtually all the world's great religious and philosophical traditions emphasize silence as a pathway to truth. In part 4—"Quiet Inside"—we'll embark on the practical work of finding silence in a world of noise, exploring strategies and ideas for how individuals can find silence in ordinary moments of daily life as well as through more rarefied, transformational experiences. In part 5—"Quiet Together"— we'll turn to the social kind of silence, exploring practices for getting beyond the noise and finding renewal in shared settings, including our workplaces, at home with our families, and among our friends. Finally, in part 6—"A Society That Honors Silence"—we'll zoom out to questions of public policy and cultural change, imagining what it would mean for our cities, our nations, and even our whole world to reclaim reverence for the wisdom of quiet.

We'll explore ideas and practices that might help you to become more patient, aware, and even effective in your work, your home life, your management of big and small challenges. Yet we want to be clear that silence isn't a "resource" you can control in a tidy or formulaic way. We can't assess its value on the basis of "what it can do for us." As the aphorism "silence is golden" suggests, silence has intrinsic value. And, as the words of Thomas Carlyle "Silence is of Eternity" imply, it can't be quantitatively measured and employed for our own purposes. Over the past couple decades, we've seen mindfulness practice often sold as a productivity tool, a performance enhancement for anything—even for sharpshooters to improve their aim or CEOs to conquer the world. Silence, we find, is bigger than self-improvement. It can't be enlisted as a life-hack to advance our personal ambitions. Silence, by definition, has no agenda.

Over the course of writing this book, the original intuition we felt has grown into more and more of a conviction. We still believe strongly in the importance of expression and advocacy and protest for what's right. We still recognize that the internet, ubiquitous communication tools, and roaring industrial technologies can bring us benefits, too. Yet in the face of that despondent feeling about the state of the world, we keep turning to this same answer: *Go beyond the noise. Tune in to silence.*

CHAPTER 2

THE ALTAR OF NOISE

Cyrus Habib never expected to have these kinds of options.

The son of Iranian immigrants to the United States, Cyrus survived a life-threatening illness and became fully blind at age eight. He learned braille, made it through high school, then through Columbia, Oxford as a Rhodes scholar, and Yale Law School. "I spent much of my life," he tells us, "convincing myself and projecting to others strength, capability, power, control . . . It was how I got to be successful in life. It was a very important kind of dogma for me." At thirty-one years old, he was elected to the legislature in Washington State and, four years later, to the position of lieutenant governor, the second-ranking public official in a jurisdiction of 7.6 million people.

In early 2020, Cyrus's options were clear: running for governor or U.S. Senate, or perhaps receiving an appointment to another high public office on the road to a prominent career in national politics. When we spoke with Cyrus later that year, though, he had just decided against all of these options, choosing a different career path instead.

He was taking a vow of poverty, chastity, and obedience as a novice Jesuit priest.

The New York Times's Frank Bruni described Cyrus's decision this way: "A Politician Takes a Sledgehammer to Own Ego."

There was no one single reason for this unexpected curve in Cyrus's career trajectory. It was a confluence of factors that both broke his heart and opened it: the sudden loss of his father, a personal health scare, a meeting with the Dalai Lama. Cyrus decided to leave politics and join the Jesuits to reduce the "complexity" in his life. "I don't mean the word 'complexity' in a bad way," he says. "Complexity just means that, for example, money has its place and is good and necessary, but it can also be a cause of stress and anxiety. Not having those attachments . . . allows you to give your life over to service in a more radical way."

When almost everyone thought Cyrus was about to scale the heights of public life, he was, in fact, facing a spiritual abyss. Amidst the overwhelming sound and stimulus of politics, he kept returning to an experience at Oxford that sparked a yearning he didn't know he'd had. During his time there, he had accepted an invitation from a friend to attend Mass at one of the university's centuries-old chapels. "The experience of the Mass . . . the music, the liturgy, the atmospheric transcendence of it—created an opening in me where I could delve deeper. It created a slowing down and a silence in me," he remembers. Cyrus started imagining what it would be like to live his life from such a place of centeredness. What a contrast that would be to the default mode of a modern politician, which is too often characterized by "dialing for dollars," tickling inflated egos, and obligatory self-promotion on Twitter.

Still, Cyrus is clear. He isn't looking for an escape.

"People think, 'He's joining the Jesuits. He's been a politician. He must be looking for more silence in his life.' And I am, I am . . . But I'm not looking to remove myself, to find silence in a palliative kind of way," he emphasizes.

"I want to deepen my own understanding of how I am meant to live, and then, having done that, go out to do the work that I've been shaped to do." Cyrus plans to continue to engage in the struggles that brought him to politics in the first place—serving people who live in poverty or in prisons, for example. But, as he takes a vow of poverty himself, he feels that he can serve in a more direct and authentic way. He tells us that "getting his heart ready" to receive higher inspiration requires "moving beyond the clutter that fills our days and our con-sciousness." It requires a certain "detox" to happen, a turning from constant distraction toward the pursuit of truth.

Cyrus knew all this would be an adjustment. When he visited the Jesuit novices early on, he offered to buy them a Roomba robot vac-uum cleaner so the brothers could spend some of their cleaning time doing other things. They were amused. "Dude, it's not about that," they said. "This is going to be an interesting transition for you."

Cyrus's adventure in egoic obliteration—from giving big speeches and shepherding legislation to sweeping floors and sitting in silence—reveals some insights about the nature of noise and what it means to find clarity. We spoke with him about how modern politics has become a knock-down, drag-out, zero-sum competition for every last scrap of attention. We discussed how it's an extreme manifestation of a society-wide addiction to drama and distraction. But Cyrus is clear about the fact that all this is just one level of the noise. While he's certainly looking forward to getting past the overstimulation of cable news blasting in the office, relentless partisan feuds, and parades of frivolous phone calls, he's ultimately making this radical shift in order to overcome a deeper form of noise—an interior noise that had been keeping him from being able to hear his own intuition and tune in to higher truth.

Yes, noise is the unwanted disturbance in the literal soundscape. Yes, it's the speed and scale of information overload. Yet it's ultimately bigger than either of those. It's all the unwelcome sound and stimulus, the loudness both inside and out. It's also what distracts our attention from what we truly, deeply want.

A TAXONOMY OF NOISE

We know; it's cliché to muse about the loudness of life. We imagine that people have always expressed the same exasperation.

In her book *The Soundscape of Modernity*, Emily Thompson looked to early Buddhist texts that describe how noisy life could be in a big city in South Asia circa 500 BCE. She describes "elephants, horses, chariots, drums, tabors, lutes, song, cymbals, gongs, and people crying 'Eat ye, and drink!'" In *The Epic of Gilgamesh*, the deities grew so tired of the noise of humanity that they sent a great flood to wipe us all out. Just over a century ago, J. H. Girdner cataloged "The Plague of City Noises," including horse-drawn vehicles, peddlers, musicians, animals, and bells. If there's such a thing as a perennial grumble, noisiness might be it.

And yet something right now *is* different from at any time in known history. These days, it's not just loud. There's an unprecedented mass proliferation of mental stimulation.

At one level, it's the literal, *auditory* noise. Even if the COVID-19 quarantines brought a temporary respite from the cacophony, the trajectory of modern life seems inexorable: more cars on the roads, more planes in the skies, more whirring appliances, more buzzing and pinging gadgetry. There are louder and more ubiquitous TVs and speakers in public spaces and open-plan offices. Across Europe, an estimated 450 million people, roughly 65 percent of the population, live with noise levels that the World Health Organization (WHO) deems hazardous to health.

It's a measurable fact: the world is getting louder. Because emergency vehicles have to be loud enough to break through the surrounding din, the volume of their sirens is a good proxy for the loudness of the overall environment. The composer and environmentalist R. Murray Schafer found that a fire engine siren in 1912 reached up to 96 decibels from a distance of eleven feet, while by 1974 siren sounds hit 114 decibels at the same distance. The journalist Bianca Bosker reported in 2019 that modern fire engine sirens are louder still—123 decibels at ten feet. This might not sound like much of an increase, but consider this: decibels are on a logarithmic scale, so 90 decibels is actually ten times the sound pressure as 80 decibels, registering as roughly *twice as loud* to our ears. It's no wonder that in big cities like New York and Rio de Janeiro noise consistently tops residents' complaint lists.

And we can't just think of the challenge in terms of the level of the volume. It's often the high- and low-frequency hums of the data storage centers and airports that cause damage. It's been found that these forms of auditory noise have a disproportionate impact on middle- and lower-income communities.

In an age when at least a third of Earth's natural ecosystems have gone quiet to the point of "aural extinction," all kinds of sounds—mechanical, digital, human—have been amplified.

There's a second kind of noise that is ascendant: *informational* noise. In 2010, Eric Schmidt, then CEO of Google, made a striking estimate: "Every two days we now create as much information as we did from the dawn of civilization up until 2003." While the tech mogul was mostly musing about the exponential growth of online content, he hit on a fundamental fact about the trajectory of human history: there is more and more mental stuff competing for your attention. The Radicati Group, a technology-research firm, estimates that 128 billion business emails were sent every single day in 2019, with the average business user contending with 126 messages a day. According to the most recent data, people in the United States take in five times as much information as they did in 1986.

Can we handle this much information? The leading experts in the science of human attention say no.

Mihaly Csikszentmihalyi (pronounced cheeks-SENT-me-high), the psychologist who first wrote about the concept of flow, summarizes the shortcomings of our everyday attentional capacities. Csikszentmihalyi estimates that when a person speaks we need to process about 60 bits of information per second to understand what that person is saying. This includes interpreting sounds and retrieving memories related to the words that you're hearing. Of course, we often add more to our informational loads—like checking the time for our next appointment or thinking about our shopping list for dinner—but cognitive scientists calculate that we'll almost always hit an upper limit of around 126 bits per second (give or take a bit here and there). We're surrounded by billions of fellow human beings on Earth, yet, as Csikszentmihalyi points out, "we cannot understand more than one of them at a time."

There's no question the growing amount of information in the world brings many blessings. We're grateful for digital contact with faraway loved ones, remote learning and work opportunities, streaming movies, and all the other bounty that the mighty interwebs bestow upon humanity. But we have to remember this: the data is increasing, but our ability to process it is *not*. Fifty years ago, the scholar Herbert Simon put it plainly: "What information consumes is rather obvious: it consumes the attention of its recipients. Hence a wealth of information creates a poverty of attention."

This points us to the third category of noise: *internal* noise. With so much stimulus consuming our attention, it's harder to find silence inside our consciousness. All the noise outside can amplify the intensity of what's going on inside us. With the increased frequency of incoming emails, texts, instant messages, and social media notifications comes an increased expectation of being *always on*—ready to read, react, and respond. This noise makes claims on our consciousness. It colonizes pristine attention. It makes it harder to focus on what's in front of us, to manage our mind's impulses, to notice, to appreciate, and to preserve open space—the space of silence.

Even in the era of sophisticated neuroimaging technologies, it's tough to quantitatively measure the levels of internal noise across humanity. Yet it's possible to see evidence of a problem through proxies: distraction, increased levels of stress, worry, and self-reported difficulty concentrating. In our interviews with academic psychologists, psychiatrists, and neuroscientists, we often heard them talk about *anxiety* as a proxy indicator of internal noise levels. While there are diverse definitions of anxiety, most include elements of not only fear and uncertainty but also internal chatter. In a 2018 study of a thousand U.S. adults, the American Psychological Association found that 39 percent of Americans reported being more anxious than they were the year prior, and another 39 percent reported the same amount of anxiety as the year before. That's more than three-quarters of the population reporting at least some level of anxiety. And that was *before* COVID. Pandemic-era studies from China and the U.K. show a rapid deterioration in their citizens' mental health. A U.S. survey conducted during the lockdowns of April 2020 found 13.6 percent of adult respondents reporting "severe psychological distress"—a 250 percent increase relative to 2018.

Ethan Kross, a professor of psychology at the University of Michigan and a leading expert on the science of internal dialogue, defines "chatter" as "the cyclical negative thoughts and emotions that turn our singular capacity for introspection into a curse rather than a blessing." Negative self-talk, like rumination about the past and worry for the future, can be merciless, even debilitating. Yet it's only one aspect of the internal soundscape. Whether its message is negative, positive, or neutral, modern internal dialogue is high velocity and high volume. As Kross puts it, "The voice in your head is a very fast talker." Based on findings that "inner speech" is condensed to a rate of about four thousand words per minute—ten times the speed of expressed speech—Kross estimates that most of us in modern times have to listen to something like 320 State of the Union addresses' worth of inner monologue on any given day.

So, how do we find peace in this hurricane of external and internal noise? How do we find clarity and wonder? How do we tune in to meaning and purpose?

One first step is to understand the nature of noise: What is it? How does it work? Why is it proliferating in our world? Today's "poverty of attention" isn't solely a by-product of the internet or workaholic tendencies or a talkative culture or challenging global events. It's the result of a complex interplay of *auditory, informational,* and *internal* interference.

Noise begets noise.

O

We don't use the word "noise" lightly.

There's a common element to the three kinds of "noise" we describe—*in our auditory soundscapes, in the informational realms,* and *in our own heads*—that makes them distinct from what we might call sound, data, or thought more generally. Noise, in two words, is "unwanted distraction." The neuroscientist Adam Gazzaley and the psychologist Larry Rosen have a useful way of defining what's happening when we encounter noise. They call it "goal interference." It's when you find focused attention, even to simple tasks, to be impossible due to nonstop banter in your open-plan office. It's when the jingle of a Twitter notification commandeers your attention just as a friend is sharing some difficult personal news. It's when we "replay" an unresolved conflict during a priceless moment, like while watching your daughter in the role of Cyclops in her first school play. These are individual, momentary experiences of auditory, informational, or internal noise. But taken together, they amount to more than a nuisance. Their cumulative impact can determine the quality of our consciousness, how we think and feel. All the noise can interfere with what might be our biggest goal of all: to consciously choose how we spend our time on this planet.

We're mindful that the word "goal" might imply a focus on productivity. But what we mean here is "goal" in the big sense—not just completing to-do lists and résumé builders—but reaching a long-range destination by the position of the North Star. What do you *really* want? What does it mean to live your life in line with what you value and what you believe to be true? What's interfering with your ability to focus on doing so?

Understanding and realizing our goals, in this sense, requires the reduction of noise. It starts with the ordinary day-to-day work of *managing the noise*. We can think of this as "turning down the dial" of interior and exterior sound and stimulus in our lives. But, as we'll see through the course of this book, this kind of clarity also requires time and space for cultivating immersive silence.

It's not just possible or preferable to get beyond the interference; doing so is one of the most important commitments we make to ourselves and to those around us. Transcending the noise that distorts our true perceptions and intentions is a deeply personal pursuit, but it has social, economic, ethical, and political implications, too.

When Cyrus Habib leaped from the public stage to a path of contemplative self-negation, he wasn't just reducing the complexity—the auditory and informational stimulus—in his life. He was reimagining his goals and his whole paradigm of success. Accordingly, he was dismantling some of the sources of internal noise in his life. Cyrus knows it's not feasible to ask every thoughtful person in politics or other noisy realms of modern life to move to a novitiate or a convent. Still, if we want our lives and our societies to embody more empathy, authenticity, and focused attention, then we do have to carefully examine the sources of noise. This might mean reducing the literal decibels. But it also might mean rethinking basic questions about what we want and how we measure success.

OUR MOST CELEBRATED ADDICTION

Take a moment to return to the deepest silence you remember.

Come back to how it *felt*: the sensory experience in your body, the quality of your attention, the depth of your listening.

In the opening words of this book, we described how profound silence isn't just an absence; it's a presence. And yet it's also worth exploring the question, when we're in a state of deep silence, *what* is absent? As we enter silence, what is it that we're transcending?

Through scores of conversations with other people on this subject, we've come to recognize that the experience of silence is increasingly endangered. The lived experience of noise—not just what's empirically measurable through decibel meters and psychological treatment statistics, but the subjective experience of external and internal distraction—is on the rise. And as we've explored the deeper qualitative dimensions of noise, we've noticed something that seems to pervade whole countries and cultures today.

Modern society doesn't just tolerate the maximum production of mental stuff; we celebrate it. It's no exaggeration to say that we're addicted to making noise.

But why?

One simple answer is that we don't think much about the costs.

Consider a seemingly mundane example from the world of work: group emails. The computer scientist Cal Newport, author of the books *Deep Work* and *Digital Minimalism*, reckons that they might cost any given small- to medium-sized company tens of thousands of employee hours of valuable thought and attention annually. Yet the underlying assumption holds that if such emails occasionally make it more convenient to access information, then they're worth it. Newport calls this modern society's "convenience addiction." "Because we lack clear metrics for these behaviors' costs," he says, "we cannot weigh their pros against their cons. Therefore, the evidence of any benefit is enough to justify continued use."

This same notion applies across society writ large.

It's rare that we stop to ask, how much noise is really necessary?

We spoke with Cyrus about how politics today is so full of sound and fury because politicians have to compete for voters' scarce attention, they have to preempt or respond to attacks, they have to win over the electorate by making their ideas and views heard. So, we're accustomed to thinking that the ruthless capture of human attention—through robocalls, text alerts, and in-your-face advertising—is just the name of the game. Because we don't often assess the toll that excessive mental stimulus exacts on our individual and collective psyches, we tend to produce and consume it with reckless abandon. We rarely perform any kind of cost-benefit analysis on it.

While the "attention economy" produces benefits to global society that now measure in the tens of trillions of dollars, we're only just beginning to comprehend its costs. Peer-reviewed studies show, for example, that the mere presence of a smartphone in a room, turned off and face down, drains people's working memory and their capacity for problem solving. Other studies show that roughly a third of eighteen-to forty-four-year-olds feel anxious if they haven't checked Facebook within two hours. The same study used MRI scan data to correlate the psychological dependency on checking Facebook with a reduction in valuable gray matter in the brain—a reduction that's comparable to one caused by cocaine usage. As Jean Twenge, a leading expert on youth mental health, wrote in the *World Happiness Report* in 2018, "95% of United States adolescents had access to a smartphone, and 45% said they were online 'almost constantly.'" While this might present benefits in terms of convenience or entertainment, Twenge found that there was a 52 percent rise in major depressive episodes among adolescents in the period between 2005 and 2017—the time during which smartphones became ubiquitous. The costs are real.

The same dynamics of "addiction" apply to the industrial soundscape, too. In her 2019 feature in *The Atlantic*, "Why Everything Is Getting Louder," Bianca Bosker writes of the struggle of Karthic Thallikar, a resident of an Arizona bedroom community who endured years of headaches and sleepless nights owing to the constant electric drone of a massive nearby data storage center. The police, the city council, and the business's representatives told him to buy earplugs and be less sensitive. An employee of the data center told Thallikar—who grew up in Bangalore—that immigrants like him "should feel lucky to live in the U.S." and not complain about such disturbances. Thallikar, in time, found out he wasn't alone in his discomfort. Scores of other local residents were suffering, too. But even as they built a sustained movement, government officials said there was nothing they could do. This was a matter of economic development, after all. Sure, the officials agreed, the noise was agitating. But it was the cost of "progress."

Cal Newport's concept of the "convenience addiction" is instructive. And yet the underlying dynamic here runs deeper than just expediency of access to information. It gets to the idea of "progress"—the set of values that constitute the organizing purpose of modern society. When former Google CEO Eric Schmidt offered his estimate that we produce as much info every two days as we did "from the dawn of civilization up until 2003," he wasn't just talking about what exponential increases in connectivity and computing power have enabled us to do.

He was talking about where we're putting our energy and attention.

He was talking about the way our social, political, and economic systems are wired.

THE ECONOMICS OF AGITATION

In the third quarter of 2020, the U.S. economy grew by a record-breaking 33.1 percent on an annualized basis. Given the realities of an out-of-control coronavirus pandemic, rampant food insecurity, raging wildfires, and massive protests against racial injustice, this supposedly wondrous and historic number seemed—to most people—like a total and utter farce.

But the disconnect between this one particular economic milestone and most people's actual lived experience was not an aberration. It was a reflection of how we tend to measure progress.

It's an illustration of why we generate so much noise.

Back during the Great Depression, few if any countries did any kind of national accounting or measurement of the sum total of all the economic activity within their borders. Without this, governments couldn't effectively mobilize their economies through fiscal and monetary stimulus measures—the kinds of actions President Franklin Roosevelt and other leaders sought to take in order to pull their nations' economies out of the doldrums. To manage the economy, you have to measure it. So the U.S. government employed a young economist, a future Nobel laureate named Simon Kuznets, to develop the first system of national income accounting. It was the forerunner of gross domestic product, or GDP.

The approach caught on. Soon, GDP wasn't just a tool for government planners. It became the go-to barometer of business cycles, government performances, and even human living standards. Public officials started using GDP as one of the most important benchmarks in crafting policies and regulations. Businesses started using it as a guide to expenditures and investments. Journalists and voters started seeing it as an indication of a president's or prime minister's success or failure. Since it became a shorthand expression of national wealth, people started thinking about GDP as the "headline indicator" of a society's progress.

GDP wasn't supposed to be used for all these purposes. As Kuznets himself indicated, "The welfare of a nation can scarcely be inferred from a measurement of national income."

His warning was prescient.

Rising GDP often runs counter to what's good for us.

During the catastrophic Deepwater Horizon oil spill in the Gulf of Mexico, J. P. Morgan analysts noted that economic activity generated by all the cleanup efforts would likely outweigh the economic losses to tourism and fishing. The largest accidental oil spill in history likely registered as a "net gain" in the country's economic output. In other words, an event of mass ecological and human destruction was a net positive event, according to our foremost metric of social "progress." The dynamics are similar in other spheres of life. Our GDP growth tends to accelerate with rising rates of crime, longer commutes, and the existence of more gas-guzzling vehicles. It also tends to slow as we take time for personal relaxation or cooking dinner at home rather than picking up fast food.

The problem is that GDP is just a measurement of raw industrial output. As the social theorist Jeremy Lent puts it, GDP "measures the rate at which a society is transforming nature and human activities into the monetary economy, regardless of the ensuing quality of life." So, if we cut down a pristine forest to collect lumber that gets sold at Home Depot, that registers as a pure positive. The worth of that pristine forest, which exists outside the monetary economy, is implicitly priced at zero. This approach to measurement gets to the heart of many of our challenges as a society—from disrespect of nature to lack of appreciation for community. It's the problem of trying to transfer everything into the monetary economy.

Speaking just a few months before his assassination in 1968, Robert F. Kennedy said the following about our headline indicator of societal progress:

> [It] counts air pollution and cigarette advertising, and ambulances to clear our highways of carnage. It counts special locks for our doors and the jails for the people who break them. It counts the destruction of the redwood and the loss of our natural wonder in chaotic sprawl. It counts napalm and counts nuclear warheads and armored cars for the police to fight the riots in our cities. It counts Whitman's rifle and Speck's knife, and the television programs which glorify violence in order to sell toys to our children. Yet the gross national product does not allow for the health of our children, the quality of their education or the joy of their play. It does not include the beauty of our poetry or the strength of our marriages, the intelligence of our public debate or the integrity of our public officials. It measures neither our wit nor our courage, neither our wisdom nor our learning, neither our compassion nor our devotion to our country, it measures everything in short, except that which makes life worthwhile.

To RFK's litany of all the cherished human values that our economic indicators ignore, we would add one more: *the peace and clarity of pure attention.*

Just as the value of the pristine redwood forest is implicitly priced at zero under our system of measuring GDP, so, too, is the value of silence.

How we measure progress and productivity in modern society explains why our systems are optimized to produce maximum noise. GDP goes up with the buzzes and roars of industrial machinery. But it also goes up when an app's built-in algorithm deduces that you're in a quiet moment of your day and swoops in with a notification that wins your attention, boosting usage statistics and juicing company earnings. GDP goes up when management finds a new opportunity to make an employee answer emails at 11:00 p.m., transforming the "unproductive" activity of rest into a verifiable contribution to the monetary economy. It's probably no coincidence that Facebook created the "like" button—one of history's craftiest means of hijacking dopamine receptors and with it human consciousness—as the company was seeking to demonstrate its potential profitability to investors in order to go public.

"Attention," says the French philosopher Simone Weil, "taken to its highest degree, is the same thing as prayer. It presupposes faith and love. Absolutely unmixed attention is prayer." The full plenitude of our conscious attention is something sacred.

And yet it's hard to assign a monetary value to anything that's sacred—whether it's a vibrant virgin rain forest or an experience of gratitude in quiet reflection. Silence gets implicitly priced at zero. The empty space beneath, between, or beyond the mental stuff gets tacitly labeled "useless." That's why we fail to guard the teenage psyche against the economic dynamo of the iPhone or why Karthic Thallikar's protest against the buzz of the nearby data center never really stood a chance.

That's why the world keeps getting noisier.

In November 2020, Cyrus Habib went straight from the lieutenant governor's office into a thirty-day silent retreat, where he prayed and examined his thoughts while learning how to rigorously practice the five-hundred-year-old spiritual exercises of Saint Ignatius of Loyola. It was the time of the presidential election, but Cyrus, the consummate politician, wasn't even able to learn the results. He had no phone or internet and no contact with family or friends.

When it came to auditory and informational stimulation, he was on a total elimination diet.

And yet Cyrus noticed that he still had to contend with hearty, heaping servings of internal noise.

"I'd have these pangs of doubt, where I started to ask myself, 'Oh my God, what am I doing? Have I made a huge mistake?'"

While Cyrus tells us that he had become a Jesuit in order to "tune his life to the key of the divine," he kept encountering discordant notes in his consciousness—internal chatter that left him agitated and unsettled.

But after a few weeks in the silence, he realized why he was facing so much internal noise: "I wasn't asking myself, 'Am I happy?' I was asking myself, 'How do other people see what I'm doing?'"

Cyrus realized he was continuing to stake his whole sense of fulfillment on other people's perceptions of him. This was especially problematic because, by this point, he had come to assume that people thought he was "totally nuts." He had just gone from being a prominent public official to a novice member of an austere religious order.

"I mean, what an off-the-wall thing to do!"

As Cyrus sat in silence with his insight about where he was looking for fulfillment, something shifted. "I reached a point where I realized what my heart actually desires. If I just asked myself, 'What do you want?' The answer was, 'To be exactly where I am.'"

Getting to this place of joyful presence required "reducing the auditory noise and the information I was receiving," he tells us. But, he says, it was also ultimately about something else. He had to decide that he "was no longer *performing*."

The constant obligation to have to think of the right thing to say, to deliver on other people's expectations, can create, in Cyrus's words, "a static that crowds out the signal. And the signal," he says, "is what is truly in the heart."

Over the past decade, a range of authors, including Alex Soojung-Kim Pang, Chris Bailey, and Arianna Huffington, have described how *busyness* is now a primary status symbol in our society. Like Cyrus, we know that feeling when quiet reflection gives way to self-doubt, even guilt. *Shouldn't I be doing something? Shouldn't I be earning my keep? Shouldn't I be getting my voice out there or staying in touch or building my brand?*

The writer and researcher Linda Stone suggests there may be even more at play in this situation than just our worship of productivity. Nearly thirty years ago, she coined the term "continuous partial attention," which, she argues, is distinct from multitasking. Whereas multitasking is motivated by the desire to be efficient, continuous partial attention is trying to ensure that we never miss out on an opportunity. We constantly scan the landscape—typically, a digital one these days—for connections, validations, and openings. It's a nonstop hustle. It's FOMO writ large. Stone says that continuous partial attention mimics an "almost constant crisis" in our nervous systems. These underlying feelings of missing out or falling behind with respect to social expectations explain, at least partially, why a reported 69 percent of millennials experience anxiety being away from a smartphone, even briefly.

Just as our economy is structured on the idea that success means GDP growth—the maximum possible production of sound and stimulus and stuff—our personal success is all too often contingent upon a similar kind of "growth": continuous accumulation of social capital, informational capital, and financial capital. On the macro-level scale of society, the message is "Production is prosperity." At the micro-level of the individual human consciousness, the message is "You can rest when you're dead."

But what if savoring silence is precisely what we ought to be doing for the good of ourselves and the good of our world?

What if there's an ethical imperative for getting beyond the noise?

Cyrus answers these questions with a metaphor. "If you want to learn how to cook," he says, "you should learn how to cook vegetarian. Because if you learn how to cook with meat, then you use meat as a crutch. If you learn how to cook with vegetables, then you're going to learn how to use spices and seasonings and sauces. You're going to notice flavors and textures."

"Similarly," Cyrus says, "when I've gone on silent retreat, when I've gotten beyond the noise, when I've stopped using the distractions and entertainment as such a crutch, I've found that the *hues of my life are brighter.* I taste the food more. When I'm washing dishes, I'm really physically feeling the plate in my hand and the sponge in my hand."

"There's an opportunity—an invitation—for each of us to become *connoisseurs of creation.*"

As we imagine what it means to transcend a world of noise, we become struck by Cyrus's phrase "connoisseurs of creation." To us, this means cultivating the capacity for delight in the senses. It's about reclaiming clarity and wonder.

Finding a way to "detox" from the noise, Cyrus says, allows us to "make more heart-driven, loving choices." It allows us to develop "an appreciation for the ways in which we are loved, an appreciation for all that's around us that's beautiful—that which we may not otherwise notice."

Way back in the seventeenth century, the philosopher and polymath Blaise Pascal said, "All of humanity's problems stem from man's inability to sit quietly in a room alone." We have to be able to transcend the noise—to withstand and even appreciate naked reality without all the commentary and entertainment and decoration—if we are to perceive what matters. We have to do this if we want to repair our relationships with nature and our relationships with one another.

Decades before the words "attention economy" entered the popular lexicon, a Swiss contemplative named Max Picard was thinking about the question, why don't we seriously weigh the costs and benefits of all the noise we generate? "Silence," Picard wrote, "is the only phenomenon today that is 'useless.' It does not fit into the world of profit and utility; it simply is. It seems to have no other purpose; it cannot be exploited." Picard wrote that there's actually more "help and healing" in silence than in all the "useful things" in the world. "It makes things whole again, by taking them back from the world of dissipation into the world of wholeness." He concluded, "It gives things something of its own holy uselessness; for that is what silence itself is: holy uselessness."

About six months after Cyrus left office and started his Jesuit training, he was already immersed in service. He was working in a group house in Tacoma, Washington, where people with and without intellectual disabilities live together and serve one another in a fraternal way. We caught up on the phone with him during a half-hour break in his responsibilities there. Cyrus was obviously making himself "useful." And yet he seemed to embody this spirit of "holy uselessness" as he engaged himself in volunteer cleaning and dishwashing that didn't register as any kind of measurable revenue-generating activity according to GDP. He had stepped out of the logic of productivity and constant connectivity, the logic of performing to other people's expectations, the logic of a world of noise. Spending time in that group house, Cyrus was hardly in monastic silence.

But his mind was remarkably quiet.

CHAPTER 3

SILENCE IS PRESENCE

"All things in our universe are constantly in motion, vibrating."

In a 2018 article in *Scientific American*, Tam Hunt of the University of California, Santa Barbara summarized a range of recent findings from peer-reviewed academic studies in physics, astronomy, and biology to present this conclusion. He writes, "Even objects that appear to be stationary are in fact vibrating, oscillating, resonating, at various frequencies." The author concludes, "Ultimately, all matter is just vibrations of various underlying fields."

"Everything in life is vibration." So goes the pithy and poignant, though possibly apocryphal, Albert Einstein quotation. Whether or not the master said it, the frontiers of modern physical sciences are showing the statement to be true.

Which raises a question: If this is the nature of reality, can anything be perfectly still?

Is there even such a thing as silence?

The twentieth-century modernist composer John Cage devoted a lot of his life's work to this question. Cage famously wrote a piece of music, titled *4'33"*, that consists of nothing but four minutes and thirty-three seconds of rest. The point wasn't to give the piano player a break. It was written for an open-air concert hall in Woodstock, New York, with the objective of bringing the audience's attention to the sounds of cicadas and the breezes in the branches. Later, when the piece was performed at indoor venues, the audience would take in other environmental sounds: the scuffling of feet, the clearing of throats, the detestable unwrapping of butterscotch candy. But the idea was always to use the music as a vehicle to expand people's attention to what's happening around them—to get people to consciously tune in to their surroundings.

Cage was inspired to create this piece years earlier when he visited the anechoic chamber on the Harvard campus. The room was designed to be soundless, built with materials to completely absorb all reflected vibration. It had been constructed with funding from the National Defense Research Committee during World War II as a way to study the extreme fatigue that bomber pilots experienced from noisy piston engines. When Cage stepped inside the chamber, he found something strange. It wasn't silent. He heard "two sounds, one high and one low." He described them both to the engineer in charge and asked why the room wasn't totally soundless as advertised. The engineer explained to him the significance of the two sounds by saying, "The high one was your nervous system in operation. The low one was your blood in circulation."

John Cage's experiences and insights point to what diverse scientific studies today affirm: we'll probably never experience silence in the pure objective sense of "a total absence of sound."

In this pulsating, oscillating, buzzing reality we live in—where even the tiniest cilia hairs inside our own ears generate sound—there's no escaping the vibration.

And that's okay.

Our conception of silence isn't the total absence of sound. It isn't the total absence of thought. It's the absence of *noise*. It's the space between and beyond the auditory, informational, and internal stimuli that interfere with our clear perception and intention.

We recently asked Joshua Smyth—the scholar and researcher in biobehavioral health who has spent decades studying these matters—for his definition of "internal silence." He thought intently, scanning his mind for what reams of relevant scientific literature had to say. In near exasperation, he put it bluntly: "Quiet is whatever someone *thinks* quiet is."

This might sound like an evasive response. But the more we explored the meaning of silence—through years of interviews, conversations, study of academic literature, and time in personal introspection—the more convincing we found Smyth's answer. We don't know if physicists or astronomers will ever someday discover a pocket of absolute stillness somewhere in the universe. But we do know it's possible for human beings to experience silence—as a personal phenomenon—on Earth, here and now.

There is such a thing as silence. It's brimming with life and possibility. It naturally inhabits a universe where everything is pulsating, oscillating, and buzzing.

IN PRAISE OF THE INEFFABLE

When we tell our friends that we're writing a book about silence, we often hear the same joke: "Oh, is it going to be a bunch of blank pages?"

There is really no such thing as an expert in that which cannot be spoken.

As Professor Smyth's answer to our question about the definition of "internal silence" suggests, it's a fool's errand to try to fit this ineffable presence into any kind of rigid box. It's up to each one of us to go inside and explore what silence really is.

For nearly forty years, the acoustic ecologist Gordon Hempton has traveled the globe to find the very quietest places to record them before they vanish. He's a devotee of silence, if there ever was one. A few years ago, we spoke with him about our intention to write this book, and he told us that our greatest challenge would be to persuade you—our esteemed reader—to supersede the *concept* of silence that lives in your mind with the *direct experience* of how silence actually makes you *feel*. "Words are not a substitute for the experience," he says.

Still, in talking with Hempton, we came to appreciate how valuable it is to explore other people's accounts. While words can only point a finger toward the reality of the experience, the guidance can be illuminating and instructive.

For example, Hempton describes his own experience of silence as "time, undisturbed."

He calls it the "think tank of the soul." He says that "silence nurtures our nature, our human nature, and lets us know who we are."

In interviewing scores of people for this book, we've been moved by so many personal insights on the meaning of silence. Here, rather than attempting one single definition, we will introduce you to a diverse range of reflections.

We invite you to pause after each one.

O

Roshi Joan Halifax—a trailblazing anthropologist, Zen priest, and innovator in end-of-life care—says, "In the presence of silence, the conditioned self rattles and scratches. It begins to crumble like old leaves or worn rock." Silence is a real and practical way to dethrone the ego from its assumed perch at the center point of everything. This seems particularly challenging for Westerners. She writes, "We have filled our world with a multiplicity of noises, a symphony of forgetfulness that keeps our own thoughts and realizations, feelings and intuitions out of audible range." She laments all we're missing when we drown out silence and adds, "Silence is where we learn to listen, where we learn to see."

O

The Reverend Dr. Barbara Holmes, a contemplative teacher and scholar focused on African American spirituality and mysticism, traces her relationship to silence through the ancestral lineage on her father's side—descendants of the Gullah people of South Carolina. "The first daughter born in the family would be the one who would see into other worlds." Rather than use the word "silence," Dr. Holmes often uses the terms "stillness," "centering," and "embodied ineffability." She uses these terms because the space of mystery has, for her, an undeniably physical dimension to it. She jokes that finding silence today is much harder than it was for mystics centuries ago. "I don't give them all that much credit—it was silence or donkeys!" But she warns that today "you can live your whole life and never have lived—running from one thing to another, not knowing what's important." She adds, "Most of the things that I thought important—weren't . . . but a moment of stillness would have said to me: 'Wait—there's more . . .'"

O

The Irish poet and theologian Pádraig Ó Tuama tells us that silence is "having enough space in yourself to ask yourself *strange questions*." Pádraig recalls working closely with a parish committee—half laypeople and half priests. "It was a great church in West Belfast that had done magnificent and important and dangerous work during 'the Troubles,' in terms of reconciliation and bringing people together," he says, referring to the violence that plagued his country for decades. There was one priest there whom Pádraig particularly admired. That priest, he tells us, wasn't afraid to ask the strange questions of himself or others. And that was an indispensable part of the work of durable and effective peace building. "I think we do all need a salting of anarchism to ask, 'Am I *really* doing the good?'" He jests, saying we might even need to ask, "What if *we're* the bastards?" Pádraig says that when you have the courage to face fears and "ask those strange questions," they can "shift the ground underneath you."

O

The Sufi teacher Pir Shabda Kahn tells us, "Silence is not silent at all— it's teeming with life and joy and ecstasy—but it is quiet of thoughts of the self, it's quiet of foolishness." He adds, with a coyote's smile, "What you call silence, I might call *freedom*." Early on his spiritual journey, in 1969—at the urging of his teacher—Pir Shabda took a vow of silence. For four months, he carried a small chalkboard for occasional and succinct communications. He jokes that while he was glad to have had the experience, he is "not a big fan," and he notes that he never passed the practice along to any of his own students. "I'm a kind of troublemaker around people who want to make a silent retreat." He laughs. "Quieting the mind is the kind of silence I'm interested in—not so much the mouth."

O

Judson Brewer, a Brown University neuroscientist and psychiatrist, is one of the world's leading experts on the brain sciences of addiction, anxiety, and habit change. We ask him about the meaning of silence, and he tells us about the last of the Seven Factors of Awakening in Theravada Buddhism, the factor that all the others lead up to in a causal chain: equanimity. It's "the absence of the push or pull," he says. Brewer explains that there's probably no such thing as "a cold, hard silence," a state of absolutely no perception or cognition, at least in a mind that's alive. But there is, he says, a "warm, soft silence" that can be attained in a living state. It's when "we're no longer caught up" in our own experience, when there's no more "craving or aversion," when we get beyond fixation on the sense of a separate self. "There can be tons of activity. And if one is not pulled or pushed by the activity, there is silence within that," he says. Through years of research studies, Brewer has gotten a sense of what it looks like, neurobiologically, to encounter profound internal quiet. He finds that there's a specific word for the feeling that corresponds to noise in the mind: "contraction." And there's a word for the feeling that corresponds to interior silence: "expansion."

○

Rupa Marya, an internationally touring musician, songwriter, activist, physician, and associate professor of medicine at the University of California, San Francisco, tells us that silence is "the place where the music comes from." For decades she's ritualized practices of silence to awaken and hone her creativity. More recently, Rupa has come to appreciate silence in her role as a medical doctor. In her work with the Lakhota, Dakhota, and Nakhota people of Standing Rock, she has realized that most of what she was taught as a physician—especially in regard to speaking with a patient, exploring a health challenge, sharing a diagnosis, or giving a prescription—runs counter to healing. The antidote, she tells us, is deep listening. She has to make space to be fully present and awake with another person. The antidote is silence.

○

Tyson Yunkaporta is an academic researcher, a carver of traditional tools, a member of the Apalech Clan in far north Queensland, Australia. "I can't think of a word that even approximates the concept of silence in my Indigenous language, because it doesn't exist," Tyson tells us. "It's *the ability to perceive a signal* that could be regarded as silence."

What does it mean to have the ability to perceive a signal? Tyson describes it as the capacity to hear what's true. "If you're tuning in to *the* signal, then you're tuning in to the law of the land—the law that's *in* the land." He notes that "whales have a genetic signal that tells them what their migration routes are, and birds, too, have these signals, and our biologists say humans don't have that, but we do have a signal that tells us how to organize in groups. It's within us, and it's *in the land.*" In our talk with Tyson, he tells us how he has a hard time sleeping and thinking clearly in Melbourne, where he now lives. "It's the hum of the infrastructure that allows seven million people to be crammed all around me. But I think about how well I sleep when I'm back in my community. At night, there's the music cacophony all around. There's dingoes howling. There are fights happening and people gambling and hollering." He adds, "Even though it's dysfunctional, it's still the signal. It's my people's true response to the incursions of the colony into that space; it's the resistance to that. I'm in it and of it, and it's real. And I can sleep. And it's *good.*"

○

Jarvis Jay Masters speaks of silence as a matter of survival. He has spent more than thirty years on death row in San Quentin prison for a crime that the preponderance of evidence now shows he didn't commit. He's been in legal limbo for years as his case works its way through a labyrinthine appeals process. Jarvis is now a renowned meditation teacher who's taken vows with Tibetan lamas and published two books. He emphasizes how the noise in prison isn't just the nonstop hollering or the party beats playing on lo-fi radios. It's the vibration of fear—the angst of uncertainty, violence, and state-sanctioned death. Still, in San Quentin, Jarvis has become adept at finding silence. He finds it in moments doing exercises in his cell. He finds it when he studies astronomy and reads Buddhist texts. But mostly he finds silence by skillfully navigating the noise in his own consciousness. "My *responses* to the noise were probably the loudest," he reflects. "I started quieting the noise by *quieting my responses to the noise*," he tells us. The deepest silence, for Jarvis, has a moral dimension. He can access it, he tells us, when he gets beyond his own personal worries and turns his focus toward compassion for others.

HIGHER SYNONYMS

In the opening words of this book, we asked you to summon a memory of the deepest silence you can remember. We asked you not only to think about it but to *feel* it. And we asked if you could sense it as not just an absence but also a presence.

These different people—through their varied backgrounds, life situations, and styles of expression—all point to an *active* experience of silence. This experience of silence clarifies our thinking and bolsters our health. It teaches us. It centers us. It wakes us up.

When we think about silence as a presence, we notice something seemingly paradoxical: this silence is quiet to the ears and quiet in the mind, and yet the experience in the consciousness can be thundering.

This kind of silence, Gordon Hempton agrees, isn't just a matter of transcending that which we don't want. It's not just the absence of noise. He calls it "the presence of everything."

Gordon's word—"everything"—is a good encapsulation of what we mean to say is present.

But, for us, there are other words, too.

"Humility" is one. "Renewal" is another. And "clarity." And "expansion." You could also call this presence the essence of *life itself.*

Silence is humility. It's a stance of not-knowing, a place of letting go. Silence is accepting that it's okay to not fill the space. It's good to just be. At the least, it's a chance to step back from the pressures of having to try to shape or direct reality. We don't have to control everything by keeping up the discourse or the argument or the entertainment. This isn't just about a personal state of relaxation. Humility is, according to

University of Toronto psychologist Jennifer Stellar, "a vital virtue at the foundation of morality and a key to living in social groups." Many wisdom traditions teach, in one way or another, that humility is among the highest spiritual virtues. There's inherent goodness in letting go of the pressures to compete and perform.

Silence is renewal. Around the time we were writing our *Harvard Business Review* article, Justin's friend Renata said, "Silence can reset the nervous system." She didn't know at the time that we were writing on this topic. She didn't know about our intuition. Renata's words remind us of early Christian Desert Fathers and Mothers who fled Rome for Egypt to lead austere lives of meditation and prayer. They focused their practice on finding a state of "rest" that they called *quies*. It's linked etymologically to the word "quiescence." But it had little to do with the kind of checked-out concession that the word "quiescence" sometimes implies today. It was rather, according to the theologian and social activist Thomas Merton, something "sublime." Their rest was "the sanity and poise of a being that no longer has to look at itself because it is carried away by the perfection of freedom that is in it," he writes. Rest, for these contemplatives, was "a kind of simple nowhereness and no-mindedness that had lost all preoccupation with a false or limited 'self.'" Transcending the auditory, informational, and internal noise, we can reset our tired conditioning. We can renew our perception of the world.

Silence is clarity. Cyrus Habib describes to us an ability to discern "what is truly in the heart." He speaks of silence as the capacity "to not say the first thing that flies into your head—even for just thirty seconds." It's like the teaching, often attributed to the psychologist and Holocaust survivor Viktor Frankl: "Between stimulus and response, there is a space. In that space is our power to choose our response. In our response lies our growth and our freedom." While we live in a culture that tends to emphasize "clarity of thought" and "clarity of logic," the truest clarity transcends plans and arguments and strategies. It lives in the "space"—the luminous in-between. This clarity beyond the mental stuff empowers us to know ourselves. It's not the basis of a solitary withdrawal from the world but a steady fulcrum from which to shift things toward what's right. The mystic Kabir says,

> Be silent in your mind, silent in your senses, and also silent in your body. Then, when all these are silent, don't do anything. In that state truth will reveal itself to you. It will appear in front of you and ask, "What do you want?"

Imagine, for a moment, that a critical mass of humanity could tune in to this kind of authentic intention. Imagine if—beyond the distractions and entertainment and games of profit and power—we could tune in to that which brings us the highest degree of flourishing. Imagine we could all have such clarity.

Silence is expansion. It's the unfolding of the attentional space. As we go deeper into it, we find more and more room to truly feel. When we arrive at profound silence, the limits of language melt away. It matters that we know not what's what or who's who but rather simply *what is.* In the deepest silence of all, we find the inner freedom to transcend the strictures of the separate self.

Silence is the essence of life itself. When there's nothing making claims on our consciousness, we can encounter the canvas of creation. In the purest attention, we can tune in to the fundamental vibration; we can encounter the essence of everything. If the sound and stimulus of speech and thought signal what needs to be done, then pristine awareness signals the opposite. It's where nothing needs to be done. When we get beneath the chatter—inner and outer—we access this awakening presence. This is wholeness.

PERFECTION IN THE MUCK

In the Buddhist tradition, there's a commonly used symbol of a lotus— a flower that comes in hues of white and pink and blue. Its petals open one by one as it sits exquisitely on the glassy surface of the pond. Yet the lotus grows in the muddiest, swampiest bodies of water. Its roots are planted in the muck. It finds nourishment in the muck. When we describe the presence of silence as "wholeness," we don't mean that it's a kind of sanitary separateness from the world of noise. Like the lotus, this flowering silence can emerge from the muck.

When we first started asking people about the deepest silence they'd ever known, we thought we'd get answers like what Jeff, the conservative manufacturing executive, told Justin in the opening pages—misty early mornings and remote youth retreats. While we cherish these kinds of spaces of auditory and informational tranquility, we've noticed that most people describe their deepest silence through situations that aren't even ostensibly quiet. We've heard about the silence that arises with the sudden end of a fierce conflict or the loss of a loved one or the sensory harmony of dunking a basketball or the feeling at the 4:00 a.m. mark of an all-night dance party. The very deepest silences that people describe are often related to depth of feeling—a kind of migration from the treetop of the thinking mind to the trunk and roots of the feeling heart and body. Often, the deepest silence arises spontaneously out of moments of doubt or distraction.

This has certainly been the case in our own experience.

Leigh met one of her deepest silences in the office of Dr. Tenenbaum. The loudness of her mind had brought her there. You could say loud interiors were Dr. T.'s psychiatric specialty.

Leigh hadn't slept for twenty-five days. Following the difficult birth of her daughter, Leigh's mind was filled with voices, each vying for the mic and the limelight. Here's a brief introduction to the tenor of just a few.

There was the "striving" voice—we'll call her "sister striving"—convinced that with the right strategy she could beat this whole motherhood thing. She could return to work without a hitch, master the art of raising a newborn, write handwritten notes, keep the grout in her kitchen spotless, host the parade of people eager to meet the baby, lose weight, keep her husband beguiled, and—as a spiritually evolved being—she would do all this while savoring the nectar of each moment. She would, she could, and she *must*. But "sister striving" wasn't the only voice in town; she was joined by a veritable Greek chorus of delusory voices.

There was the "belligerent genius," quick to dismiss anyone who couldn't keep up with her intellect and wit. She was the one who reprimanded an EMT from the back of the ambulance for the gross mischaracterization of her condition as postpartum depression, "I'm not depressed, moron. *I'm elated!*" She was enlightenment—in a blender. Then there was the "tragic poet" who could foresee every grisly catastrophe that could befall a newborn. She inherently understood this life could end only in tragedy, so, naturally, she obsessively kept watch over her sleeping baby. There was the "paradox chaser" with a gift for finding the Gordian knots of everyday conversation, the "mad scientist" who likened insanity to an escape room you simply had to *think* your way out of, and his loyal assistant who painstakingly recorded every observation and revelation—and there were thousands—on cassette.

And while not an exhaustive list, we'll stop here with one last voice—the most troubling of all—the voice of "unbridled paranoia." Fortunately, this voice got the mic on only a few occasions, for within a split second this voice could corrode all trust and reason. In its presence, Leigh questioned the motives of friendships that spanned decades and the very ground on which she stood. It was ruthless beyond measure.

Having heard plenty from the chorus, Dr. T. posed this question: "Have you ever lost your witness?"

And it was when he asked this question that—for the first time in weeks—*time stood still and everything went quiet.* It was like what those Desert Mothers and Fathers called *quies*—that sudden place of luminous rest: "the sanity and poise . . . the simple nowhereness and no-mindedness." Leigh remembers the voices parting like clouds to reveal a vast expanse of pristine awareness.

Then came a clear answer. "Yes, but only once."

In that brief exchange with Dr. T., Leigh encountered a silence both mystifying and familiar. This presence had been holding her all along. For Leigh, that revelation meant that she would be okay. In fact, everything would be okay: she would not be institutionalized, her sanity would return, she'd be a good mother to her daughter, her marriage would endure, and her being would be, somehow, better for it. Eight months later, when the last milligrams of antipsychotics and tranquilizers were lifted, it was as if Leigh emerged from being underwater. Silence was her companion through her darkest of journeys.

One of Justin's deepest silences happened at a time when he and his dearest loved ones were being bombarded with noise.

Justin and his wife, Meredy, had just had their twin babies in late February 2020. The babies came early. Thankfully, they came healthy. Still, the medical protocols demanded that they spend a few weeks in the hospital at the newborn intensive care unit (NICU) and then an intermediate care nursery. It was just before the very first cases of COVID reached New Mexico, where they live, and they were anxious to get out of the hospital with the newborns and get home before the lockdowns would start. Because they were separated from their three-year-old, who was left home with grandparents an hour away, Justin and Meredy were also anxious because they felt like neglectful parents. It was a noisy time internally.

But mostly, it was noisy externally—in the auditory sense. For Justin, who was already steeped in the literature about the impacts of noise pollution on human beings and particularly young babies, the relentless soundscape of the NICU was an almost surreal source of stress.

There were the droning pulses of the oxygen monitors.

The piercing bells of the heart rate and respiratory rate alarms.

The digital jingles, reminiscent of 1980s arcade games, that went off with the conclusion of bottle warmings and automatic feedings.

Each of the babies in the facility wore little ankle bracelets to alert the staff if they were ever taken out of the unit without authorization. One bracelet apparently got lost in the laundry, so every half hour or so (mostly at night), the security system would go off—with a roaring alarm that resembled some combination of a British World War II–era air-raid siren and an oversized squeaking carnival balloon, overwhelming the sounds of all the various other beeping instruments. The nurses couldn't figure out how to shut it off.

While Justin never wanted to seem as if he were telling anyone how to do their job, he occasionally gently offered a nurse or a doctor an idea for reducing the gratuitous noise. Without fail, the staff member would point him to a bizarre-looking monitoring device hanging on the wall. It was an outline of a human ear. When the outer lobe was lit up green, the noise levels were supposedly safe. Yellow lines in the middle were a warning. And red lights at the center of the ear would illuminate to signal dangerous decibel levels. It was a positive indication that the medical system recognized the importance of managing noise. However, Justin and Meredy noticed that most of the monitors, even amidst the most withering noise imaginable, never changed colors. They seemed to be either broken or rigged.

The noise of those three weeks was overwhelming. But there was unexpectedly profound silence, too.

One afternoon, Meredy finished nursing and stepped out briefly. Justin was holding his baby girl, and his baby boy started moving around. For the first time, the nurse offered Justin the opportunity to hold both babies simultaneously. She moved the chair over between their cribs and helped him get into "double football hold position." He unbuttoned and took off his shirt, then he held both babies on his chest, skin to skin.

After a few cozy moments, Justin started feeling his breathing synchronizing with theirs. Then it started feeling as if all three heart rates were somehow synchronized, too.

The beeping and buzzing sounds were still happening all around, and the concerns about COVID and getting home to the babies' big sister—and all the countless other contingencies—were still there. But in the pulse of the synchronized heartbeats, in the gently harmonized rising and falling of the three connected chests, none of the beeping or buzzing or worrying had any potency. It was as if none of it could penetrate. His mind became quiet. Suddenly everything felt whole.

Neither of us could have engineered these experiences of silence. Neither of these situations could be quantitatively measured as quiet according to any kind of objective analysis. And yet, out of so much sound and stimulus, there was silence. Out of the muck, there was flowering perfection.

NADA

If "everything in life is vibration," can anything be silent?

Is there even such a thing as silence?

We say, *yes, there is.*

But not necessarily in the sense that we're sometimes trained to think of it.

In some Romance languages, including Spanish and Portuguese, the word for "nothing" is *nada.* Strangely, in Sanskrit, one of the root languages on the other side of the Indo-European language family, the word *nada* means "sound." Nada yoga is the spiritual discipline of meditating on the inner sound, the "unstruck sound," sometimes called the "sound of silence."

When we enter the most profound silence, we're not extinguishing the vibration that is the essence of life. We're dropping the distraction and ego and restlessness so we can better tune in to it. The "nothing" we're talking about is this: *No noise. No interference. A direct encounter with the essence of what is.*

This meaning of silence isn't static. The Buddhist teacher Thích Nhất Hạnh calls it "the sound that transcends all sounds of the world." The depth psychologist Robert Sardello describes silence as "the mother of possibility," a living wholeness that contains *currents* that "pulse" and "whir" with rhythm. "Silence," says Rumi, "is the language of God."

This isn't a book about silence for people who live in monasteries.

We're not so interested in how to flee or extinguish the vibrations of reality.

What interests us is the question of how to find silence in a world that is—thankfully—pulsing and vibrating and singing and dancing.

CHAPTER 4

THE MORAL DIMENSIONS OF SILENCE

Standing before a crowd of tens of thousands of people on the National Mall in Washington, DC—as tens of millions more watched on live television—the poet Amanda Gorman, then twenty-two years old, summarized a simple and challenging lesson at the conclusion of the 2021 U.S. presidential inauguration:

"We've learned," she said, "that quiet isn't always peace."

She's right.

When Leigh was in her early twenties, she worked for a battered women's shelter answering a hotline that served northeast Georgia. One day, she heard from a woman who'd been "mail ordered" from China, as the woman explained in her newfound English tongue. The man responsible had been holding her hostage on his family compound for *eight years*. He'd kept her in near-total isolation. The few people they'd come into contact with hadn't bothered to ask questions. With unimaginable perseverance, the woman taught herself English through closed-captioning on television. She was waiting for the day her abuser might forget to unplug the landline phone and take it with him to work. When that day finally came, Leigh was on the other end of the line. Leigh remembers the steadiness in the woman's voice as she described an impossibly complex situation. "No police," she said. "His best friend, chief of police." They'd have to find another way. Thanks to the woman's courage and judiciousness—they did. There's no doubt that a kind of silence enabled her unconscionable imprisonment. Her quiet was the antithesis of peace. "Break the Silence" is still, today, a rallying cry of the battered women's movement.

For at least half a century, the notion of silence as complacency, complicity, or even violence has been a prominent cultural current.

In 1977, the legendary Audre Lorde—self-described Black, lesbian, mother, warrior, poet—asked, "What are the tyrannies you swallow day by day and attempt to make your own, until you will sicken and die of them, still in silence?" In the same essay, she described her agonizing three-week wait between diagnosis and breast cancer surgery. In the space of such uncertainty, she reflected on her life and said, "What I most regretted were my silences." She warned, "My silences had not protected me. Your silence will not protect you."

If you walked around New York City a decade after Lorde's writing, in the late 1980s, you'd find her sentiment operationalized in one of the most important and effective campaigns in modern history. You'd see the iconic "Silence = Death" poster wheatpasted everywhere, its stark white lettering emblazoned on a pitch-black background beneath a pink triangle. It was the galvanizing image of the AIDS movement. Activists worked tirelessly to shake the world awake to the scope and scale of the epidemic that would go on to kill thirty-three million people worldwide. Silence, in this context, was a shorthand for failure *or refusal* to wake up to action.

We can find this sentiment in the origins of the environmental movement, too. The title of Rachel Carson's world-changing *Silent Spring* is a reference to the despairing landscape of a John Keats poem, a kind of apocalyptic silence, where "the sedge is wither'd from the lake, / And no birds sing." Carson was well aware of how chemical industry profiteers would attempt to discredit her and squelch her voice. She wrote to a loved one about the moral requirement of her life: "Knowing what I do, there would be no future peace for me if I kept silent."

Today, the notion of silence as oppression is as relevant as ever. The actress Lupita Nyong'o's 2017 *New York Times* op-ed described how Harvey Weinstein attempted to assault, harass, and manipulate her. She wrote about the "conspiracy of silence" that enabled the "predator to prowl for so many years."

This kind of "silence"—*the refusal to speak and act in the face of injustice*—is real. And we oppose it to the core of our beings.

Yet, we've come to an understanding that the "silence" of closed-lipped complacency is not silence in the truest sense. Why? Because the refusal to perceive and address abuses is the polar opposite of clear perception and intention. When our eyes and hearts are open—when we have the space in our consciousness to pay attention—we can't be ignorantly satisfied to look elsewhere. The silence of apathy is a function of fear. It's a distortion of perception and intention that's born of anxious clinging to one's narrowest self-interest. This kind of so-called silence is, we believe, both a cause and a consequence of noise in our consciousness.

Consider how a noisy world enables injustice. If we're caught up in thinking about Instagram likes, reality TV stars, and socially unproductive profit seeking, how can we deeply understand inequities and concentrate on addressing them? If we're fixated on our own inner chatter, then how can we hold the interior space that's necessary for empathy—for experiencing the hurt and joy and inspiration that lie outside our own skin?

We started writing this book because we were feeling despondent about the state of the world. The intuition we felt was that the most intractable problems of the current era have their root, at least in part, in the problem of noise. To identify and enact more effective and durable solutions, we need the humility to listen, we need a capacity to continually renew our energy, and we need the clarity to be able to discern, on a personal and collective basis, the signal of what is true and what we truly want.

While complacency in the face of injustice is a genuine evil in our world, it's more accurate to call it noise rather than silence. True silence—the kind that enables presence and discernment and sympathetic understanding of nature and humanity—is an antidote to the noisy distortion that drives self-centeredness and apathy. It's a resource for uncovering our hidden biases, understanding other perspectives, and more skillfully addressing what's wrong.

Silence, in itself, can be a force for justice.

In April 1968, Martin Luther King Jr. was scheduled to join Thích Nhất Hạnh and Thomas Merton for a joint retreat—a few days of interfaith prayer, quiet contemplation, and conversation focused on ending the Vietnam War and building a fair society. Dr. King made the last-minute decision to postpone his participation so he could go to Memphis to stand in solidarity with striking sanitation workers there. It was, of course, a fateful decision to go to Memphis. It was on this trip that he was assassinated.

When Merton arrived at the monastery for the retreat, the *New York Times* contacted him about writing a commentary on the assassination. He declined. He entered into a period of deep silence. In his letter of condolences to the newly widowed Coretta Scott King, he wrote, "Some events are too big and too terrible to talk about." The Reverend Dr. Barbara Holmes contrasts Merton's then high-profile silence to the empty and exasperating dynamic of public figures offering "thoughts and prayers" in the wake of school shootings today. "The only responsible choice is to be silent," Holmes says, reflecting on Merton. "I can say nothing to this evil."

While Merton was a prolific public intellectual and a prominent voice against racism, militarism, and greed, he saw the immersive silence of contemplative life as part of a struggle for justice. As he wrote at the height of the civil rights movement and Vietnam, "I make monastic silence a protest against the lies of politicians, propagandists, and agitators, and when I speak it is to deny that my faith and my church can ever be aligned with these forces of injustice and destruction."

Gandhi had a similar view of the moral dimensions of silence. In a recent article in *The Hindu*, one of India's largest newspapers, Rajeev Kadambi, a political scientist at O. P. Jindal Global University, explores the question of why Gandhi didn't immediately condemn the United States for the use of the atomic bomb on the Japanese cities of Hiroshima and Nagasaki in 1945. Might this have been, Kadambi asks, "a tactical silence that waited for events to play out"? As unfathomable as it seems, Kadambi says, Gandhi's refusal to offer a verbal response, at the time, fed rumors that the "global apostle of non-violence and a critic of Western imperialism" somehow endorsed the use of the atomic bomb. Gandhi broke his silence to say only this: "The more I think of it, the more I feel that I must not speak on the atomic bomb. *I must act if I can.*"

Gandhi was a master of what Kadambi calls "the magical quality of unspoken-action." Kadambi suggests that Gandhi's silence—rooted in the yogic principle of *ahimsa*, nonviolence in intention, thought, and deed—was an act to "break from the circulation of violence and counter-violence."

Every Monday, Gandhi observed a "day of silence." In addition to meditation and contemplation, he continued his correspondence by letter, he selectively took visitors, and he listened closely in meetings and attended important summits without speaking. He kept to his weekly "day of silence" even during moments of intensity and upheaval in his multi-decade work to dismantle the British Empire's occupation of India. When others, including close friends, pleaded for him to make an exception and speak, he refused. His weekly "day of silence" was a centerpiece of all his work. "It has often occurred to me," he wrote, "that a seeker after truth has to be silent."

When Tuesdays arrived and Gandhi returned to speaking, he'd often deliver especially deliberate and eloquent speeches, without notes, in a kind of rapturous flow. He would bring his quiet consciousness to bloated and windy political arenas. In his autobiography, Gandhi wrote, "A man of few words will rarely be thoughtless in his speech; he will measure every word." Gandhi lamented the character of most meetings he attended, with "people impatient to talk" and the chairman "pestered with notes for permission to speak." He observed that "whenever the permission is given the speaker generally exceeds the time limit, asks for more time, and keeps on talking without permission. All this talking can hardly be said to be of any benefit to the world. It is so much waste of time."

Once, after a period of fifteen days of silence, just months before his assassination, he offered a reflection:

One cannot help feeling that nearly half the misery of the world would disappear if we, fretting mortals, knew the virtue of silence. Before modern civilization came upon us, at least six to eight hours of silence out of twenty-four were vouchsafed to us. Modern civilization has taught us to convert night into day and golden silence into brazen din and noise. What a great thing it would be if we in our busy lives could retire into ourselves each day for at least a couple of hours and prepare our minds to listen in to the Voice of the Great Silence. The Divine Radio is always singing if we could only make ourselves ready to listen to it, but it is impossible to listen without silence.

In the sound and fury of today's politics, we've been thinking about Gandhi's example as a quiet force of social transformation. He, too, lived in a point-and-counterpoint culture, and he employed silence as a way to break through seemingly impossible binaries and help resolve cycles of conflict and outright violence. Gandhi tuned in to "the golden silence" not as a means to withdraw from the struggle but as a means to transform it. He saw his political life as an extension of his spiritual work as a "seeker after truth," and, accordingly, silence was a source of both practical and spiritual clarity for him.

You can find the power of the socially engaged silence of Merton and Gandhi in our world today. In fact, you can often find it in unexpected places.

In the summer of 2020, Sheena Malhotra—an author and professor of gender and women's studies at California State University—was at a Black Lives Matter demonstration in northern Los Angeles in the wake of the murder of George Floyd. The demonstration came just after the first months of lockdowns in the COVID-19 pandemic and just weeks into one of the biggest protest movements in U.S. history. "When the events evoke so much anger, when things are at boiling point, it's hard to go from there to silence," she says, describing the way the demonstration proceeded. "But we did—we went from all shouting slogans, to taking a knee, in silence." The hundreds assembled stopped and knelt for nine minutes, observing the nine minutes that Derek Chauvin held his knee on George Floyd's neck before his death.

Sheena recounts how the silence unfolded: "You felt despondent. You felt the physicality of it. You felt how long those nine minutes were in your body. At some point as you keep kneeling, you're just struck by how interminable this is, like lifetimes passing, and this is not ending. But then," she remembers, "you start looking around, and there's this crowd around you. People of all colors are there. You're noticing young Black boys there with their mothers. What must this feel like? How existential is this threat to their being? It sinks in."

In the crucible of silence—shared by hundreds of people—Sheena surfaced layer upon layer of latent thoughts and feelings. "I went through this gamut of emotions. Sadness. Anger." And then, she recalls, "anger transformed into compassion for the people around me. It went to a space of elation, like 'We're all here. We're all here together. And it's meaningful to be here together.' Then, in that space, I remember looking at the police officers standing around the perimeters and thinking, what are they feeling?"

"Silence is kind of like an ocean," Sheena tells us. "It can change forms. Silence gives you the space for a shape-shifting of emotions. It gives you the space to absorb the energy of people around you." Reflecting on that summer day in Los Angeles, she remembers a kind of positive transformation of the collective: "You could sense this shift in the energy of the whole crowd. It's the silence that allows the space for that to happen."

Sheena, along with her colleague Professor Aimee Carrillo Rowe, edited an anthology called *Silence, Feminism, Power: Reflections at the Edges of Sound*, which they dedicated to the late Audre Lorde. While they honor the advocates and scholars who have called out censorship and oppression for decades, they also reflect on the importance of breaking free from a "purely oppositional stance," of viewing "silence as an unexamined force of oppression that must be thrown off." They underscore that "silence allows us the space to breathe. It allows us the freedom of not having to exist constantly in reaction to what is said."

The volume contains an essay by Sheena in which she reflects on her own struggle through ovarian cancer. She describes how her treatment opened a series of realizations about the place of wordlessness in the work of justice. "Just as fire signifies the transformation of form from matter into air, silence too," she writes, "opens the space to imagine the unimaginable, allows us a place for reflection, re-articulation, and un-articulation so that we can come into another way of communicating that's beyond language."

SANCTUARIES

Working on Capitol Hill is a master class in the art of discerning the signal from the noise.

During Justin's years as legislative director for three members of

Congress, he worked to learn how to navigate the ever-present din of ringing phones, background gossip, alarm bells signaling votes on legislation, buzzing alerts to attend to absurdly flooded email in-boxes, and glad-handing lobbyists passing out invitations to boozy and boisterous nightclub receptions. But, over time, Justin found that some of the loudest, most jarring voices he'd encountered couldn't actually be classified as noise. Instead, these were signals. He'd often talk with advocates who would register high-volume indignation about polluted rivers and the plights of refugees fleeing Aleppo. These voices weren't unwanted distractions; they were signaling necessity. They had to be heard.

For Justin, to disregard these kinds of signals would have been an abdication of responsibility. Of course, what he's describing isn't just a fact about federal service. It's the reality for therapists, firefighters, teachers, medical personnel, and people in countless other service-oriented callings. It's the reality for all of us who have children or take care of aging parents and loved ones. We can't ignore time-sensitive signals. So, how do we maintain clarity and energy amidst so much agitation and urgency?

The radical philosopher Slavoj Žižek once criticized mindfulness by asserting that it allows people to get away from their stress without dealing with the underlying causes of their stress. It allows you to be *in the world but not of it*, he explained. We appreciate his point. We can't let the drive for inner serenity obstruct our outward duties.

So what, then, is the alternative?

We believe that it's possible to weave silence into a fully engaged life. If we want to live in the current reality—and if we want to cultivate the strength and focus necessary to make the current reality better—then we need spaces of immersive rest, spaces of minimum sound and stimulus, spaces where we simply don't have to say anything.

We've come to believe that silence is essential for renewal. It's a requirement for doing what's right on a sustainable basis. In the chapters to come, we'll offer scores of recommendations for how to find auditory, informational, and internal quiet while simultaneously fulfilling the obligations of life. But here's one thing we've learned that we'll share right now: *Look to the pros.* Turn to those who have been successfully navigating these questions through fraught circumstances for considerable lengths of time.

Cherri Allison is one such person. She's been on a journey of more than five decades, seeking the righteous balance between speech and silence and between responsibility and renewal.

"For me, as an African American woman growing up in these United States, the constant pressure was to *be* silent," Cherri tells us in a recent interview. She did her best to not succumb to the pressure. "You could fire me; you could dock my pay. But you cannot take my truth from me," she says in earnest. Still, Cherri recognized early that silence *did* have something to offer her—the kind of silence that came through her own volition. "I didn't realize how much *strength* it took to be in that silent place," she tells us. "Finding that silence enabled me to not have to whup nobody's ass, curse nobody out, or get fired from my job—so that I couldn't continue to do the work." The work she wanted to continue—that she was destined for—was the work of justice for victims of violence. It's work for which Cherri, now in her seventies, recently received a lifetime achievement award.

Cherri is the former executive director of one of the largest Family Justice Centers in the country. The center, based in Oakland, California, provides a safe haven from domestic violence, sexual assault, child abuse, elder abuse, and human trafficking. It's a vibrant space, usually scented with lavender and filled with lively conversation, laughter, and music, as well as tissue boxes for the tears that come with the territory. Cherri has always welcomed the full range of expression that lives here—especially the expression that comes from the heart. "You gotta be real brave to go there," she tells us. "I'm talking about sitting, feeling, and *listening* to your heart. And if you do that, those are the times when you're brought to real tears."

Cherri wants to stay connected to those real tears, although she didn't always see how she could do that *and* perform her job. She used to "power through" her workday as she was taught to do in law school, a typical modus operandi in crisis work as well. But she found that the effort of that approach—maintaining that distance from the "deep hurt" in her heart—was unsustainable:

> You're looking at a victim in her face and you're feeling her damaged spirit and her hopelessness, and then she's gone and the next one is right there . . . No pause to let her story sink in . . . It's just Bam! Bam! Bam! Bam! All day.

Her staff might have resorted to the same "power through" strategy, but Cherri was determined that they not make the same mistakes she once made. Cherri says that sitting in silence and listening with the heart bring her and her staff in *direct relationship* with the people they're there to help—lest they forget they are in a role of *service*, not of savior. She advises her staff to "be silent and listen and *witness them into their being.*" She reminds her team to explain all the choices available to them and "sit back and watch them stand in their power." She recalls coming to this realization: "When I finally stopped and talked to a victim *like a person*, instead of being like, 'Oh, *I'm the lawyer.*' Oh my God! So much was revealed to me!" She continues, "They had so much knowledge and information and experience to bring to the table. It made me a *much* better provider of services."

When Cherri took the reins at the Family Justice Center in 2011, she embarked on an experiment. Before she and her senior staff launched into their daily meeting, she asked them to sit in quiet reflection together. Sometimes, they'd start the meeting with a poem or an inspiring quotation. Someone might ask a stirring question. Or they might simply sit and breathe together. She suggested that they mix it up and rotate the leadership. They made space for silence. They made space for their humanity. These practices were *far* outside the operating culture at the time. But Cherri decided—despite feeling vulnerable as a new director—to take that chance. "I've really started to embrace the role of elder," she says. "And what I found is that it comes with a lot of being quiet."

Reflecting on the importance of silence, Cherri says, "I don't care *what* field you're in. Silence is a powerful tool." The daily practice she instituted deepened their cohesion as a team. It fostered a culture of self-care. It helped them to remember to listen with their hearts. The team continued this practice throughout Cherri's tenure, and even after her retirement they continue to do so to this day.

O

Even in the noisiest spheres of life, even amidst the most constant barrage of sound and stimulus, the paths to silence are often surprisingly simple.

When Tim Ryan first ran for the state senate in Ohio, the priest at his Catholic church offered him a set of keys to the sanctuary. While Tim appreciated the gesture, it wasn't until the election got ugly that he came to really appreciate the value and foresight of this gift. The local party bosses decided he was too young to make the jump to the upper house of the legislature. As attack ads, gossip, and campaign roadblocks started to mount, he took advantage of the sanctuary's quiet space as a daily refuge to replenish energy and maintain motivation. He needed it. The church had always been an important place to him; it was where he had grown up, where his grandfather had once been an usher, where he developed his "original connection to quiet time." But it was his experience on the campaign trail that made him recognize the fundamental need for silence as a connection to source.

When we spoke with Tim Ryan, now a senior Democratic member of Congress, he told us about the power of silence in his life today. He describes it as an essential source of energy and patience that fuels his capacity to respond to the important signals in a sustainable way. "When you're quiet, you get that inner conviction that's essential to taking on big challenges . . . and to living the life you want to live. It's got to come from the inside out," he tells us. "If you have nothing but noise in your head and around you, it's tough to get tuned in. It's beyond reason. It's beyond your brain."

THE TYRANNY OF THE GRIND

The noise of the world is on the rise.

But so, too, are the signals. So, too, are the indicators of what really requires our attention.

There's not just a growing amount of unwanted interference but a rise in genuine and important cries for help. Whether it's alarming news about refugees or environmental crises or personal outreach from loved ones feeling mired in depression and despair, so much of the sound and stimulus of the modern world *is* justified. It's not "distraction." It's signaling the need for change.

Looking at the world today, there's a little-examined linkage between the signal and the noise. The more noise we generate, the more numerous and desperate the signals for help become. What's at risk when we're agitated by the jagged soundscape? What's the cost when our attention is overwhelmed? What's at stake when we're primarily consumed with the chatter in our heads? There's one common answer for sure: We're less capable of caring for one another and being good stewards of nature. The ethical imperative for quiet time isn't just personal. It's planetary.

The performance artist, theologian, and activist Tricia Hersey draws a clear link between a culture of noise and the problems of apathy, burnout, and even trauma. She's organized a "Rest School"—in the spirit of the legendary Freedom Schools of the 1960s—to train activists on the front lines of today's justice struggles to pause for centering and renewal. She evangelizes quiet time as a bold and beautiful act of resistance to what she calls "grind culture." "Let's see if we can work a human being like a machine and have them work up to twenty hours a day, every day, for centuries," she says, drawing a line from slavery to a modern domination paradigm that devalues our needs for silence, for rest, for sleep, and for dream time. "Grinding keeps us in a cycle of trauma. Rest can disrupt this cycle," she says. Looking at the culture we live in—one that celebrates an addiction to the maximum production of mental stuff—she lauds the power of silence as a "veil buster" and recommends the cultivation of an oft-overlooked life skill: napping. "The guilt and shame you feel about napping doesn't belong to you. It's misplaced. Rest is a primal need and a divine right."

In her breakthrough book, *How to Do Nothing: Resisting the Attention Economy*, Jenny Odell points out how a culture that glorifies busyness and maximum noise keeps us separated from nature, ultimately driving ecological crises. As she puts it, a growth-obsessed economic system and "colonialist thinking, loneliness, and an abusive stance toward the environment all coproduce one another." The modern obsession with mental stuff—massively amplified by the rise of online life—means a shift from physical "presence" on Earth to a disembodied "presence" on the internet. Odell prescribes the remedy of "placefulness," or what she calls "bioregionalism." It's the practice of paying attention to the place you live—the flora and fauna, the climate, the terrain, the ways the landscapes interact with the cultures. Odell finds placefulness through birding. Whatever way you find it, one thing is certain: it requires quiet attention. In a conversation with Liv O'Keeffe of the California Native Plant Society, Odell says, "Bioregionalism gives us a sense of home, a way to engage and feel a part of something at a time when everyone is pitted against each other and atomized." Speaking personally, she adds, "It's the only way I know of to reliably get outside of this myopic and narrow and overstimulated and fearful, isolated self that is cultivated online."

So, what is the place of wordlessness in the work of justice? How do we balance the necessity of decisiveness with the necessity of calm and clear seeing? How do we respond to the cries of the world with timely earnestness, nonetheless avoiding the distortions of noise and urgency? How do we drop beneath the artifice of intellectual concepts so that we can feel another person's pain—or even our own?

Hersey, Odell, and other contemporary voices echo what Gandhi emphasized seventy-five years ago: finding silence is an ethical necessity. As Saint Bernard, the patron saint of the Cistercians, once reflected on the message of the prophet Isaiah: "Silence is the work of justice."

But this work requires continual care and attention.

THE FINE ART OF DISCERNING

We asked Cyrus Habib, who you met in chapter 2, about the link between silence and justice. He points us to a single word: "discernment."

He likens it to how, "when you're in an argument with a person you love, it's best to not say the first thing in your head. The stillness and silence," he says, "even if it's just thirty seconds, can be so helpful in figuring out how to proceed." This same logic, Cyrus points out, applies to the macro-level work of making systemic change. As a high-profile politician, Cyrus was accustomed to a mode of social action that's all about moving quickly, responding to events instantly, and optimizing how you appear in a press release. But discernment, he emphasizes, is about the slower, often invisible work of determining what's true. It's about envisioning what it means to fix something—*really* fix something—rather than applying a Band-Aid. He's been focused on building his capacity for discernment through deep silent practices as a Jesuit, finding the true signal amidst the static. He emphasizes discernment as a kind of meeting point between contemplation and action.

Cyrus shares with us the example of how the Jesuits have been grappling with the question of reparations for slavery. In 1838, a group of Jesuits in Maryland sold 272 Black persons as slaves to Louisiana plantation owners in order to pay off the debts of the then fledgling Georgetown University. Over the past decade, there's finally been a reckoning for these atrocities. The religious society and the descendants jointly created the foundation to facilitate fact-finding and dialogue in 2019, laying the groundwork for a reparations program. In 2021, they announced an initial $100 million commitment for investments aimed at improving the lives of the descendants of the 272 men, women, and children.

While these efforts are way ahead of the U.S. government and the vast majority of educational and religious institutions in addressing the legacies of slavery, Cyrus emphasizes that the Jesuit initiative has been criticized for a simple reason: it's slow. Even after four years of study and dialogue, they're still in a learning phase. It'll be years more before any real action commences. While Cyrus, who was trained as a lawyer, admits he still sometimes gets antsy with the pace, he tells us, "This is part of the point."

The process is happening through "a lot of silence," he says. A key pillar of the reparations work is quiet listening. It's listening to the descendants of the people who were enslaved, understanding how to be fair and effective and how to build genuine partnership and trust. It's listening internally, too. Cyrus emphasizes that the process is happening through a lot of prayer and contemplation—a rigorous inner search for signals about the right way to proceed.

"Why does it take so long?" Cyrus asks. "It's the need for *discernment*."

In the Quaker tradition, this process of discerning is often called threshing—separation of the wheat from the chaff. While the Quakers are known for the silent religious meetings wherein they're counseled to *only speak when the spirit moves you*, they, too, emphasize a practical dimension to silence. The Quakers have a particular kind of gathering called a Meeting for Worship for the Purpose of Business, where they search for answers to worldly questions, like how to deal with disputes among members or how to make financial decisions as an organization. When things get heated or stuck or confused, the person chairing the meeting, the "clerk," will call for a period of group silent contemplation. This is a primary tool for threshing.

"For some, it's potentially uncomfortable in that quiet," says Rob Lippincott. "But I would suggest that the power of that moment is exactly when it becomes uncomfortable." Rob is a birthright Quaker who has been a lecturer in education at Harvard as well as a senior vice president at PBS, among many other roles in public and nonprofit service. He notes how a common default in times of conflict is more and more talk and posturing and positioning. Disagreement usually turns up the volume. But the Quaker tradition encourages a reverse response: shared silence. They employ silence to transform the dynamic in the search of "unity." Rob elaborates, "It's not really a consensus, exactly. It's sort of mutual consent. It's not a deep 100 percent agreement. It is more like 'I will not stand in the way.'"

"When the clerk calls for silence," Rob says, "I allow myself to get centered. I take a breath. Then I'm able to focus. What's the real issue? What's the real conflict? Am I upset about something? Is there a defect in reasoning somewhere?" When the period of silence is done right, he says, everything stops. You won't even hear the rustling of papers. "The silence allows me to back off from my 'jump right in' instinct," Rob says. "It allows me to wait, maybe even for someone else who may feel a little more clear to speak, which is often the most shocking and interesting to me," he says. He tells us it's not uncommon for someone else to say exactly what he was thinking, only clearer. "It's like, 'Wow! We're making progress.' It's an exercise in togetherness."

TRUTH AND POWER

In his book *Consolations: The Solace, Nourishment, and Underlying Meaning of Everyday Words*, the poet David Whyte offers the following:

> In silence, essence speaks to us of essence itself and asks for a kind of unilateral disarmament, our own essential nature slowly emerging as the defended periphery atomizes and falls apart. As the busy edge

dissolves, we begin to join the conversation through the portal of a present unknowing, robust vulnerability, revealing in the way we listen, a different ear, a more perceptive eye, an imagination refusing to come too early to a conclusion, and belonging to a different person than the one who first entered the quiet.

In the world of geopolitics, the phrase "unilateral disarmament" usually signifies an abdication of the responsibility to defend yourself, laying down the arms that you need in order to assert your sovereignty. Often, we do, indeed, use words to uphold our identity, to assert our individuality, to defend our point of view. And sometimes we need to, in order to signal what's necessary and hold our ground in the inevitable skirmishes that happen in a world of point and counterpoint.

But what happens when we simply lay down these arms? What happens when we let go of having to have an opinion or defend a viewpoint in order to prove our worth? "Robust vulnerability," says Whyte. "Present unknowing." A refinement of perception. A revelation of our deeper nature.

When Rob Lippincott describes the conscious intervention of silence in a contentious meeting, he's not describing a kind of censorship. He's talking about the introduction of spaciousness. What needs to be spoken can be spoken, but without the perfunctory pressure. In the claustrophobic gridlock of opinions, a hidden door opens. You feel a fresh breeze.

It's like the clarity and presence that Sheena Malhotra describes—the one that flowered in those nine minutes of silence at the Black Lives Matter demonstration in Los Angeles. Or, as Cyrus discussed, the slow and quiet work of discernment being taken on by Jesuits today. Wordlessness has a place in the work of justice. It is essential to resolving challenges, both big and small.

While the Quaker faith is all about the practice of silence, the Quakers also cherish the principle of "speaking truth to power." The first known use of this phrase in print is from a 1950s publication called

Speak Truth to Power: A Quaker Search for an Alternative to Violence that sought to inspire people to challenge nuclear weapons development and Cold War militarism. In conversation with Rob, we explored this simple proposition: *the hardest part of speaking truth to power is discerning truth itself.* "To listen for truth is something that's really a discipline; it's the fundamental of meditation," Rob tells us. "If it's so clear to me that something is true as I've plumbed the depths in silence, then it's worth sharing."

As with the galvanizing speeches Gandhi delivered on Tuesdays after coming out of his weekly retreats, there's a certain moral dimension to the words that emerge from silence. Gandhi used a particular Sanskrit term, *satyagraha*, to describe the spiritual power of the movement he helped to lead. It's a word that conveys this particular quality of speech that arises out of the wholeness of the ineffable.

Like the Quaker value of "speaking truth to power," the word *satyagraha* is translated as "the force which is born of truth." Clear perception. Clear action. It's the bridge between silence and justice.

None of this is to say that quiet time will automatically solve the problems of the age. It is, of course, vital to do the worldly work of justice, too: to challenge oppressive systems, to radically reduce greenhouse gas emissions, to build equitable economies. All of these shifts are necessary. And yet, on their own, they're not sufficient. Unless we deal with the underlying urgency and agitation in human consciousness, even the most enlightened policies won't resolve the social and ecological crises we face today. Unless we reimagine our conceptions of "success" and "progress," rethinking the paradigm of GDP obsession and the maximum possible production of sound-stimulus-and-stuff, the tyrannies of what Tricia Hersey calls "grind culture" will persist.

PART II

THE SCIENCE OF SILENCE

CHAPTER 5

FLORENCE NIGHTINGALE WOULD BE PISSED

When Faith Fuller was a little girl, she loved losing herself in the dense forests of the Berkshire mountains of western Connecticut. "We didn't really have neighbors," she tells us, "and life at home was . . . complicated." As the youngest—by far—of four kids, she grew up functioning as an only child. "The woods were my companion. I felt seen, recognized, and known by the woods." Faith immersed herself in daylong excursions: wading into ice-cold streams, foraging for treasures, resting on her belly to behold the bright red clover mites that speckled the forest floor. "From the age of six to about ten, there was no real difference between me and the woods," she recalls.

As she entered adulthood, Faith turned to meditation and found another reliable route to immersive silence. For more than six decades, she has sought and savored these states. Silence has been a source of companionship and renewal.

But she never expected it to be the medical prescription that would someday save her life.

One day in 2015, on her way home from work, Faith was hit head-on by an oncoming car. That car, she's told, jumped the median, forcing her car up onto the sidewalk, through some foliage, and into a cement wall. "My shoulder was pulverized, like little clumps of gravel," she tells us. But her brain had also been badly injured. "Coming back from a bad brain trauma is like being reborn in this sense; you're infantile, initially, you don't have much language, you have trouble following directions, and if they're complicated"—she shrugs—"You just say, 'Fuck it, *I can't*.'" Faith described her brain at the time as tender and raw.

Initially, Faith's brain injury was too severe for her to speak with the medical staff directly. She lacked not only words but a sense of time and place, even identity. She recognized only her own name and the presence of her wife, Marita, who was managing everything. The medical team assessed Faith's progress throughout each day. "I would claw my way up to answer or be responsive. But it was *exhausting*," Faith remembers. "Then I would drop and let go into nothing. But it wasn't a scary nothing. It was supportive and nurturing. It's where I needed to be."

Faith describes the period leading up to the accident as "busy, busy, busy, busy—but not trivial busy, *meaningfully* busy." Still, Faith knew there were limits to what she could sustain even then. "You can think of me in the world as a sort of a bubbling stream," she says, harkening to the streams of her childhood. "But the stream has a source. The source is the huge, vast silence, and the bubbling stream comes right out of that huge, vast silence. And if I bubble along in the stream too long—and don't get back to that silence—the stream dries up."

As co-founder and president of an international training and coaching firm, Faith had been continuously traveling the world—from San

Francisco to Dubai to Tokyo to Istanbul—advising organizational leaders and teaching and managing teams of consultants. She was doing her best to make time for meditation and time in nature, but her stream was running dry. "I went to see the scars and skid marks where I'd been pushed off the road," she says. "It's funny, I didn't *really* get it for some time. But I was shoved off the road I had been on—quite literally *and* metaphorically."

Faith's medical team emphasized a protocol to avoid overstimulation of key regions of the recovering brain. She rested in a space with low light and little sound, where caretakers kept their voices to a whisper. For weeks after the injury, Faith's doctors discouraged her from working, socializing, using her smartphone, or generally taking in a lot of information. But, for Faith, there seemed to be something more to the prescription than the simple physiological rationale that the doctors gave her. The first few days after the accident—before Faith had any sense of time or place—were, as she put it, "rather lovely, because there was no internal dialogue . . . no narrative of the self." She laughs and says, "Sure, I was brain damaged and heavily drugged. But the quiet was *profound*. It was an oceanic experience."

Faith believes that the respite from ordinary sound and stimuli created space in her consciousness. It was the aperture through which healing arrived. When we spoke recently with Faith, she was unequivocal: "Silence allows the brain to recover."

Faith's healing after the accident revived in her a reverence for and commitment to silence. That "oceanic experience" was new, but not altogether unfamiliar. Over time, it became an inspiration to return more regularly to "the source"—to make ample time for quiet reflection, meditation, and jaunts in the woods like the ones she took as a girl. She, Marita, and their two beloved dogs moved from the bustling Bay Area to a rural part of Oregon, a place of plentiful songbirds and fewer distractions.

Faith's healing also provoked in her a question that no single physician or scientific expert has been able to satisfactorily answer:

What is the biological basis of the power of silence to heal the body and clarify the mind?

It's a question that researchers are just beginning to explore.

EXPECTATIONS IN THE MIND

Silence—at the auditory level—has historically been of little interest to mainstream science. It's been a control variable in laboratory research rather than a primary subject of investigation. In fact, most scientists who have uncovered useful insights about silence have done so accidentally.

Consider Dr. Luciano Bernardi. A professor of internal medicine at Italy's University of Pavia and an enthusiastic amateur musician, he took on a passion project in the early years of the twenty-first century: investigating classical Greek philosophers' notion that music supports good health. He studied the effects of six types of music—all with varying tempos, rhythms, and melodic structures—on the cardiovascular and respiratory systems of his test subjects. He randomly ordered the tracks from the six selected types of music and inserted two-minute "pauses" of silence to bring the subjects back to baseline. But something strange happened. When the subjects listened to these pauses, they didn't return to baseline. They relaxed. In fact, they relaxed so much more profoundly during the silent pauses than during even the slowest, most soothing pieces of music that Bernardi had to rethink the whole premise of his experiment. He ended up concluding that silence was a more potent contributor to good cardiovascular and respiratory health than music. In 2006, Bernardi's study was the most downloaded article in *Heart*, a peer-reviewed journal of cardiologists. While it might seem intuitive that silence would calm the circulatory systems, no one had empirically demonstrated it before. Bernardi, inadvertently, helped to prompt a shift. It is now generally accepted that silence is more than just a control variable.

In fact, today, silence is an increasingly prime-time area of scientific investigation. Since Bernardi's study was published, neuroscientists at Stanford have determined how those silent intervals between pieces of music activate the parts of our brains associated with the kind of relaxed attention that boosts working memory. Building upon a growing interest in the science of mindfulness, researchers at universities around the world have used fMRI equipment—imaging technology that makes it possible to follow blood flow through the brain—to demonstrate how silent meditation practices help to improve attention and mitigate factors related to depression and anxiety. A range of studies have demonstrated how silent meditation helps us to better discern between important and superfluous stimuli—"The signal and the noise." While physicians have in the past disagreed about the value of "cognitive rest" for recovery from concussions and other traumatic brain injuries, new findings reinforce the importance of protocols like the one Faith undertook. There's increasing recognition that avoiding "cognitive strain"—too much mental stimulus—allows the regeneration of neurons and the restoration of brain functions.

These leading-edge scientific findings reinforce what grandmotherly folk wisdom has passed on for millennia. And more than 150 years ago, one of the world's most prominent medical professionals advocated powerfully for silence as a necessity for good health.

In the autumn of 1854, Florence Nightingale, the gifted daughter of a wealthy English family, volunteered for an assignment in one of the most squalid and depressing settings imaginable. She led a staff of nurses at Scutari Hospital, in present-day Istanbul, serving injured and infirm soldiers in the Crimean War. The hospital was built above a sewer that routinely burst open, leaving seriously ill patients wading in sewage. Ten times more soldiers died of diseases contracted in the hospital—including typhus, typhoid, cholera, and dysentery—than from injuries incurred in battle. Gangrenous wounds went unattended, and even the most basic hygienic standards of the day were ignored. British army bureaucrats were mostly indifferent. They had a war to win.

In those days, conditions in a military hospital were mostly the concern of voluntary religious institutions and charity organizations. Nightingale—who was the first female fellow of the Royal Statistical Society—bypassed the army bureaucracy by masterfully presenting visual data. In a colorful one-page pie chart, she demonstrated a plummet in preventable diseases and infections under her patient care protocols. She was then able to quickly implement sweeping reforms like cleaning and handwashing requirements while ensuring the provision of basic nutrition for patients. Conditions improved dramatically. Amidst the death and stench of Scutari, it's almost inconceivable that anyone would prioritize auditory noise as a top-tier concern. But Nightingale did.

In 1859, reflecting on her experience in the Crimean War, Nightingale wrote, "Unnecessary noise, then, is the most cruel absence of care which can be inflicted either on sick or well." In treating soldiers for symptoms that she described as "palpitations, sweats, deep fatigue, sighing respiration, a persistent quick-acting heart"—conditions now generally considered related to PTSD—Nightingale advocated for silence as the most important cure. Following her time in Crimea, she wrote thousands of letters and dozens of books, reports, and plans focused on building more humane and effective systems of care, especially for the urban poor. In these documents, she frequently described how "alarming noise" in hospitals produced a specific set of conditions that undermined health and blocked healing: raised blood pressure, sleeplessness, heightened anxiety.

While Nightingale was concerned about overall volume levels, she had a sophisticated way of distinguishing between different kinds of noises. Above all, she railed against the kind of "noise that creates an expectation in the mind," like the sounds of whispered conversations, hallway chats just out of range of intelligibility. These are noises that keep the mind racing, or, in her words, deny a patient the feeling of "closure." She refers to the kind of noise that makes a claim on our consciousness—the kind that lingers in both the body and the mind.

So, why did Florence Nightingale—in a putrid abyss of amputated limbs and mind-boggling filth—focus so much on the seemingly measly problem of noise? It's because she recognized something about the nature of noise. It pulls us from the presence that's necessary for healing. It's the strain on our adaptive capacities, a driver of fight-or-flight response, an almost universal threat to the felt sense of well-being.

Noise, in essence, is stress.

Modern research backs up this proposition.

Twenty years ago, Rosalind Rolland, a scientist at the New England Aquarium, was trying to understand how environmental factors impact reproductive and endocrine functions in endangered ocean mammals. She and her team trained dogs to detect the smell of whale feces in the ocean while riding on boats. Then, in Canada's Bay of Fundy, divers collected samples of whale poop to analyze hormone levels. Rolland's team looked at how various conditions in the aquatic surroundings, including noise, changed the chemical compositions of the samples. In 2001, they witnessed an extreme—almost overnight—drop in the presence of stress hormones in their study samples. The following season, however, they found that the stress hormone levels had gone right back up to their previous norms. Rolland examined all the possible factors, including measurement—by hydrophone—of sound levels transmitted through the bay waters. She and her team came to see just one plausible explanation for the sudden drop in stress: a temporary pause in ocean shipping traffic with the suspension of global trade that followed the September 11 attacks. Something similar happened in the spring of 2020, when global ocean traffic rapidly declined amidst the COVID-19 pandemic. While no one took the initiative for another whale-feces-sniffing-dog expedition, maritime scientists all over the world listened in on their hydrophones. Many heard a resurgent chorus of whale songs—a leading indicator of health—that had long been suppressed in noisy, high-traffic waters.

We're a lot like our fellow mammals in the ocean. And for us there's a clear physiological explanation for the link between noise and stress. When sound waves hit our eardrums, they vibrate the bones of the inner ear, causing ripples and waves in the fluids of a pea-sized, spiral-shaped cavity called the cochlea. Tiny hairlike structures inside the cochlea convert these movements into electrical signals that the auditory nerve transmits to the brain. Neuroscientists have found that these signals go to the amygdalae, the two almond-shaped clusters of neurons that arguably form the main biological basis of our emotional lives, including our quick-action impulses like the fight-or-flight response. When signals hit the amygdala, it starts the process through which we secrete stress hormones. Too many stimuli result in excessive stress, as evidenced by the presence of stress chemicals, like cortisol, in our blood. But the toll of stress doesn't end there. Under what are called "safe and social conditions," our tiny middle-ear muscles are activated, allowing us to tune in to mid-range frequencies, like those of the human voice. However, when we're in a fight-or-flight mode, these tiny muscles deactivate; we primarily hear lower frequencies, like those of past predators, and higher frequencies, like those of another person or creature screaming in pain. The mid-range frequencies become harder to hear. In other words, under duress, we actually *stop hearing* one another.

"Noises cause stress, especially if we have little or no control over them," explains Mathias Basner, a professor at the University of Pennsylvania who specializes in auditory processing and rest. "The body will excrete stress hormones like adrenaline and cortisol that lead to changes in the composition of our blood—and of our blood vessels, which actually have been shown to be stiffer after a single night of noise exposure," Basner says, describing the classic pathway of noise-induced stress. For years, our concern has been that excessive noise can cause hearing loss—a serious issue that can also lead to social isolation and loneliness. But a broad set of peer-reviewed papers over the past few decades have shown risks that include cardiovascular disease, arterial hypertension, stroke, obesity, diabetes, decreases in cognitive function and learning, depression, and sleep disturbances, as well as the diverse complications that happen downstream of any of these.

Like those stressed-out whales in the Bay of Fundy, we're bearing real physiological impacts from rising noise levels. Globally, the World Health Organization now ranks noise pollution as second only to air pollution in terms of costs to human well-being. A recent study by the WHO calculates a loss of 1–1.6 million life years annually in western Europe alone due to illness, disability, and early death. In 2019, Bruitparif, a French nonprofit organization that monitors noise levels, published a report analyzing "noise maps" generated by a network of acoustic sensors. The report concluded that an average resident of any of the loudest parts of Paris and its surrounding suburbs loses "more than three healthy life-years" to some combination of conditions caused or worsened by the noise of cars, trucks, airplanes, trains, and other industrial machines. Paris ranks ninth in a recent index of the fifty loudest cities in the world. This makes us wonder: How many healthy life years are lost by the average resident of the three loudest cities in the world—Guangzhou, Delhi, and Cairo—for which no such statistics exist? How about the increasingly noisy fast-growing cities in the developing world for which there are few, if any, decibel-monitoring activities?

As with other kinds of pollution, the impacts of noise fall disproportionately on people without economic or political power. As the journalist Bianca Bosker puts it, "Noise is never just about sound; it is inseparable from issues of power and powerlessness." A recent nationwide study in the United States suggests that poorer urban neighborhoods are typically two decibels louder than affluent areas. On a logarithmic scale, this registers. The findings also claim that cities with larger proportions of Black, Hispanic, and Asian residents consistently face higher noise levels.

Regrettably, more noise also means less sleep, and less sleep is turning out to be a far bigger issue than perhaps any of us had imagined. The sleep researcher and neuroscientist Matthew Walker puts it bluntly: "The shorter your sleep, the shorter your life span." With the advent of personal fitness tracking devices, like Fitbit, a breakthrough 2015 study found sleep disturbances are five times more likely to plague Black research participants. This "sleep gap" contributes to numerous downstream health effects that, according to Walker, include heart disease, obesity, dementia, diabetes, and cancer. In his best-selling book, *Why We Sleep: Unlocking the Power of Sleep and Dreams*, Walker writes, "The best bridge between despair and hope is a good night's sleep." But, when we live in unremittingly loud environments, it can be hard—if not impossible—to cross that bridge.

It's not that Florence Nightingale's warnings are uniformly ignored in the modern world. Faith's doctors, for example, recognized the reality that auditory noise is stress in the body and mind and that it's necessary for a healing patient to avoid it. But these kinds of protocols are the exception. In spite of what modern research is showing about the stress effects of excessive auditory stimulation on human health, most of our hospitals are off-the-charts noisy, as Justin's experience in the newborn intensive care unit illustrated. The average intensive care unit (ICU) frequently registers on par with "a lively restaurant" rather than the thirty-five decibels recommended by the World Health Organization. One study found "peaks above 85 dBA occurred at all sites, up to 16 times per hour overnight and more frequently during the day." According to a 2005 Johns Hopkins study, the decibel levels of its hospitals have climbed an average of four decibels per decade since 1960, which they suspect to be true of nearly all modern hospitals today.

Spikes in decibel levels are often due to sounding alarms. Of course, alarms are necessary in a hospital setting. Ideally, they're *signals* to clinicians about what has to be done. And yet there's also a problematic "convenience addiction" at play, wherein we're failing to consider the true costs of excessive alarms. We recently learned about a heart monitor that has eighty-six different sonic notifications. *Eighty-six.* It would take an acoustic savant to distinguish one from another, and even if that were possible, leading research shows that anywhere from 72 to 99 percent of clinical alarms are false. This gives rise to a condition of alarm fatigue—when a medical professional misses or delays response to an alarm due to sensory overload. While it's possible to study the impacts of rising noise on medical staff, it's harder to quantify the far-reaching physiological and psychological consequences in patients.

What would Florence Nightingale say?

NOISE BEGETS NOISE

Faith knew she was in good hands. Her medical team was keenly aware of the importance of a serene auditory soundscape. Faith described the feeling of this time as being "gently packed in the softest possible material—like a soft cotton wool." Silence was a healing presence. And yet, as she recovered, Faith still struggled mightily with other kinds of noise—informational and internal.

Despite decades of Buddhist training and practice in the art of managing mental chatter, Faith quickly found herself overtaken with the impulse to pick up her phone, open her laptop, and, most of all, ruminate over all the responsibilities she'd left unattended. "I wasn't allowed to work," she recalls. "The doctors were always pissed off at me because I couldn't stand it—not doing things!" She reckons she could have been easier on the medical team: "They just want to give your brain a freakin' rest." But instead, just weeks into her recovery, she was fixated on the preparation and logistics for a planned work trip to Europe. She was still going, she told everyone. "It was comical," she admits now. "I had this inability to disengage. It was the hardest part of the prescription."

While it might seem as if Faith were just an incorrigible workaholic, she was acting out a tendency for which we're all hardwired. We're information-seeking creatures. It's natural that we incessantly grasp for mental stuff. In chapter 2, we introduced you to Adam Gazzaley and Larry Rosen, the neuroscientist-psychologist duo who have extensively studied how our "ancient brains" operate in a modern world. They explain how we're "driven for information rewards in very much the same systems that drove other animals to seek food and juice rewards, even though it's not critical for survival." In other words, the physio-logical mechanisms of the human brain don't always distinguish much between clicking a juicy hyperlink underneath a news story or picking a ripened blackberry while foraging in the forest. "Information alone triggers these same ancient reward mechanisms," Gazzaley and Rosen explain. It's no wonder that we devour news feeds and email and gossip. For our ancient brains, it's irresistibly tasty.

As Faith's condition improved, her doctors steadily let up on the rest protocols. And, with the leniency, her information-foraging ten-dencies went full throttle. Faith returned to what she calls the "default reality" of information saturation. "I was bound and determined to get right back to normal, to underplay any symptoms, including the nine months of double vision I had." As she returned to the external crescendo of sound and stimulus, Faith noticed an increase in her own ruminative thinking. "My internal silence *diminished* as I recovered," she remembers.

Faith's experience brings us back to the notion that there are subtle linkages between different kinds of noises. Auditory, informational, and internal distractions all reinforce each other.

To understand how this reinforcement works, Gazzaley and Rosen say it's important to consider a push and pull of two competing forces: *top-down* and *bottom-up* attention. The first, *top-down* attention, is our focus on individual goals—like fetching water or food for the fam-ily or writing a novel or following the doctor's recommendations for recovery from a head injury. The second is *bottom-up* attention—the stimulus we react to, whether it's a falling tree branch or a honking car horn or our name being called out in a crowd. Gazzaley and Rosen say that constant connectivity has made us more sensitive to bottom-up interference than ever before. It's made our worlds noisier—*both inside and out.* "Tech device notifications and societal expectations that have conditioned us to respond more reflexively to external bottom-up dis-tractions have also led to more internally generated distractions," they argue.

In our conversations, Gazzaley and Rosen describe this state to us as an "interference dilemma."

We think of it as a *noise dilemma*.

In the modern world, "bottom-up interference" usually starts with something beeping or vibrating in your pocket. As innocuous as a gentle buzz or custom ringtone may seem, they conjure mental projections that bloom like algae in the mind. Whether or not we realize it, that bottom-up interference often devolves into a feedback loop of both external and internal noise.

Here's an illustrative example from Gazzaley and Rosen. Say you're driving through busy traffic on a highway, and you get a text (a bottom-up interference). You stay focused on driving safely to your destination (your top-down goal). But, as hard as you try to ignore it, the vibrating begins to feel, in their words, "like a burning ember in your pocket that is accompanied by rising anxiety—'who is texting at this hour, and what do they have to tell you?'" (This is a bottom-up distraction from your own mind.) With your attention diverted, you miss your exit, and you have to interrupt your safe driving yet again to pick up your phone and reroute your course. All of this has to happen in order to get back on track toward your original top-down goal.

That one simple buzz—that bottom-up distraction—produces a cascade of internal and external interference. Noise begets noise.

Understanding this dynamic helps us better understand the role of noise in cognition. In the 1970s, the pioneering environmental psychologist Arline Bronzaft found that the reading test scores of Manhattan middle schoolers whose classrooms faced high-decibel elevated subway tracks lagged up to a year behind those of students in quieter classrooms on the opposite side of the building. Since the stress response to noise is well established, it was clear that intermittent spikes in decibel levels—almost on par with a heavy metal concert—were inherently problematic. But the issue was more than agitated amygdalae. Looking through the Gazzaley-Rosen lens, we can see that the fleeting bottom-up interference of the screeching trains probably broke students' concentration, sending them off into their discursive thoughts, undermining the top-down goal of listening to the teacher. External noise likely fed internal noise, damaging attention, and in turn challenging cognition and memory.

While the subway track study is an example of simple auditory interference, Gazzaley and Rosen's example of the driver's buzzing smartphone goes deeper. This kind of decidedly modern digital simulation reminds us, strangely, of Florence Nightingale, writing by candlelight in her stately home in Victorian London. Why? Because the common denominator to the buzzing, pinging, chirping forms of bottom-up noise that we encounter in the modern soundscape is "expectation in the mind." Like the whispered conversations and hallway chats just out of range of intelligibility in a nineteenth-century infirmary, news alerts and notifications of Instagram likes charge up our ruminating minds, denying us what Nightingale called the feeling of "closure."

A recent study of several hundred teenagers in the Netherlands found high levels of social media usage were significantly linked to reduced attention and increased tendencies of impulsivity and hyperactivity a year later. Another recent study of sixteen hundred American adults found that just a one-month break from Facebook resulted in substantial improvements in emotional well-being, including reductions in self-reported loneliness and increases in self-reported happiness.

"It's the inside noise, the inside interference, that is the most insidious," Larry Rosen tells us in a recent conversation. For young people especially, the use of tech platforms comes with a host of what he calls "social obligations"—the need to regularly check in, keep up your persona, and reply to messages promptly, lest you leave someone "on read," waiting for a response. These obligations might seem trite, but they fill the consciousness with distracted chatter. Rosen sees them as a preeminent cause of rising modern anxiety—what he describes as "stress in the mind."

We spoke recently with Judson Brewer, the neuroscientist and psychiatrist, about the relationship between anxiety and internal noise.

"It's a direct link," he tells us. "Anxiety," he says, "is not only having a bunch of repetitive thoughts; it's getting caught up in them." Brewer emphasized that those "repetitive thoughts" arise when we don't have enough information to accurately predict the future. We're subject to perseverate on them, to get stuck in worry.

"Fear + Uncertainty = Anxiety," he summarizes.

With the exponentially increasing volume of information in the world, it seems, in theory, that there should be *less* uncertainty and in turn less anxiety. But it doesn't quite work that way. "It's like drinking out of a fire hose," Brewer says when describing the modern information stream. We don't have nearly enough working memory to make use of it all. What's more, with the rise of rampant misinformation and disinformation, the increase in inaccurate content means more uncertainty, reduced trust, and, accordingly, more anxiety. Brewer underscores how clickbait news, algorithm advertising, and other cunning means of continuous engagement tickle our dopamine receptors—our reward centers that are supposed to promote life-sustaining behaviors like eating and procreating—in ways that no one had ever previously imagined. "The dopamine pathways have always been there," Brewer says. "They're our oldest survival mechanism. But they've never been tapped this way before." In an effort to address one important piece of misinformation, he adds, "A lot of people write about dopamine as this happiness molecule. It is *not*. Ask any of my patients who are addicted to cocaine. It makes them restless, paranoid, contracted; there's no happiness in that."

Our economic and social systems increasingly seem to be built on vicious feedback loops of inner and outer noise.

Today, there's a growing understanding of the implications of all the noise for our mental clarity and well-being. As Ethan Kross, a University of Michigan psychologist, writes in his best-selling book, *Chatter*, "Verbal rumination concentrates our attention narrowly on the source of our emotional distress, thus stealing neurons that could better serve us." He explains that "we jam our executive functions"—our capacities to attend to top-down goals—"By attending to a 'dual task,' the task of doing whatever it is we want to do and the task of listening to our pained inner voice." Internal noise—at any age—includes all of the pained chatter of the self *about the self* in its past, present, and future circumstances, be they real or imagined.

There's also increasing recognition of physiological consequences of internal noise. Steve Cole, a professor of medicine at UCLA, has documented how the sense of chronic threat that often comes with overactive internal dialogue leads to an overexpression of inflammation genes. As he and his colleagues point out, this can also mean a decrease in expression of the cells that are needed to defend against viruses and other pathogens. Kross summarizes the leading edge of the research this way: "When our internal conversations activate our threat system frequently over time, they send messages to our cells that trigger the expression of inflammation genes, which are meant to protect us in the short term but cause harm in the long term." As Kross emphasizes, "Genes are like keys on a piano." When we get caught in ruminative chatter, we hit discordant notes.

So, given all that we now know about the causes and consequences of noise, what can we say about the biological basis of the power of silence to heal the body and clarify the mind?

There's one common element to all the unwanted interference in the inner and outer soundscape. It is, in a word, stress. Noise drives the fight-or-flight response, pulling our physical and cognitive systems out of equilibrium. Different kinds of noises feed each other, creating pernicious feedback loops that strain our felt sense of well-being and tax our bodily health—down to the cellular level.

While decades of research demonstrate the importance of transcending noise for achieving good health and cognition, we recognize that there's another aspect to Faith's question that's still left unanswered. Her intuition that silence enabled her to recover—that it provided the aperture through which healing arrived—was about more than simply transcending noise. It was something active, too.

THIS IS YOUR BRAIN ON THE OCEANIC EXPERIENCE

Professor Imke Kirste of Duke University Medical School led an unusual study, placing mice inside anechoic chambers for two hours a day—miniature versions of what John Cage entered at Harvard in 1951. She and her team tested for responses to five types of sounds: mice pup sounds, white noise, Mozart's Sonata for Two Pianos in D, ambient sound, and silence. Inside the anechoic chamber, the mice could hear only the direct sound of pups, white noise, or the classical virtuosos without interference from ambient sounds. As for the exposure to silence, researchers let the chamber work its magic, eliminating outside noise while absorbing all reflections of sound and electromagnetic waves inside. Following the application of each sonic variable, the team measured cell growth in each mouse's hippocampus—the region of the brain most associated with memory. Kirste and her team ultimately rejected their hypothesis that pup sounds would yield the strongest results. Silence, in fact, elicited the strongest response from the mice, yielding the highest number of newly grown and sustained neurons. *Listening to silence* demonstrably accelerated the growth of vital brain cells.

Yet in Kirste's analysis the power of silence didn't have to do with relaxation. Counterintuitively, she noted that the salutary silence actually presented as *a kind of stress.*

Of the four stimuli, she wrote, silence was "the most arousing, because it is highly atypical under wild conditions and must thus be perceived as alerting." While she agrees that most everyday stress undermines the growth and healing of the brain, Kirste sees the particular "stress" of novel silence as something different—something that might even be considered "good stress" or "eustress." This term, eustress, was coined in the 1970s by the endocrinologist Hans Selye to describe intense exertion that actually *enhances* functioning. Kirste clarifies what's going on here. "Functional imaging studies indicate that trying to hear in silence activates the auditory cortex," she says, "putting 'the sound of silence,' the absence of expected sound, at the same level with actual sounds."

So, in short, there's something active about *listening to nothing*. It's not just "zoning out." It is, rather, a positive sort of exertion.

We keep coming back to Kirste's words—"Trying to hear in silence"—because they imply something profound for us bigger mammals as much as for mice. They remind us of the practice of Nada yoga, of listening to the "unstruck sound." They remind us, too, of the results of fMRI studies of deep meditation practitioners, who assiduously pay attention in spaces of virtually no sound and stimulus. The intense state of focused receptivity is a kind of exertion, too. It requires concentration. It's the *good* kind of stress.

This idea of silence as an active force, not a passive one, resonated for Faith. "It's the creativity of the universe streaming through your mind. You wouldn't ever want to stop it!" she says. But when your mind finally settles down, she observes, we find ourselves actively absorbed in focused concentration, really *meeting* silence. Just as she had as a little girl.

CHAPTER 6

A MUTE BUTTON FOR THE MIND

"What is silence in the mind?"

We've posed this question to neuroscientists, physicians, and academic psychologists, and we've gotten answers that sound strikingly similar to those offered by modern physicists and Vedic mystics: A living mind, like a living universe, is always vibrating, firing, buzzing, churning. It's always gathering and synthesizing sense data. To be literally "silent"—in the sense of no thought, no perception, no activity—is to be, in a word, dead.

Still, many of the technical experts we've talked with agree there is such a thing as "silence" in a living human consciousness. There is a condition of presence that's beyond the noise. How do they know? Because they've experienced it for themselves.

When we've shared with academic researchers and clinicians how many if not most people describe their deepest silence as having occurred in conditions that aren't auditorily or even informationally quiet, no one has been surprised. It was Joshua Smyth, the professor of biobehavioral health and medicine, who told us about a participant in one of his stress-reduction studies who finds unmatched inner quiet by carving wood sculptures with a roaring chain saw.

Silence in the mind is a real phenomenon. But it's really hard to define.

So, given the limits in how the medical and scientific communities can describe and categorize this state of internal silence, we'll turn first to a different kind of authority to explore the contours of the phenomenon: our friend Jamal, a fourteen-year-old middle school basketball star.

Why is Jamal an expert? Adolescence, you might recall, is a time of peak internal noise—a period of life when most of us derive our sense of self from a fickle outside world. Around middle school age, most of us rely on other people and outside circumstances to tell us who we *are* and who we *are not*. There's a tendency to always be "performing." The middle school norm of constant conforming to external expectation is a high-powered engine of internal noise.

But even though he's in this phase of life, Jamal knows internal silence intimately.

"When I'm hot, I feel like I can't miss a shot . . . like every shot I make is going in," he tells us. "And *I* know I'm hot, and my *teammates* know it, and they feed me the ball, and when they're hot, I do the same. That's how it works." He takes us right into the final quarter of a championship game—heart thumping, sneakers squeaking, crowds cheering. "You take it like possession by possession, instead of focusing on what happened in the past or what's about to happen. You gotta stay present." When he's in this state, he tells us, "my mind is silent."

Consider free throws. Jamal describes them as "essentially free points." But he recognizes that he might miss those free points if he doesn't get into that quiet place inside himself. "I'll take a deep breath to just focus in on what's going on . . . to get my heart to stop pounding," he tells us. "I wanna take my time on it." Jamal has a ritual for finding his quiet in these moments: "I usually do one dribble, and then I spin the ball in between my hands, and then I shoot." The feedback is instantaneous. If he rushes it, if he lets outside factors distract him, if he entertains even a nanosecond of concern about other people's opinions, the ball bounces off the rim. If his mind is silent, *swoosh*.

We asked Jamal if he could remember a time when "hot" was unattainable. "Yeah, that was the last game of the season," he says, with slight resignation. He's talking about the abrupt ending of his 2020 season just four days before the California schools declared a shelter-in-place period for COVID. "I was in my head a lot for that game." Amidst the uncertainty of the moment, the gym was packed with his classmates and their parents—people who never ordinarily came to games. They wanted to be together and support the home team. There was a frenetic energy in the building. But at that time no one suspected we were facing a full-blown pandemic. Early in the game, he remembers missing a shot and a voice inside him saying, "What are people thinking?" He felt the pressure to perform; his image was at stake. He couldn't get "hot," because he couldn't shake the internal chatter.

So, even if the leading neuroscientists of the world lack a concise way of describing the nature of an internal state of silence, Jamal has one. It's being "hot" on the court. Jamal's heroes, Stephen Curry and LeBron James, have their phrasing, too: "in the zone." In psychology, the term that comes closest to describing this active aspect of "silence in the mind" is "flow."

Mihaly Csikszentmihalyi—the trailblazing scholar of positive psychology who popularized the term "flow"—once led a large-scale study of perceptions of flow around the world. He and his colleagues found that irrespective of differences in age, gender, culture, or native language people used some variant of the term "flow" to describe a specific kind of state. "The flow experience was not just a peculiarity of affluent, industrialized elites," Csikszentmihalyi wrote. "It was reported in essentially the same words by old women from Korea, by adults in Thailand and India, by teenagers in Tokyo, by Navajo shepherds, by farmers in the Italian Alps." Csikszentmihalyi and his team have provided us with a word for a subjective phenomenon that's hard to study or define but that's nonetheless been central to the human experience since the dawn of human life.

There's an intuitive link between silence and flow. When Jamal describes hitting a free throw or receiving the ball from a teammate, he's clearly transcending the noise. But there's also a less obvious commonality. Csikszentmihalyi and other scholars note that flow happens when we're in eustress. Like the mice immersed in the anechoic chambers in Professor Kirste's study, we enter the state of flow in the "sweet spot" between distress and boredom, when we're engaged in a challenge but not overwhelmed—like when Jamal and his teammates are well matched against an opposing team. Csikszentmihalyi and his longtime colleague Jeanne Nakamura describe this "sweet spot" as "perceived challenges, or opportunities for action, that stretch (neither overmatching nor underutilizing) existing skills." It's when we turn all of our conscious awareness over to the task at hand, thereby entering a state of pristine attention.

When we first started asking people "What's the deepest silence you've ever known?" we thought we were doing something wrong. Why, we wondered, were they telling us about sweaty raves and scaling mountains in severe weather conditions? "Perhaps they didn't understand the question," we thought to ourselves. "That sounds noisy." But over time we realized *we* were mistaken. They were describing the inner experience of silence.

While our own mental states are subjective, there are some clear characteristics that we can identify across different people's experiences. Csikszentmihalyi describes several defining features of flow, one of which gets to a core aspect of internal silence. It's what he calls "loss of reflective self-consciousness." As he writes, the "loss of self-consciousness does not involve a loss of self, and certainly not a loss of consciousness, but rather, only a loss of consciousness of the self." He clarifies: "What slips below the threshold of awareness is the concept *of* self, the information we use to represent to ourselves who we are." This is a source not just of fun but also of personal growth. "When not preoccupied with ourselves," Csikszentmihalyi writes, "we actually have a chance to expand the concept of who we are. Loss of self-consciousness can lead to self-transcendence, to a feeling that the boundaries of our being have been pushed forward."

So, here's another way to describe what happens in the state of inner quiet: we stop talking *to* ourselves *about* ourselves.

This is partly out of necessity. When we're immersed in the eustress of flow, we don't have the attention reserves to doubt or fret or self-congratulate. According to Csikszentmihalyi's estimates, our attentional filters will bypass something like 99.999 percent of gathered bits of information, in order to screen the roughly 0.001 percent of relevant stimuli. With limited attention to go around, researchers speculate that more sophisticated forms of thought—such as reflective self-consciousness—are too dear a price to pay. We don't have the spare cognitive capacity to fixate on the past or the future or the status of the ego.

This isn't to say that immersion in flow leads to an extinction of the sense of self. Csikszentmihalyi describes what happens as a kind of evolution. There is a self that recedes and a self that emerges. The self that recedes is the one that's imprisoned by its self-concept and self-interests. It's captive to noisy interrogators that constantly ask "How do I rank? What will they think? What does this mean for me?" That's where Jamal was stuck after missing that shot during that last game of the 2020 season. The new self—the one that emerges through flow, the one that's "hot" on the court—is both more "differentiated," carrying a healthy individuality and uniqueness, and more "integrated," able to perceive unity with others and communion with what extends beyond the skin. When Jamal is making shots and shaking defenders, he's still Jamal, but he's a more present and connected version of himself. Even at the apex of anxious self-absorption—middle school—Jamal can, like Houdini, slip through the bars of "reflective self-consciousness" and enter a mental state that feels expansive, almost eternal.

This is silence in the living mind.

MAPPING MENTAL NOISE

In the *Wall Street Journal* in 2014, the author and researcher Michio Kaku declared, "The Golden Age of Neuroscience has arrived." As he put it, "We have learned more about the thinking brain in the last 10–15 years than in all of human history."

Scan the major newspapers, podcasts, magazines, and academic journals over the past decade, and you'll find similar triumphalist conclusions. Advances in physics, computer science, statistics, and other fields have enabled an extraordinary range of new technologies with a dizzying array of acronyms—fMRI, PET, EEG, CT scans, DBS, TES—that have cumulatively enabled scientists to not only observe physical architectures of the brain but also study the neurobiological implications of thoughts and nervous system functions. These developments have tremendous implications for our understanding of the brain as well as our practical ability to deliver improvements in human lives—including emerging medical treatments like a "brain pacemaker" for Alzheimer's patients and a robotic exoskeleton to allow paraplegics to walk.

Still, amidst all the advances, we shouldn't deceive ourselves into believing that we're unraveling any of the big mysteries of human consciousness. When we spoke with neuroscientists about the potential of neuroimaging technologies to decipher the mental states of internal silence, they were generally adamant about their disclaimers. For example, we still don't have anything like a "moving fMRI machine" to non-intrusively track the brain in an active flow state, like the one Jamal is in when he's dunking a basketball. Even when you can view real-time brain activity, it reveals little about what a person is *actually experiencing* in the moment, says Adam Gazzaley. Someone might have a life-changing insight or a debilitating flashback, but these events "could be quite subtle neurally," Gazzaley tells us. At the same time, a person might light up the machine with what appears to be a major "event" that doesn't even register in their awareness. We asked Gazzaley if it might be possible to use today's most advanced neuroimaging technologies to identify signals or proxies for a mind that is "quiet."

"*Quiet-ish*," he clarified with a chuckle.

While we're still a long way from being able to directly link specific measurable brain activity to corresponding lived experience, neuroscience is, nonetheless, getting a better understanding of the "geography" of the brain. We're closer to being able to tell which regions and networks of the thinking organ have the most to do with anxiety, worry, and self-referential thought. These advancements have important implications for understanding the meaning of noise and silence in the mind.

Mark Leary, professor of psychology and neuroscience at Duke University, once mused, "Had the human self been installed with a mute button or off switch, the self would not be the curse to happiness that it often is." Inspired by Leary's observation, we've set off to answer this question: Is there a neurobiological mechanism that might come close to a "mute button" for the brain? If so, then where do we find it?

We spoke recently with Arne Dietrich, a neuroscientist at the American University in Beirut who specializes in the neurocognitive mechanisms of a brain like Jamal's when he plays ball. He coined the term "transient hypofrontality" to describe what's happening in the internal quiet of the flow state. "Transient" describes the temporary state of this form of consciousness. "Hypo" describes a slowing of activity in the "frontality"—or, the prefrontal cortex (PFC) of the brain, where we formulate our sense of a separate self. According to Dietrich, flow states and other expanded forms of consciousness—including mental states brought about by psychedelic and entheogenic substances—facilitate an experience of oneness because the areas of the brain where we formulate our sense of self and time dissolve. Dietrich is quick to point out this irony: while these states are often heralded as "a more evolved form of consciousness," they arise through *diminished* activity in our most evolved, most celebrated region of the brain, the PFC.

Evolution or devolution aside, what Dietrich's talking about is a pathway to silence in the mind. He's talking about a biological mechanism for transcending the internal distraction that plagues so much of the modern world.

He's talking about a potential "mute button."

Yet this isn't the only idea of what constitutes the neurobiological basis of a silent mind. While the prefrontal cortex deactivates during some flow activities of physical exertion, other flow activities—like arithmetic or jazz improvisation—seem to require more executive controls and an *increase* of activity in the PFC. So, the "mute button," in fact, might not simply be about resting one part of the brain. It might be more about launching an intricate ballet throughout the whole organ.

In the last chapter, we shared Adam Gazzaley and Larry Rosen's description of the push-pull forces of attention—top-down and bottom-up. Rather than a simple diminishment of the PFC, some studies of flow describe a kind of synchronization between different *attentional networks*—like, for example, Jamal setting his sights on landing a three-point shot (top-down goal) while still keeping tabs on an incoming defender (bottom-up). These studies also highlight the role of *reward networks*, involving neurotransmitters like dopamine, which seem to reinforce focused attention while decreasing impulsivity and distraction. This "synchronization" theory suggests that an elegant sequencing of different functions and activities quiets a noisy mind.

Some of the biggest clues about the location of a potential "mute button" have come through research over the past few decades on our minds' *default states.*

Until recently, most experts considered the brain "at rest" to be like a relaxed muscle: alive but mostly stationary and using little energy. In 2001, Marcus Raichle, a neurologist at the Washington University School of Medicine, and his colleagues turned this assumption upside down. They discovered what some scientists had suspected: that the brain is always highly active and expending lots and *lots* of energy. In fact, the set of regions in the brain associated with passive states—the default mode network (DMN)—is a particularly egregious energy hog.

It's also noisy.

In his book *How to Change Your Mind*, Michael Pollan succinctly recaps the recent science, saying, "The default mode network appears to play a role in the creation of mental constructs or projections, the most important of which is the construct we call the self, or ego. This is why some neuroscientists call it 'the me network.'" Pollan is speaking of reflective self-consciousness and all the worry, rumination, self-narration, and self-importance it encompasses. This makes for a disconcerting commentary on human nature: *our "default," the DMN, is defined by noisy thoughts of "me."*

Recent studies have found that the DMN is negatively correlated with the attentional networks of the brain. In other words, when the DMN is activated, the structures and processes that underlie our attentional capacities go quiet, and when attentional networks are active, there's a reduction in the DMN. Pollan offers a seesaw as a metaphor. On one end sits your DMN; on the other, your attention. This suggests that activities that require our attentional networks, like ones that produce a sense of flow, would diminish the activity of the DMN and, with it, all that self-referential thought and preoccupation.

Judson Brewer has found through his research that the noisiest aspects of human consciousness correspond to activities in two primary parts of the brain associated with the DMN: the PFC and the posterior cingulate cortex (PCC). While the PFC is responsible for the verbalized sense of your name and intellectual identity, the PCC is more responsible for the "felt" sense of self. The PCC is associated with the ineffable noise of self-consciousness—the kind of bodily sense of *ugh* that's associated with pangs of guilt or uneasiness around self-image. Brewer, an experienced meditator, is keenly aware of the gap between first-person experience and third-person reporting on neural activity. So, he's led studies that apply an innovative "grounded theory" methodology, combining neuroimaging with firsthand personal descriptions of what's happening. For example, he'll have study participants do "short runs" of just a few minutes of meditation practice in an fMRI or EEG machine and then ask them, "What was happening in your experience?" Overwhelmingly, he's found that the default mode network lights up at the points where study participants describe getting into a mental or emotional state of *constriction*—like when they're meditating and they get frustrated and then try really hard to "power through it." In contrast, he finds that the DMN, and particularly the PCC, ease when subjects enter mental and emotional states associated with *expansion*—feelings of ease, effortlessness, and loving-kindness.

In his studies, Brewer has used *non*-meditators as control subjects. These participants were taught a meditation practice in the morning and then slid into the scanner to try to practice what they'd learned in the afternoon. "They were actually more interesting than the experienced meditators, in many ways," he told the meditation teacher and author Michael Taft in a recent interview. According to Brewer, several of the novice meditators were "literally flipping their brain activity" in the PCC region from red (activating) to blue (deactivating). They'd learn to do this after only nine minutes—"Literally three runs of three minutes each"—of neuroimaging feedback. They were adapting on the spot. Brewer speculates that they were learning what it feels like *to get in and out of their own way.* These subjects were able to temporarily reduce PCC activity, implying some promising potential for managing "the me network."

While just one single meditation session seems to result in *mental states* that transcend our noisy default setting, long-term practices of meditation and other forms of concentration may produce more lasting *mental traits* of quiet. In a 2021 study, Kathryn Devaney, a postdoctoral researcher at Harvard, and a team of researchers gave experienced Vipassana meditators and control group subjects two kinds of tasks: focusing tasks (requiring heavy lifting from the attentional networks) and resting, with no explicit task (inviting the DMN to activate). They found that meditators showed less DMN activity while at rest than the control group did. Devaney and her co-authors summarize their findings this way: "Long-term meditation practice contributes to brain health and mental wellness by gaining effective suppressive control over the ruminative DMN." Brewer, too, has found that seasoned meditation practitioners are able to rewire their brains over time to make the DMN less active, even during periods of rest.

This is good news. *We can make our default state less noisy.* We can build the skills to do so and, with practice, the capacity for our inner environment to be less constrictive and more expansive. By working with our PFC and PCC, we can find not just an occasional, temporary "mute button" but a way to turn down the everyday noise in the ambience of our consciousness.

All of this research points to something counterintuitive about silence in the mind. Our ordinary idea of "rest" isn't necessarily quiet. Imagine you've powered off your phone, turned off your TV, your computer, and every other source of external auditory and informational distraction that surrounds you. That's a good start. But if you're still sitting on the couch with a tub of ice cream, indulging your worst paranoias and letting self-centered fantasies run amok, then that's not really silence in the consciousness. Zoning out can be the noisiest state of all.

We're not knocking good old-fashioned daydreaming here. As Harvard's Kathryn Devaney and her co-authors concede, "Not all mind wandering is ruminative." There are kinds of blue-sky thinking—say, reflecting on memories, imagining new possibilities, watching puffy clouds turning into bunnies and dragons and bunnies again—that have little in common with the gloomy detours of self-obsessed, ruminative mind. But Devaney and her colleagues conclude that a practice like meditation or simply paying conscious attention to silence is helpful for regularly and reliably transcending the noise. "The primary findings," they write, "are consistent with positive effects of meditation training on suppression of the DMN."

So, even if there's no perfect "mute button," we can learn how to dial down the noise.

THE NEUROSCIENCE OF SELF-TRANSCENDENCE

"A sense of flow, being with the breath." That's how one participant, an experienced meditator, in one of Brewer's real-time fMRI neurofeedback studies described a particularly glowing moment of practice. According to the readings on the monitor, this one specific moment corresponded to a notable reduction in activity in her PCC.

While we typically associate flow with physically active states—like Jamal dunking a basketball—the link to sitting meditation makes sense. Flow, like breath concentration practice, is about grounding in the present moment. It's about the integration of mind and body. Csikszentmihalyi has, in fact, often written about meditation as a way of training for flow.

In fMRI studies, Brewer and other researchers have often had study participants engage in different kinds of meditation—including "loving-kindness" practice, one in which you focus on your feelings or intentions of compassion for other people. On the surface, such practices don't necessarily seem to have the same flow-like physicality as, say, breath awareness. Still, in the studies, they've resulted in a similar reduction in activity in the PCC.

In a recent conversation, Brewer pointed out to us that awareness and loving-kindness practices do, in fact, share a core element—one that links directly to flow.

"What does it feel like when you think of a time when somebody has been kind to you?" Brewer asked us, referring to a key reflection in loving-kindness practice. "Does it feel contracted or expanded?"

"And what does it feel like when you're just resting in awareness of breath or an object and not being caught by the chatter of your mind? Is the feeling contracted or expanded?"

For us, the answer to each question was clear: expanded. Brewer's research shows that there is a shared quality that emerges in the consciousness when a person does any of these practices. It's not just the eustress of physical flow—when the brain has to be so utterly focused on the task at hand that it lacks the attentional resources to entertain even a modicum of self-cherishing or worry. It's a feeling of expansion beyond the tight clinging to a sense of the separate self.

Expansion quiets the mind.

There's an emerging area of multidisciplinary academic study focused on self-transcendent experiences (STEs), a category of experience that encompasses mental states of flow, mindfulness, awe, and mystical encounters, to name just a few.

David Bryce Yaden of Johns Hopkins Medical School and his collaborators in a recent paper describe STEs as "transient mental states of decreased self-salience and/or increased feelings of connectedness." They specify two subcomponents to STEs: an "annihilational" component, "which refers to both the dissolution of the bodily sense of self accompanied by reduced self-boundaries and self-salience"; and a "relational" component, "which refers to the sense of connectedness, even to the point of oneness with something beyond the self, usually with other people and aspects of one's environment or surrounding context." Self-transcendence is a kind of "right sizing." It's a diminishment of the importance of the egoic self while our sense of interconnectivity to the world around us is heightened. We are simultaneously smaller *and* larger—a mere drop in the ocean but nevertheless a part of its vastness.

STEs—almost universally—bring us this subjective feeling of *expansion*.

They also typically do something else: *they shut our mouths.*

Consider awe. The UC Berkeley psychologist Dacher Keltner, founder of the Greater Good Science Center, and his colleague Jonathan Haidt define awe as a combination of two factors: "perceived vastness" and the "need for accommodation." The first, perceived vastness, is when "you're around things that are vast or that transcend your frame of reference—either spatial or temporal or meaning-based." It's marveling at a dazzling lightning storm. It's gazing at the otherworldly ruggedness of the Grand Canyon. Sometimes, it's a realization of the immensity and grandeur of the universe through participation in a sacred ritual or contemplation of a concept like string theory. The only vocalized response that suffices is "ahhh" or "ohhh" or "mmmm" or, perhaps best of all, a full-bodied surrender to silence.

The second characteristic of awe, the need for accommodation, is when an experience or realization "transcends your knowledge structures. You can't make sense of it." As Keltner explains, "You are left speechless and wordless." It's an inability to put reality into neat and tidy categories. Ludwig Wittgenstein, the Austrian logician and trailblazer in the fields of philosophy of math and philosophy of mind, offered this summary at the end of his magnum opus, *Tractatus Logico-Philosophicus*: "Whereof one cannot speak, thereof one must be silent. What we cannot speak about we must pass over in silence." His words are like the blessed collapse of a turbocharged engine of logical computation into the loving arms of the cosmic mystery.

This encounter with knowledge structures that surpass our current frameworks is reminiscent of the work of the Swiss psychologist Jean Piaget, who noted that development in children occurs when there's a need for their worldview to expand. They transcend their previous paradigms because they must. Or, more accurately, they transcend *and* include them. In short, when we cannot accommodate an observation or experience with our existing mental structure, we grow. This doesn't just happen in adolescence, as Piaget and others from his era believed; it happens throughout our lives. This has been affirmed by a new wave of theorists and psychologists.

Summer Allen, a colleague of Keltner's at the Greater Good Science Center, writes that awe experiences "shift our attention away from ourselves, make us feel like we are part of something greater than ourselves, and make us more generous towards others." Psychologically, she writes, the benefits of self-transcendence through awe seem to "give people the sense that they have more available time, increase feelings of connectedness, increase critical thinking and skepticism, increase positive mood, and decrease materialism." All of these attributes speak to the kind of *expansion* that Judson Brewer finds with the diminishment of activity in the PCC. With nothing to say and no overbearing sense of self, our constrictive tendencies melt away. As Keltner underscores, an awe experience can "calm your stress physiology, activate the vagus nerve, trigger the release of oxytocin, activate the dopamine networks in your brain." He continues, saying that this biological response can "help you explore the world, make you kinder and more filled with wonder."

The deactivation of "the me network" brings us back to the moral dimensions of silence—to Gandhi's notion that "nearly half the misery of the world would disappear if we, fretting mortals, knew the virtue of silence." Or the sentiments of Sheena Malhotra, who described silence "like an ocean" that shifts energy and transmits empathy even through a crowd of thousands. Or what Rob Lippincott describes in the silence used in Quaker business meetings that seek to find unity in their "exercise in togetherness." When we step back from the ordinary brain's experience of noise and constriction and division and step into states of silence and expansion and connection, we enable the transformation not just of our individual selves but of our relationships, communities, and societies.

In their 2017 paper, Yaden and his co-authors write about the most intense variety of the STE: *mystical experience.* "Some people report that during mystical experiences the sense of self can fall away entirely, creating a distinction-less sense of unity with one's surroundings." Such experiences go by many names, including primary religious experiences, cosmic consciousness, Christ consciousness, satori, samadhi, non-dual and transcendental experiences, to name just a few. While each of these experiences has its own character and nuanced meaning based on the tradition from which it's derived, neuroscientists and psychologists point to the experiences' shared qualities, like the propensity to generate a long-term shift in a person's perspective.

More than a century ago, William James, the Harvard scholar who is today widely recognized as the father of American psychology, described the unifying characteristics of the mystical experience. According to James, they share four qualities. One is a *noetic quality*. The experiences feel real and true, and they "carry with them a curious sense of reality for after-time." Another quality is *transiency*. These experiences are brief, but if the experience recurs, an element of "continuous development" is possible. Yet another quality is *passivity*—a feeling of overwhelm or surrender. The subject feels as if they have been "grasped and held by a superior power."

The fourth and most important, according to James, is *ineffability*: the sense that the experience "defies expression."

For James, the mystical experience was something not just salutary for the mind but awakening for the whole being. Speaking about mystical experiences to a packed audience at the University of Edinburgh at the turn of the twentieth century, James said, "The only thing that [a mystical experience] unequivocally testifies to is that we can experience union with something larger than ourselves and in that union find our greatest peace." The quest for this "greatest peace" remained one of James's primary academic research interests until the end of his life.

Still, James, like other scholars, found the science of mystical experience extremely difficult to study. That's because mystical experiences tend to happen spontaneously in environments far removed from our scientific scanners and instrumentation. Even the kinds of innovative "grounded theory" experiments that Brewer describes aren't much help when it comes to deciphering the neurobiological mechanisms at play in a genuine mystical experience. As James recognized, *they're ineffable.*

O

We recently asked Grace Boda about the deepest silence she's ever known.

Her eyes filled with tears, and she said, "I remember this like it was yesterday because it changed the course of my life.

"I'm six years old. I'm in first grade. It's recess," she recalls. "They've just mowed the grass, and so we're all doing what we always do when they've just mowed the grass: we're scraping up all the grass clippings into a big circle to make a nest and play birds.

"So, all these little kids are flapping around and squawking. The boy birds are jockeying for turf, and the girl birds are hunting for worms, and my job, because I'm the littlest person in first grade, is to be the baby bird," she remembers. "So, I'm just standing there squawking, and I'm supposed to chirp, but I'm really just daydreaming and looking for four-leaf clovers, and I'm just doing that, and then all of a sudden, unprovoked, *poof!* I am not in my body anymore."

Grace slows down: "I experienced myself, my awareness, as distributed through absolutely everything. I remember the moment of shock, like, 'Oh, I'm everything.' There isn't even a word for it. In my six-year-old meaning making, I thought, 'This must be God' . . . and I just realized, 'I'm in that presence.'"

Grace describes a presence of pure goodness, and since she was *everything*, she was also that presence. She had transcended "self" and connected to wholeness. Though something *was* being asked of her. "There was a question present too," she says, "not in words, but I knew it was, 'Are you willing? Are you *really* willing?'" Her answer at the time was lucid: "I knew, with every cell of my being, with every fiber of anything in me, it was absolute, all out: *Yes.* I mean, *Yes! Yes!*

"And then the next thing I know, the recess bell rings: *POOM!* I just snap. It was a sensation like a rubber band snapping. I just snapped back into awareness of my body and myself as a little girl on the field at recess, and all my friends are screaming and squawking and chirping and running past me to go line up on the dots to go back into our classroom.

"And I remember thinking to myself, 'I'll never be the same.'"

She wanted to understand what this mystical experience was showing her. "I was raised in the Catholic Church, so I thought I was being called to be a priest. But I told the priest at my church, who patted me on the head and, of course, said, 'Girls can't be priests.'" This could have been a devastating moment for her. It wasn't. "I just stopped talking about it," she tells us. "I *never* doubted it, because it was such a direct strong, powerful experience," like William James's description of the noetic. "I *never* for a second doubted its reality."

Grace, now sixty, has gone on to become an accomplished executive coach, both a professional and a spiritual adviser to people looking for clarity, direction, or meaning in their lives. "It was an initiation and a dedication," she says of that experience as a first grader. "There have been many experiences since then, but that first one oriented my life and changed my being in a way I can't begin to describe, in a way that allowed everything else to follow."

She can't "begin to describe" it, because the experience was, as William James would say, ineffable. "Because it blew my heart wide open, none of these words are adequate. All words fall apart, because a word is, by definition, in contrast to a different thing."

Speaking of this deepest silence, Grace can only call it "a place in consciousness." For more than fifty years, it has been the well she draws from, this place of "inner stillness and inner fullness and inner wholeness and inner oneness." The "place" that Grace experienced was a *rapturous silence in the mind*—a fundamental cleansing of the noise at every level of perception.

So, here's a question: Is there any point in trying to come up with a neurobiological explanation of such an event?

Probably not.

In our view, the meaning of a mystical experience like this one can't be solely attributed to externally observable phenomena. And yet it's nonetheless possible to respect the mystery while engaging in a meaningful exploration for signs of what's happening in the brain and nervous system in such a state.

While it's clearly not possible to use any kind of neuroimaging to study the brain activity of a person in a spontaneous mystical experience like the one Grace had on the playground, new developments in neuroscience are bringing us surprisingly closer. In particular, the renaissance of research in psychedelics is presenting new insights on the neuroscience of self-transcendence.

In 2009, Robin Carhart-Harris received U.K. approval to study the effects of psilocybin on the brain. Volunteers in the research study slid into fMRI machines, received their synthetic mushrooms, and took off on their magic carpet rides. Carhart-Harris hypothesized that brain imagery would reveal lots of activity. It would look "like the dreaming brain," he told Michael Pollan. Instead, he and his teammates recorded decreased blood flow in the DMN, signaling a relative deactivation of "the me network."

This makes intuitive sense. Like Grace's experience as a six-year-old, a common element of experiences with psychedelics and entheogens is a loss or diminishment of the sense of a separate self or a rigid ego identity. As in Grace's childhood experience, this radical transcendence of internal noise can yield lasting change. Not just altered *states*, but altered *traits*.

In the 1962 "Good Friday Experiment," a group of twenty theological school students were divided in half for a study. One group of students was given psilocybin (which was legal at the time); the other was given an active placebo. They all attended a Good Friday church service together. The prominent civil rights leader, author, and theologian the Reverend Howard Thurman gave the sermon along with his blessing for the study.

One man who received psilocybin, Mike Young, said that when he volunteered for the experiment, he was unsure of his future in the ministry. While under the influence of psilocybin, he had a mystical experience of dying and being reborn. He described it as being both "very painful" and "glorious." When he returned home to his wife, she immediately knew something substantial had happened. Nearly fifty years later, he remains affected by the experiment. As he said in an interview, "I'm a Unitarian Universalist minister as a result of"—he pauses to amend his statement—"*partly* a result of that drug experience." It wasn't the *only* reason. But something in him was forever changed.

The renowned scholar of religion Huston Smith was also a study participant, and he, too, received a dose of psilocybin. He frequently wrote and spoke of the experience as having been formative. He has said that he felt "renewed gratitude" each time he's thought of it. Thirty-five years later, he said that the experiment "round[ed] out my experience of the holy by enabling me to experience it in a personal mode." He continued, "This permanently enlarged my experiential toolbox . . . [E]ver since then I have been able to understand experientially that classic mode of mysticism."

Of course, this isn't just a testament to the psychedelic experience. We can have mystical experiences through fasting, chanting, breath work, prostrations, sensory deprivation, or—as Grace's experience attests—pure spontaneous mystery. However, psychedelic work can be an especially helpful vehicle to understanding the science of mystical experience because it's conducive to randomized control studies. These fMRI experiments demonstrate that mystical experiences do strongly correlate with a reduction of activity in the noisiest parts of the brain.

When Judson Brewer first started studying the brains of seasoned meditators in expanded states of awareness, he tells us that he and his team "looked everywhere for increased activity." But they didn't find it. "I think our brain is more efficient during a self-transcendent experience," he tells us. Brewer's use of the word "efficient" implies something important. There's a surprising "utility" to what we might call mystical awareness.

There's nothing more cognitively wasteful than noisy thoughts of "me."

O

So, what is silence in the mind?

Is it a reduction of activity in the prefrontal cortex? In the posterior cingulate cortex? In the whole default mode network?

Is it an active state of flow on the ball court—leaving all defenders and all self-referential thoughts behind?

Is it the passive state, where we feel the vastness of existence and have to abandon our old mental models to accommodate it?

Is it the rarefied mystical encounter, where we get a cosmic "right sizing" that corrects our sense of separateness and egoic self-importance?

Yes. The science points to *all of the above.*

Thanks to substantial advances in neuroimaging and in our understanding of the biological bases of mind and consciousness, we're able to explore many more aspects of the meaning of silence—especially internal silence. This is a good thing. It can help us make sense of the world.

But just because we're living in the "golden age of neuroscience" doesn't mean we've arrived at any kind of mechanistic understanding of the mysteries of silence in the mind. As Ludwig Wittgenstein, one of the most rigorously logical minds in human history, said, there are things that we will never be able to analyze, things we will never be able to verbally or logically explain. There are limits to what the decibel meters and hydrophones and fMRIs and EEGs can ever tell us.

And that's okay.

As he puts it, there are some things we must "pass over in silence."

PART III

THE SPIRIT OF SILENCE

CHAPTER 7

WHY SILENCE IS SCARY

Take a moment to join us in a thought experiment. Or really, more of a feeling experiment.

Imagine you just committed to spending the next five years of your life in total silence.

There's no need to take care of any logistics. No concern about how you're going to earn a living or provide for loved ones. All the practical arrangements have been made.

What's your first thought?

When you imagine this is actually happening, what feelings arise? How does your body respond? Is there a foreboding of loneliness? Is there a feeling of relief? Or do you experience something else entirely?

With nothing to say, how do you imagine your inner landscape would shift? With no words, where might your mind gravitate?

As you imagine yourself actually venturing out into this sea of silence, there's one more question we want you to consider, even though—at least at some level—we're pretty sure that we already know the answer: *Is it scary?*

THE FIRST RUDIMENT OF CONTEMPLATION

The name Pythagoras might evoke fearsome flashbacks to middle school math class. For many, the Greek philosopher's namesake these days is that geometric theorem for finding the long side of a right triangle. But Pythagoras has a lot more to teach us.

About twenty-five hundred years ago—around the same time Gautama Buddha and Confucius walked the earth—Pythagoras of Samos did what some of us would consider impossible today. He transcended the apparent chasm between science and spirituality, combining numinous contemplation with rigorous investigation.

In addition to deriving the famous theorem that bears his name, Pythagoras pioneered understanding of numerical proportions and the five regular solids in geometry, still foundational concepts in modern-day math. He invented a system of musical tuning wherein the frequency proportions between notes are based on a three-to-two ratio—a system that many scholars consider uniquely harmonized with proportions in nature. Pythagoras was the first person to divide the globe into the five climatic zones that are still used in meteorology today. He correctly identified the morning star and the evening star as the same planet, Venus. He is widely believed to be the first person in recorded history to teach that Earth is spherical rather than flat.

Yet Pythagoras wasn't what we would today call an empirical researcher. He was the leader of a mystery school—a society for training initiates to examine esoteric questions about the nature of reality. The members of the school studied the spiritual science of metempsychosis, or the "transmigration of souls," a framework for understanding reincarnation. They developed intricate doctrines around numerology and astrology that all pointed to order within nature, a measurable cosmic harmony. For example, Pythagoras posited a *musica universalis*, the notion that the planets move according to specific mathematical equations that produce a beautiful, though inaudible, melody in the heavens.

The Pythagorean school was revolutionary. It broke through the rigid patriarchy of the day and was the intellectual home of the first known woman mathematician and astronomer, Hypatia of Alexandria. The school lasted for hundreds of years after the death of its founder, and it laid the groundwork for much of Western philosophy, influencing the ideas of Socrates, Plato, and all the teachers who would follow them. The school, in turn, influenced the mathematicians and astronomers, including Copernicus and Newton, who would come to shape modern science.

Some say Pythagoras was the first person to fulfill the formal vocation of philosopher: "a lover of wisdom." According to Manly P. Hall, a scholar of the mystery schools of the world, Pythagoras meant something specific by the term "wisdom": "understanding of the source or cause of all things." As he saw it, attaining wisdom required "raising the intellect to a point where it intuitively cognized the invisible manifesting outwardly through the visible," reaching the point where it could become "capable of bringing itself *en rapport* with the spirit of things rather than with their forms."

If you wanted to become a student in the inner circle of the Pythagorean school, you had to commit to a host of guidelines, including dietary restrictions, study regimens, personal ethics, and lifestyle choices. If you wanted to gain access to the esoteric teachings, you had to undertake one commitment, though, that was bigger than the rest: *you had to pass through a five-year period of not talking.*

"Learn to be silent," Pythagoras advised his students. "Let your quiet mind listen and absorb the silence." The fifteenth-century humanist John Reuchlin explained that Pythagoras saw silence as "the first rudiment of contemplation"—the prerequisite of all wisdom. According to Hall, Pythagoras maintained his own practices of profound silence. He would regularly retire for months or more to his cloistered temple without scrolls, writing instruments, scribes, or companions. He took only his proprietary health concoction of poppy and sesame seeds, daffodils, mallows, the dried skins of sea onions, and a paste of barley, peas, and wild honey.

Why did Pythagoras see silence as the key to wisdom? Why did he require his inner circle of students to spend five years not talking before beginning their formal studies? There's no known record of his exact thinking on the topic or the specific rationale behind the requirement for members of the inner circle of the school.

But let's see if we can home in on his reasoning.

Return, for a moment, to the "feeling experiment" from the start of this chapter. Imagine you're one of the initiates.

How might five years in silence change the architecture of your mind?

In meditation retreats, extended times in nature, and other periods of contemplative practice in silence, we've gotten some clues. Silence, of course, forces us to face ourselves. Without distraction, we have to learn how to deal with our own internal noise. This enables us to tune in to what's really happening both within ourselves and outside ourselves. In the absence of judgment and conjecture and performance, the mind turns magnetically, like a compass, toward the truth.

But we don't want to imply this is an easy process. In profound silence, we first burn through heaps of habitual patterns and thought forms and fantasies and ambitions and lusts and delusions. In silence, we've both felt an intense desire to run away, to do anything to fill the space.

In English, we have the word "diversion" for entertainment. In Spanish and other Romance languages, the similar word *divertir* means to "amuse" or "entertain." This word raises a question: What is it that we're *diverting* ourselves from in the pursuit of a good time? Boredom?

Loss? Mortality? To get comfortable with deep silence is to sit in a room alone with all of these discomforts and pull energy away from those parts of the brain—like the medial prefrontal cortex and the posterior cingulate cortex—that specialize in protecting and decorating the distinct sense of "me."

In *The Genealogy of Morals*, Nietzsche writes of the *horror vacui*, the "horror of the vacuum," or the dread that a human being feels in the absence of sense data or mental stimulation. This phenomenon is real. In a 2014 study, Timothy Wilson, a social psychologist at the University of Virginia, left undergraduate and community member volunteers alone in a sparse room with no cell phones or entertainment for fifteen minutes. The participants had a choice: they could either sit in silence alone or push a button that would administer a painful electric shock. While all participants had initially stated that they would pay money to avoid being shocked with electricity, 67 percent of men and 25 percent of women eventually chose to shock themselves rather than sit in silence.

That was fifteen minutes. Imagine five years.

In the Christian mystic tradition, there's a term for an encounter with the impatient wildness of craving and aversion in a long period of deep silence. It's called "the dark night of the soul." In Buddhism, we've heard the same phenomenon described as the "pit of the void."

Silence, in this sense, *is* scary.

But what do we find on the other side?

THE BASIC PHENOMENON

The Swiss writer and philosopher Max Picard says that silence is a "primary, objective reality, which cannot be traced back to anything else. It cannot be replaced by anything else; it cannot be exchanged with anything else. There is nothing behind it to which it can be related except the Creator Himself."

The German poet, playwright, and philosopher Johann Wolfgang von Goethe has a specific term for just this category of reality: "a basic phenomenon." Goethe emphasized that the other items that fit in this category of "basic phenomena"—phenomena that don't depend on anything else—include "love, death, and life itself." Even amidst this impressive company, silence should be listed first. Silence is the phenomenon from which everything else is born. Picard writes, "One cannot imagine a world in which there is nothing but language and speech, but one can imagine a world where there is nothing but silence." He goes on to say that silence "is a positive, a complete world in itself," that it "contains everything within itself," that it "is not waiting for anything," and that "it is always wholly present in itself and it completely fills out the space in which it appears."

As Goethe explained, "When the basic phenomena are revealed to our senses, we feel a kind of shyness and even fear itself." And how could it be any other way? All those "basic phenomena" that Goethe described—love, death, life—can be frightening in their own respects. Our small selves—satisfied with diversion and delusions—claw and scratch and tremble when confronted with the full immensity of reality. Silence, the mother of the basic phenomena, might be the scariest. Especially since we are used to the veritable 24/7 all-you-can-eat buffet of sensory diversions that is the modern world.

Goethe's "basic phenomenon" and Nietzsche's *horror vacui* are rather abstract ways of describing the relationship between silence and fear. Let's look to a more accessible explanation: horror movies.

Let's say you're watching your sympathetic protagonist being chased by rapacious carnivores or deranged guys with chain saws through a pitch-dark pine forest. Filmmakers and sound editors often employ the total absence of sound and information in these kinds of scenes as a tool to evoke a particular degree of terror. That's because silence creates a *loss of reference points*. In silence, there are fewer guardrails to hold on to, fewer hints to help you make sense of what's going on.

In Alfonso Cuarón's Academy Award–winning 2013 film, *Gravity*, high-speed debris strikes a space shuttle, leaving Sandra Bullock's character tumbling alone in a space suit through the pitch-black vacuum of space. The scariest thing about the spectacular destruction of the spacecraft—her only lifeline—is that it happens in total silence. The sound waves of the explosion don't carry in space. The scene is not just eerie because it's unusual; it's eerie because it gives you the sense that you have no idea what's really going on.

The fear of silence is the fear of the *unknown*. But it's also the fear of what might *become known*.

This applies to mundane everyday situations as much as to extraterrestrial cinematic terrors. Ask a fifteen-year-old, for example, to name an everyday sort of fear, and you're likely to hear about "awkward silence." You know, being caught face-to-face with another person with nothing to say. No script. No agenda. Just the heavy poignancy of someone else's un-diverted presence. We don't necessarily get over this discomfort when we reach adulthood, either. Leigh's brother, Roman Mars, the creator and host of the podcast *99% Invisible*, tells us that capturing "room tone"—tape used to smooth transitional moments in editing—is usually the most uncomfortable part of any interview. It requires everyone in the room to be silent for about one minute. Invariably someone—and he confesses it might be him—will break the silence to say, "Well, that's probably enough," when barely thirty seconds have elapsed.

It's hard to be with another person in the vacuum.

But it's harder to be utterly alone in it.

About seventeen hundred years before the first horror movie was produced, Saint Anthony, the original Desert Father and forerunner of all Christian monastic traditions, gave Freddy Krueger a good run for his money. The third- and fourth-century mystic spent twenty years by himself in the Egyptian desert. While he almost certainly experienced the bliss of self-transcendence, some of the records of his experience of silence are reminiscent of a 1970s surrealist horror film. *The Temptation of Saint Anthony*, a painting that's part of Matthias Grünewald's sixteenth-century *Isenheim Altarpiece*, shows the sage with his blue cloak and hardy beard being brutally dragged on the ground by ferocious beasts with gnashing teeth. They're tugging on his hair and poking him with intimidating rods, all before an apocalyptic scene of burned branches and hazy skies. Looking at the *Temptation* painting, the spiritual psychologist Robert Sardello comments on the symbolism of the beasts: as we enter silence, we "encounter anxiety, fear, fantasy, stupid thoughts, and buzzing impulses." In the depths of silence, these thoughts and impulses can be excruciating.

It's important to note that Saint Anthony doesn't attempt to kill these psychic beasts in the painting. He doesn't even run away from them. Looking at Saint Anthony, you get the clear message that there'd be no point in trying to escape or fight off the fearsome creatures. "We [the viewers] suspect," Sardello says, "they are somehow a necessary part of our wholeness."

In intense silence, we surface our ferocious beasts. We summon the hungry predators that have been lurking in the understories of our own psyche. If we live our lives in noisy distraction—in diversion—then we let the beasts surreptitiously run amok, wreaking havoc from unseen places. When we enter profound silence, we're not necessarily seeking to slay these beasts. We are raising them up from the depths so we can bring them to the light—maybe even to befriend them.

When we spoke recently with Roshi Joan Halifax, she emphasized how simultaneously scary and nourishing silence can be. In *Being with Dying*, she writes, "When we stop our habitual mental and physical activity and sit quietly, difficulties often become more visible. We can become even more sensitive to suffering and feel at risk for a breakdown." She continues, "What is probably breaking down is the ego—our identity as a small, separate self—and the healthy part of us should welcome this." She considers the direct encounter with silence a healing medicine. As she writes in her book *The Fruitful Darkness*, "If we have courage, we take silence as medicine to cure us from our social ills, the suffering of self-centered alienation. In silence, sacred silence, we stand naked like trees in winter, all our secrets visible under our skin. And like winter's tree, we appear dead but are alive."

SILENCE IN GRIEF

Sometimes, entering the challenging kind of silence is not a choice. Sometimes, life thrusts silence upon us.

On the morning of April 7, 2021, Justin got the news that one of his dearest friends had died unexpectedly in his sleep, just shy of his thirty-fifth birthday. This was a friend with whom Justin had a whole shared personal language, a whole way of being. He could make Justin laugh harder than anyone, from the center of his belly—so hard that he'd forget about all his defenses and worries. They'd been best friends since third grade, when they first started singing Beatles songs together in the backyard and engaging in friendly contests over who could formulate the lengthiest, most over-the-top description of a perfectly cooked fried fish sandwich. For decades, they had shared an unusual ability to be present with each other and not say anything.

When Justin got the news, in the early morning, standing out in his robe by the big juniper tree in his backyard, he felt this indescribably strong desire to speak to his friend, to say one last thing, to make him laugh, to express his love. But the option was unavailable. The door was shut. There was nowhere to go but into the silence. So Justin stood there in it. In minutes that seemed to stretch into hours, the silence was palpable. It was thick. It filled up to the point of feeling like almost bursting—with sorrow and appreciation and restlessness and thanks. It was as if the silence had its own color—a brownish-green mixture of hues. There was nothing for him to do but hold it. Feel it. Wail into it.

Silence is a primary container for grief. It's the space where we can be most fully present in feeling and memory. While it's tempting to run away and find diversion, silence—if we can stay with it—has a way of metabolizing loss. When we let words fail, meaning emerges. The writer, psychotherapist, and Jewish mystic Estelle Frankel offers insight into why cultures all over the world honor the role of silence in our individual and collective grieving:

> In Jewish law, one who visits the bereaved is instructed to be silent—to not speak unless spoken to. Holding the sacred space of silence for mourners makes it possible for them to be present in their grief. In silence, we do not run the risk of trivializing the mourner's experience with our well-intended but often awkward words.

Leigh also suffered an unexpected loss in the course of writing this book. Her father died of COVID-19 in November 2020. It was during a surge in Ohio, when the death toll in the United States had just crossed 250,000. Like so many, he died alone in the ICU.

During the days preceding and following his death, when it was clear that air travel and hospital visits were out of the question, Leigh sat motionless in her living room staring into a crackling fire. Her daughter, Ava, and husband, Michael, would periodically curl up with her on the couch or the floor. Few words were spoken. Leigh's dad had been estranged from her since she was four years old. Her father had been absent for her whole life. There were *too few* stories to tell.

Acquaintances offered generous reflections about losing a parent. But not knowing the nature of this particular father-daughter relationship, those "well-intended but often awkward words" that Frankel describes were painful reminders for Leigh that she'd actually been grieving her father her entire life. In the silence, Leigh realized that she was now grieving the loss of a relationship that had *never been* and *would never be*. Eventually, the language would come to describe that grief. But the first to comfort Leigh was silence.

William Blake wrote, "The deeper the sorrow, the greater the joy." He counsels us to experience the full range of grief so that we are able .

to experience our full range of joy, too. This is one of the ways that the presence of silence is the presence of *life* itself. To feel it is to take the "medicine" that Roshi Joan describes. To feel it is to open up to the full range of the experience of being human. This isn't a "shadow side" of silence. It's an expression of our wholeness, as Sardello says of the tribulations of Saint Anthony. Though it's intensely uncomfortable—full of anguish and even fear—grief, tended in silence, can become fertile ground in which joy may bloom.

THE STILL, SMALL VOICE

The inscription on the Temple of Apollo at Delphi in ancient Greece comprises two words that are sometimes attributed to Pythagoras: "Know thyself." We've found that Jewish, Christian, Muslim, Buddhist, and Taoist scriptures, among many others, enshrine this same teaching in various ways. They all advise studying your own thoughts, words, and actions as preparation for understanding that which lies beyond you.

In chapter 2, we described how Cyrus Habib endured weeks of anxiety and doubt during his first silent retreat as a Jesuit novice. He examined himself through the silence and found the source of his suffering. He was basing his own fulfillment on what he thought other people thought of him. When he absorbed the silence, the question arose spontaneously in his consciousness: "What do you want?"

Then came the authentic answer: "To be exactly where I am."

As the study of the University of Virginia students who eagerly electroshocked themselves in less than fifteen minutes demonstrates, time in silence isn't always a straightforward path to self-knowledge. Delving straight into silence can amplify internal noise. Meeting the deepest silence is, as Cyrus puts it, an active process of discerning the "signal" of "what's really, truly in the heart," in contrast to the "static" of the socially conditioned brain. There's a reason we so often avoid this work. It takes courage.

Pablo Neruda writes,

If we were not so single-minded
about keeping our lives moving,
and for once could do nothing,
perhaps a huge silence
might interrupt this sadness
of never understanding ourselves.

What Neruda calls "this sadness of never understanding ourselves" is, we find, a pervasive defense mechanism against a primordial fear: *that we're not who we think we are.* The poet is describing how we tend to protect ourselves from what we might discover if we truly *pay attention.* It's not necessarily that we might discover something "bad" in the depths of our psyche. We might just encounter something strange or inconvenient, something we can't easily explain or control. Often, we'd rather divert our attention with some form of the electroshock button than really look inside and ask ourselves the challenging questions about what's in our heart, what we really want. Yet, as Neruda implies, the journey toward "understanding ourselves" is necessary for "interrupt[ing] this sadness." Perhaps it's even a prerequisite of finding joy.

In the Judeo-Christian tradition, there's a mysterious phrase that describes what we encounter when we pay profound attention internally. Estelle Frankel writes about it this way: "Scripture also refers to God's voice as a speaking silence, *kol dmamah dakah.*" She elaborates: "This Hebrew phrase, most often translated as 'the still, small voice,' expresses the essential paradox of divine revelation: God's voice, *kol,* is the voice of *dmamah,* silence and stillness."

The passage in the Old Testament from which this expression is derived goes as follows:

And behold, the Lord passed by, and a great and strong wind rent the mountains, and broke in pieces the rocks before the Lord, but the Lord was not in the wind; and after the wind an earthquake, but the Lord was not in the earthquake; and after the earthquake a fire, but the Lord was not in the fire; and after the fire, a still small voice.

—1 Kings 19:11–12, RSV

There's a hypnotic quality to this verse, even in translation. There's percussion to it. There's the added poignancy of the description of the earthquake and the fire and the winds, given that we are in the throes of climate change and so much upheaval today. Elijah encounters the adversities, and they wear down the layers of his ordinary mind. Then, after everything, he discerns where the divine presence is: in "a still small voice." Biblical scholars sometimes also translate this presence as "the voice of fragile silence."

Sister Simone Campbell is a lawyer, antipoverty advocate, nonprofit executive director, and Catholic nun who has, in high-profile ways, challenged her own church on issues of women's reproductive health and economic justice. She knows what it's like to be worn down by conflict and unrelenting worldly events. She describes a simple practice as a source of resilience and clarity in her life. She sits in silence, lets her guard down, and listens for what she calls the "wee small voice." But this, she notes, isn't a typical mindfulness practice. It's an unpredictable act of faith. "Deep listening," says Sister Simone, "is risky business because it often calls on each of us to change in some way." And change can be scary.

This, too, is part of the "medicine" that Roshi Joan talks about. Facing ourselves in silence means having the courage to become more aware of what's been hidden. While talk of "a still, small voice" implies a biblical kind of divine revelation, what we're really talking about here is something more familiar and accessible: *intuition*. Elijah was a great prophet, but each one of us has the capacity to perceive quiet signs and insights within our own consciousness. It's what Cyrus described as the ability to discern "what is truly in the heart." It's an essential part of coming to know ourselves.

INSTANT MONASTICISM

When we've asked people to tell us about the deepest silence they've ever known, we've often heard stories of transcendent but fleeting experiences: spontaneous mystical events like six-year-old Grace Boda glimpsing infinity on the playground, unexpected rapturous absorption in the church pews, or sensations of egoic obliteration in psychedelic states. These are moments when the heart starts beating hard and fast, not necessarily because of any kind of cardiovascular exertion. It's the bodily response to the loss of the familiar self. In these transient experiences, many describe a kind of silence that's almost like a lifting of the cosmic veil. There's brilliant clarity and bodily trembling.

As we've explored the scientific, psychological, and spiritual implications of self-transcendent experiences—including mystical encounters, flow states, and moments of awe—we've noticed striking similarities between these brief events and periods of long-term silence, like what Pythagoras required of his inner circle of students. There's the inward turn and the impossibility of diversion. There's the extinguishment of our typical impulses to perform for other people or to try to control circumstances and events. There's the "right sizing," what David Bryce Yaden of Johns Hopkins University School of Medicine calls "decreased self-salience"—a diminishment of the importance of the egoic self. And there's what William James called the noetic quality, or what he described as "insight into depths of truth unplumbed by the discursive intellect." Just like in the long-term work of silence, these conditions are often present in the fleeting experiences of profound silence.

It's just that they're *radically condensed*.

On a panel with Michael Pollan and Dacher Keltner at the Wisdom 2.0 Conference in San Francisco in 2019, Roshi Joan explored one of the lesser-recognized aspects of awe. "I think a feature of awe that is not always addressed is *fear*," she says, "when we are opened to the unknown, the unknowable, the mystery, the inchoate. We actually have a moment of threat to our egos," she continues. "The ego is deconstructed and it will do everything possible to avoid that happening." In other words, it's only natural to be afraid. Through his extensive research on awe, Keltner estimates that about 21 percent of people's awe experiences are defined by a feeling of fear. The etymology of "awe"—a word rooted in Old English and Old Norse—points toward "fear and dread, particularly toward a divine being." As the meaning of the word evolved in English, sources of awe began to encompass more secular meanings as well, such as "solemn and reverential wonder, tinged with latent fear, inspired by what is majestic in nature."

Awe—what Keltner described in the last chapter as the conditions of "perceived vastness" and the "need for accommodation"—gets to the essence of why silence is scary. Awe challenges the very foundations of what we know. It calls on us to change. As we saw in the previous chapter, the neurobiological common denominator to diverse self-transcendent experiences is a significant diminishment of activity in the medial prefrontal cortex and the posterior cingulate cortex, the parts of the brain associated with our sense of separateness. This raises an important question: *What part of the self is actually getting frightened in such experiences?* It's not necessarily *you* that's getting scared. It's the noisy default mode network, the limited ego-self. It's "the me network" that senses impending annihilation.

Estelle Frankel, the seasoned teacher of Jewish mysticism, is also a musician. She looks to music as a metaphor for how to understand and work with fear. "There are different octaves of fear," she tells us. "The lower octave is self-preservation. It's a survival mechanism. And the higher octave is transcendence. You're taking your personal fear, and then in prayer, in meditation, you bring it to the majesty. It's still a kind of fear, but it's the trembling of the disassembling of the self."

"Fear," at the lower octave, "shrinks our universe," she says. "Awe, the higher octave, expands it. The individual self transcends self. Instead of our yammering mouth talking, the jaw drops. We're speechless." So, whether it's a spontaneous and fleeting experience of vastness and wonder or a slow and deliberate five-year retreat that prompts awe, the result is surprisingly similar. There's a frightening silencing of the familiar noise and an opening and attuning to a level of experience that's bigger, fuller, and more real.

A DIFFERENT KIND OF WISDOM

If Pythagoras were alive today, he probably wouldn't be considered a suitable candidate for tenure at a major university. With his astrological and numerological doctrines and his unusual dietary recommendations, he doesn't fit the mold of an establishment empiricist. And yet he was able to translate an awareness of the workings of nature into insights that yielded real improvements in human lives—in a way that basically no one seems to be able to do today. The mystic-scientist-teacher showed what it means to merge the sublime and the mundane, the spiritual and the material, and still show up in virtually all contemporary eighth-grade math textbooks.

Pythagoras's insights run counter to the modern vision of wisdom. In the most dominant worldview today—the paradigm of GDP growth and the maximum production of mental stuff—understanding of reality results from collecting and analyzing reams of data, debating ad infinitum, publishing in peer-reviewed journals, and pontificating in the public square. Even in the realms of spirituality and religion, we often demonstrate wisdom through analysis of scripture and philosophy: preaching, teaching, televangelizing. There's a common denominator to what we regard these days as wisdom: *thinking, writing, talking.*

For the Pythagoreans, there are different core elements to the process of becoming wise: *emptying, opening, receiving*. The Pythagoreans were, of course, defined by extremely rigorous order and practice. They did debate and analyze. And yet their general theory of clarifying consciousness is more like mystical rapture than like the vaunted productivity secrets of modern innovators.

This is a timely and important lesson.

We're living in an age when humanity is tiring of the superficial. We're weary of medicines that attack symptoms rather than addressing deep causes. It's dawning on us that lasting solutions to climate change, polarization, and mass malaise won't emerge from even the most killer app or wonder drug or intricate algorithm. We're running up against the limits of the latest "life hacks" and losing trust in the cleverest zero-sum political strategies. Today, it's becoming evident that we need what Pythagoras prized most: *insight into the source of things*. We need answers that bubble up from this depth.

With that in mind, we should consider the recommendation from Pythagoras, one of the most generative geniuses in all of recorded history:

Go deep into the silence.

Absorb it.

Let it scare you.

Let it reshape you and expand your awareness.

CHAPTER 8

LOTUSES AND LILIES

"Speech is silvern, Silence is golden."

In the opening pages of this book, we shared the Scottish philosopher and mathematician Thomas Carlyle's interpretation of the maxim "Speech is of Time, Silence is of Eternity."

While the talk of silver and gold, of time and eternity, might sound like a comparison—as if one were more valuable than the other—that's not necessarily how we understand it. Carlyle isn't denigrating the sacredness of speech. Just as silver is a precious metal, time is a holy mystery. Yet time is a mystery that we human beings measure and manage, in practical ways, in the course of our day-to-day lives. Speech, like time, is immanent. And silence, like eternity, is transcendent.

Today, amidst the mass proliferation of mental stimulation, it's clear that we're facing a deficit of silence. How do we find the counterpoint to so much thinking and talking? How do we imbue our urgent, noise-soaked lives with a healthy dose of eternity?

Throughout the world, spiritual and philosophical traditions emphasize the balance of speech and silence as a state of flow between the worlds. While religious traditions often hold that written scriptures—like the Bible, Quran, and Buddhist sutras—are sacred, the vast majority also recognize the sacredness of the space where words and concepts dissolve into unknowing. For example, Jewish mystics cherish the "black fire" of the Torah's written word, but they give equal weight to the open white spaces of the Torah—what is called the "white fire"—the timeless realm of wordless silence.

We've noted that many of the great religious and philosophical traditions don't just look to silence as a *path to wisdom*. In the deepest contemplative practices across traditions, we find a recognition of silence as the *essence of wisdom itself.* Rumi called silence "the voice of God" and all else "poor translation." Black Elk, a great visionary medicine man of the Oglala Lakhota people, asked, "For is not silence the very voice of the Great Spirit?" The *Tao Te Ching* says that "the name you can say isn't the real name," and analysis of the Kabbalah speaks of the "silent, fertile void" as the "Source" and "the divine womb of all being."

From the sadhus of India to the rites of passage in Aboriginal Australia, virtually every religious and spiritual tradition enshrines silence as sacred spiritual encounter. Why is this? Why do the wisdom traditions emphasize silence not only as a vehicle to illumination but, ultimately, as illumination itself?

THE FINGER AND THE MOON

In the Laṅkāvatāra Sūtra, a Mahayana Buddhist text that holds an important place in the Zen traditions, the Buddha teaches "not to get attached to words as being in perfect conformity with meaning, because the truth is not of the letter." He says that "when a man with his finger-tip points at something to somebody, the finger-tip may be taken wrongly for the thing pointed at." If we want to grasp "ultimate reality," he says, we have to consider the possibility that there's more to it than that which can be spoken.

The Zen master Thích Nhất Hạnh interprets the sutra this way: "A finger pointing at the moon is not the moon. The finger is needed to know where to look for the moon, but if you mistake the finger for the moon itself, you will never know the real moon. The teaching is merely a vehicle to describe the truth," he says. "Don't mistake it for the truth itself." While these Buddhist teachings still recognize that words have a valuable place in our lives, they honor a more expansive level of being.

There's a science to how our words work. They separate that which is named from that which is not named, so that we can tell what's what. In fact, in Hebrew the word for "word" is *milah*, meaning "to circumcise or cut." With our words, we divide and dissect in order to describe and indicate. Our whole human world depends on being able to *point to what we mean*—like the finger to the moon. And, still, there are other levels of reality—beneath, between, and above that which we can articulate—that transcend the distinctions of naming things. We asked Estelle Frankel to take us deeper into this concept. "When I'm in my thinking mode, in words, things are broken up. I'm in my 'knowing.'" She continues, "But when I'm in silence, I'm in my *'not knowing'*; it's beyond conceptual thought."

Imagine seeing and sensing the world like a baby.

Imagine encountering a big slobbery dog or fluffy blossoming tree, unmediated by labels or preconceived notions of what's in front of you. A baby's experience is defined not by *what's what* but by *what is*. In your life today, when you sense a shift in the weather or hear an unfamiliar sound, can you tune in to a level of experience that—like a baby's perception—goes deeper than all that you "know"?

It was Michael Taft, the meditation teacher and author, who first offered us the term to capture this phenomenon: "conceptual overlay." He describes it as what happens when we encounter most objects: we *think* about them rather than using our senses to fully *observe and experience* them. We do this, most notably, when an object is familiar. "This is how the human brain evolved—to save energy," Taft reassures us. "If you were walking to work and tried to encounter every object on the way to work with full sensory clarity . . . you'd never get to work; you might be a very happy person, but you'd never get anywhere on time." Taft describes the value of getting beyond our "conceptual overlay"— our mental shorthand—to where we can find a higher degree of what he calls "sensory clarity." If we suspend ourselves, even briefly, in a state of "not knowing," we can encounter the moon *directly* through our senses. We won't settle for our "concept of moon." We won't mistake it for the finger pointing to it.

When we pause in a state of "not knowing" and engage in sensory clarity, we find ourselves in a more direct relationship with *what is*—not what we think it to be, *remember* it to be, *fear* it to be, or *prefer* it to be.

Perhaps no one has captured the heart of this teaching more succinctly than Bruce Lee in his film *Enter the Dragon*. Lee offers one of his pupils a teaching and asks what he's learned. His student brings his hand to his chin and says, "Let me think." Lee whacks the pupil upside his head and says, "Don't think! *Feeeeel*. Don't concentrate on the finger or you will miss all that heavenly glory." Lee directs his apprentice away from his conceptual overlay and toward his sensory clarity.

Justin first encountered the finger and moon metaphor when he picked up an old book about Zen at the age of nineteen. He was intrigued by meditation, but he was still unsure of how to break out of the paradigms of a hyper-talkative suburban American upbringing that was soaked in heady political activism, skeptical secularism, and lots and lots of TV. The image of the finger and the moon was an invitation to a deeper level of silence. It was a rare affirmation that it wasn't necessary to perform or prove things or constantly make progress on preconceived life objectives. Having lived with an often-present buzz of anxiety as a kid—ruminations about the past and worries about the future—he found this teaching a solace. For a mind conditioned to fret about time, this was an invitation to relax into eternity.

When Leigh first started attending meditation retreats, some of her teachers would emphasize the importance of setting clear and firm intentions before going into a long period of practice. She took note. In fact, she took it a little too seriously. She journaled for hours. For each retreat, she fully articulated a topic for consideration—toxic patterns in romantic relationships, the pros and cons of becoming a parent, next steps on her career path, and so on. On the day that a fly made it into the otherwise motionless meditation hall, Leigh had an ironclad intention. But the fly landed on her head, then a neighbor's, then another's, then back to Leigh's head. It was infuriating. Whatever equanimity she'd mustered was foiled each time the fly returned. Leigh's consciousness was consumed by fantasies of how to bat away the buzzing little menace (preferably without anyone noticing). After a while, she realized she had made no progress on addressing her intention of the day at all. The fly had ruined everything. Suddenly she stopped and let the absurdity of it all penetrate her heart. She smiled at her own hubris. Once again, she had tried to let some overanalyzed, future-oriented personal aspiration be the whole point of a retreat that was supposed to be about the present moment. She had been focusing on what she verbally and intellectually thought the retreat was about rather than the living reality of the experience.

The fly pulled her out of her noise.

FLOATING IN THE CLOUD OF UNKNOWING

"Meditation" almost always connotes silence. Buzzing flies notwithstanding, the word evokes images of sitting quietly on a cushion—endeavoring to transcend the "conceptual overlay" in the mind and seeking harmony with *what is*.

"Prayer" evokes something more active: clasped hands and spoken verses. It's usually understood as a verbal act of asking, or at least the formulation of a request within our inner monologue. This word can provoke strong feelings. Even among the most pious, there are varying views on whether it's prudent to ask the higher power for what we personally want. Who are we, after all, to influence the ultimate order of things.

In 1945, the British novelist and philosopher Aldous Huxley published a book called *The Perennial Philosophy* in which he sought to identify the mystical core of the world's great religious traditions. In the book, Huxley describes prayer as not just one practice but four practices. They are (1) *petition*, when we ask for something that we want for ourselves, (2) *intercession*, when we ask for something for somebody else, (3) *adoration*, when we give praise to the divine, and (4) *contemplation*, when we empty ourselves and simply listen. Huxley describes contemplation more specifically as "the alert passivity in which the soul lays itself open to the immanent and transcendent divine Ground of all existence." Contemplation doesn't presuppose that we can in any way change the order of things. It's all about dropping the "conceptual overlay" and tuning in to what is. While contemplation is, in a sense, akin to meditation, it's somewhat different from watching our thoughts or our sensations or the waves of our breath rise and fall. It's about finding quiet in the self as a preparation for handing our personal agency over to a greater mystery. It's not just distinguishing the finger from the moon, but perhaps also letting go into its light. Reflecting on the meaning of contemplation, Huxley offers a takeaway: "The highest prayer is the most passive."

The anonymous fourteenth-century spiritual masterpiece *The Cloud of Unknowing* gives advice on how to enter into a state of immersive contemplation like Huxley's vision of the most passive kind of prayer. "The first time you practice contemplation," the anonymous author says, "you'll only experience a darkness, like a cloud of unknowing." Rather than trying to find your bearings and navigate with your senses and intellect, you should *forget everything*. The author says to simply tune in to the "gentle stirring," to let go into the feeling. Abandon any concepts of the situational and material contents of your life and float in total adoration of the essence of life—the source of life itself.

The message of this spiritual text is that ultimate reality—what you might call nature, the divine, God—is beyond our intellect. The highest reality is knowable only through the directly felt experience of love. Not through speech or thinking, but rather through deeply receptive attention.

The Franciscan friar and socially engaged mystic teacher Richard Rohr underscores that floating in the cloud of unknowing isn't about disrespecting or devaluing the "thinking mind" that "functions by means of concepts, images, words, and so on." It's simply about recognizing that our time-bound minds can't take us all the way up to the eternal. "God is beyond the grasp of concepts," he says. To reach higher, we have to embrace "paradox, mystery, or the wisdom of unknowing and unsayability."

In the Zen tradition, there's a story of the Buddha arriving to give a sermon at Vulture Peak. Monks, bodhisattvas, devas, heavenly beings, and animals are all assembled to hear it. They all stand in focused, serious anticipation of what he has to say. The Buddha rises up and holds a single white flower in his hand so everyone can see. Then he twirls it between his thumb and forefinger. And that's it. The whole sermon consists of a simple gesture with a flower.

A disciple, Mahakashyapa, listening, breaks the serious mood and flashes a slight smile. In that moment, a teaching is transmitted to him. Without a single word, he becomes illuminated.

About five hundred years after the time of the Buddha, Jesus stands before his disciples by the Sea of Galilee at a time when many of them are preoccupied with finding food and other material needs. As recorded in the Gospel of Matthew, as part of the Sermon on the Mount, Jesus says, "Consider the lilies, how they grow: they neither toil nor spin; and yet I say to you, even Solomon in all his glory was not arrayed like one of these."

Jesus is calling on his disciples to not be anxious, but rather trust in the abundance of creation. And he's showing specifically how to do so: *Look to the lilies. Be like a flower.*

We might need more than sunlight and water to survive. But our truest essence is in the same divine simplicity.

What a radical idea. If you want to glimpse the highest wisdom, look to beings that don't even speak. Make them your role models.

Throughout religious history, there's been a balancing act between the *kataphatic* way of knowing—through words, ideas, and distinctions—and the *apophatic* way: through silence, symbols, and unity. Like speech and silence or time and eternity, both the *kataphatic* and the *apophatic* ways have their place and their importance. But since the Reformation and the Enlightenment, there's been a turn toward prioritizing words, images, and distinctions in most Western religious traditions. The European Enlightenment's emphasis on rationalism and the primacy of the printed word arguably drove church leaders toward a *kataphatic* emphasis on sermons and scriptural analysis over the rapturous encounter with the ineffable. In a world of empiricism and rationality and verbal competition, how could the ethereal, intuitive way of silence compete?

The teachings of the Buddha and Jesus we described above—teachings of lotuses and lilies—point to the *apophatic* essence at the heart of the world's wisdom traditions. Richard Rohr emphasizes how religion needs this living connection to the ineffable. It's these "open-ended qualities" that make mystical spirituality "dynamic, creative, and nonviolent." They contrast dramatically with the rigid certitudes and noisy judgments of fundamentalist and fanatical religions.

THE MOST ACTIVE OF ALL LISTENING

The teachings of lilies and lotuses illustrate Aldous Huxley's notion that the "highest prayer is the most passive." These teachings—with such gentleness—point the way to presence and show us how to transcend the noise of self-referential thought and our preoccupation with past and future.

And yet, with immense respect to Huxley, we're not so sure about the word "passive."

Of course, there's receptivity in wordless contemplation. The flower isn't "active" in the sense of creating sound or motion. But emulating a flower is a truly radical departure from the ordinary human condition. It's hard to call that action "passive."

Pythagoras's advice to his students—"Let your quiet mind listen and absorb the silence"—reminds us, strangely, of Professor Imke Kirste's findings with the mice. She described how "trying to hear in silence activates the auditory cortex," how the act of listening to the absence of anything stimulates brain cell development. The mind expands when we enter the most intense receptivity. In profound states of quiet attention, we've experienced the eustress Kirste describes. Even if listening to deep silence is a receptive practice, it's active. As Josh Schrei, a mythologist and host of the podcast The Emerald, put it to us recently, "The silence of focused attention is both alert and relaxed at the same time."

Earlier, we reflected on the word nada: how it means "nothing" in some Romance languages and "sound" in Sanskrit, another Indo-European language. The practice of Nada yoga is a practice of intense active listening—turning down the dial of inner and outer noise, ideally to nothing, in order to make it possible to hear the essence of everything, the pulse of life. According to some understandings, this is the supreme creative act for a human being.

Within the Hindu traditions, the most sacred kind of knowledge, including the four Vedas, is shruti, the product of divine revelation. Later texts are considered smriti—analyses and elaborations. While smriti means "that which is remembered," shruti means "that which is heard." The primacy of shruti implies that the process by which the most revered foundational knowledge came to Earth was not through thinking or even a flashing insight in meditation. It was through listening. It was by letting the quiet mind absorb what is. It was by paying the deepest imaginable attention to nature, to the air, to the essential vibration of life. The ancient rishis *tuned in*.

A centerpiece of the Jewish service is the prayer called the Shema, the affirmation that "God is One." The word *shema* literally means "listen" or "hear." During the prayer, worshippers are instructed to cover their eyes to "close down the visual fields so you don't see the ten thousand things," Estelle Frankel tells us. "Listen. Listen to the oneness. Hear it," she says. That's how you perceive the unity of God. The point of actively tuning in to the auditory, says Frankel, is to focus all attention on "dissolving into divinity." Judaism, Frankel says, "is an auditory religion." The highest realization in Judaism happens through the most alive hearing, just as it does in Hinduism, through *shruti*. "In sound, you may hear multiple sounds," she says, "but they all become one in your experience." This perception of wholeness is another way to describe the highest form of prayer.

We won't pretend to understand exactly how the highest sages of ancient India or the greatest kabbalistic teachers have been able to tune in to the point that they're able to receive timeless revelation or "dissolve into divinity." But here's an educated guess: *practice*.

They rigorously prepared themselves to be in silence.

As Schrei says, "The rishis lived in nature. They sang a lot. They kept a certain diet. All these things brought *attunement* . . . They had a regimen of practice to prepare the vessel to hear the divine sound." Schrei explains that virtually all the wisdom traditions emphasize ethics and morality, avoiding, for example, lying or being excessively materialistic or hurting other people—for reasons that go beyond the maintenance of social order. "Ethical practice is necessary for a being to experience harmonious silence," he says. "If you're lying a lot, you'll be caught up in internal noise."

It isn't as if the ancient sages of India or the great teachers of Judaism—or the contemplative masters of any tradition—just plopped down one day to hear divine revelation. They prepared themselves.

Across diverse traditions, sages have structured their whole lives around the purpose of arriving at the place beyond any and all noise, the place where there's no more servicing the ego, the place where, in Schrei's words, the whole body can become *like a tuning fork.*

The deepest kind of listening is, in a sense, passive. It is an act of receiving. It is, to paraphrase Huxley, about "laying oneself open" to the cosmos. Yet the practice of ordering one's whole life to be able to overcome the noise, to be able to concentrate fully on the grandeur of the present moment is, inarguably, *active.*

MA

Take a moment to come back, once again, to the "feeling experiment" we presented in the last chapter.

Imagine how five years of silence would shift the architecture of your mind.

When we personally imagine this depth of silence, we, of course, imagine devoting a whole lot less energy to formulating arguments and opinions. We imagine less emphasis on the "conceptual overlay" of distinctions and naming things—less attention to the pointing finger and more to the felt sense of the moon. Five years, we imagine, would take us a little closer to the rishis of ancient India who could hear the fundamental vibration of life.

Even through a comparatively short time in silence, we often notice how our minds start to gravitate away from our own preferences and labels and what-if scenarios and toward a higher degree of presence. Sometimes, we find a glimpse of this "reset" in just a brief moment of silence—in the appreciation of the ordinary spaces "in between."

This value of tuning in to the empty spaces—the silent spaces—is, in many ways, a centerpiece of traditional Japanese culture. You'll find it in their aesthetics, architecture, ceremony, and communication. It's not just a stylistic preference; it's an expression of the apophatic way of knowing.

In Japanese, the word *Ma* combines the kanji characters for "gate" and "sun." Together, these written ideograms create an image: *golden light streaming through the slats in the entrance to a temple.*

A common definition for *Ma* is "negative space." It's also described as a "gap" or a "pause" or even as silence itself.

Ma—like silence—is something more than absence. *Ma* is perhaps better described as "pure potentiality." It emanates through both space and time. It expands perception.

Ma describes the intervals between the notes in music—the spaces that make rhythm and melody perceptible. It's the temporal and vibrational presence from which all sounds arise and return. John Cage's *4'33"* is a pure expression of *Ma*.

In the Japanese traditional art of ikebana flower arrangement, *Ma* describes the dynamic balance between the shapes, colors, and textures of the flowers and the empty spaces between and surrounding each meticulously placed item. The objects—the branches and flowers—and the space—the *Ma*—are of equal importance. The admirer is encouraged to step back and take in the wholeness of the creation.

Similarly, *Ma* is a key element of Japanese calligraphy, haiku, painting, gardens, traditional storytelling, dance, and theater. The aim is to make the "invisible energy" of *Ma* as dramatic or breathtaking as the dialogue or design that delineates it.

The formal tea ceremony, which commences with a silent bow and continues for up to four hours of quiet attention, is a ritual of *Ma*. It's about the shared appreciation of silence. As the scholar Okakura Kakuzō emphasizes in his classic 1906 essay *The Book of Tea*, the formal ceremony works with silence as a way to bridge the mundane and the sacred. It's about imbuing the ordinary acts of eating, drinking, and washing with the reverence of exquisite awareness.

Ma is held so central that in the Japanese language a person *without Ma* is called a *manuke*, a fool.

The roots of *Ma* run deep. It's derived, in part, from the principles of emptiness and selflessness that are common to various schools of Buddhism. It's also derived from the Indigenous religion of Japan, Shintoism, which emphasizes both harmony in relationships and balance with nature. Shintoism is an animistic religion, wherein all of the elements—the waters, the trees, the rocks, the winds—are spirits with agency. Without sufficient *Ma*, a spirit may decide not to descend to Earth.

Ma has roots in agriculture, too. If you plant seeds too close together, the crops won't grow as well. You'll have to perform *mabiki*, a thinning and removal of excess foliage to make space for *Ma*. Empty space is a necessary precondition for life to flourish. It allows each of the needed elements—water, sunlight, soil, and air—to reach the growing seedling. And, of course, space is especially valuable in a small and highly populated archipelago.

We're not looking to put Japanese culture on a pedestal. If you've ever walked the packed, buzzing, hyper-commercial, anime/Hello Kitty streets of central Tokyo, you'll know it's one of the most auditorily noisy, informationally overwhelming places on Earth. Yet in today's Japan you can still find elements of a traditional culture that holds silence as sacred. You'll find signs of a society deliberately organized for people to tune in to the empty space "in between."

Years before the car accident, when Faith Fuller was still in her go-go workaholic phase, she was traveling regularly to Japan to give trainings. She remembers meeting her students and asking a perfunctory question: "How are you this morning?"

Her question was usually met with a long period of silence before an eventual answer.

"I always thought, 'They're not understanding me. Let me say it a different way,'" Faith tells us. Her Japanese colleague Yuri Morikawa would give Faith a friendly jab with her elbow. She was telling Faith to wait. "Take a moment to be in the silence with the person you're greeting."

Yuri was instructing Faith in *Ma*.

When Faith asked, "How are you this morning?" students would often take her question as an opportunity to go inside and feel into how they were *actually* doing in that moment. This took some time. Since there were no hang-ups about being silent in conversation with a person they'd just met, they let the wordless space be part of the conversation.

Faith laughs about it now. Even as someone who'd traveled the world and extensively studied intercultural communication, this was—in practice—radically new to her. She got a lot of elbow jabs.

Over time, Faith came to appreciate how this ostensible cultural quirk was, in fact, an expression of something profound. Being comfortable in the silence of another person, she found, brings presence and authenticity to an encounter. It's an antidote to the tyranny of the fastest and loudest. If she could get over her culturally conditioned impulse to jump in and fill the space, she could let golden sunlight enter these encounters. She could make way for pure potentiality.

○

Society hasn't always been as noisy as it is today. But our inquiry, *how we can know silence amidst the internal and external din,* is nonetheless ancient.

"Interior noise," says Pope Francis, "makes it impossible to welcome anyone or anything." Welcoming humanity and nature—affirming life—requires a willingness to float in unknowing, to be like a flower, to stand in the mystery of silence.

You don't have to be a religious person or an adherent to a secret philosophical society to imbue your life with a little bit of eternity. In the chapters to come, we'll embark on the practical work of finding silence in a world of noise. We'll look at how to find both "everyday quiet," informed by fields like psychology and organizational design, and "rapturous silence," applying teachings with mystic origins to modern life.

PART IV

QUIET INSIDE

CHAPTER 9

A FIELD GUIDE TO FINDING SILENCE

Trash talk.

Steel bars clanging.

A gaggle of old TVs and lo-fi radios, adding up to a withering cacophony of party beats and sports commentary.

Nothing but a layer of wire mesh to keep it all out.

In 2007, mounting evidence suggested that Jarvis Jay Masters hadn't committed the crime for which he was imprisoned on San Quentin's death row. The California Supreme Court issued an unusual order for prosecutors to reappraise all the evidence in his case, laying the groundwork for an eventual new trial. A group of activists had built and publicized a rigorous case showing that Jarvis was, in fact, innocent—that he had been the fall guy in a conspiracy to murder a prison guard more than twenty years earlier.

Meanwhile, behind bars, Jarvis had come to be regarded as something of a mensch, a source of calm and counsel—even to the warden's staff.

As his case went on appeal, Jarvis was transferred from solitary confinement—"The Adjustment Center," to use the official Orwellian terminology—to the East Block, a place where inmates were afforded relative freedoms, including more outdoor space, occasional telephone usage, and access to a commissary that sold candy bars and packs of ramen noodles.

Jarvis had been in solitary confinement, the "AC" for short, for twenty-two years—longer than anyone in San Quentin's history. Being moved from the AC to the East Block was a personal victory years in the making.

But when Jarvis got to the East Block, the noise overwhelmed him. He had a seizure—his first in decades and the worst of his life. While he wouldn't have wished solitary on anyone, he realized the solid cell doors had helped manage the outside racket. On the East Block, he had no such sound barrier. He'd need to deepen his practice.

Jarvis is known today as "the Buddhist on Death Row," as the title of his recent biography calls him. He took vows with the Tibetan teacher Chagdud Tulku Rinpoche in 1991. For decades, he's been a principal student of the American Buddhist nun and popular author Pema Chödrön, whom he lovingly calls "Mama." Jarvis has published his own autobiography as well as PEN Award–winning poetry about the work of taming the mind under difficult circumstances. As an aspiring bodhisattva, he works to do what he can to extinguish the suffering of all sentient beings. Over the years, he's come to the realization that San Quentin State Prison's austere 170-year-old maximum-security campus might be as auspicious a place for doing this work as any.

When we spoke with Jarvis, whose case is still on appeal, he emphasized how the noise of San Quentin isn't just auditory. It's a vibration of fear—some of the most pernicious internal noise imaginable. It's fear of upcoming hearings, behavioral reviews, and everyday interactions with prison guards and ornery inmates. For some, it's the existential angst of an impending death sanctioned by the state. For almost everyone there—Jarvis included—it's reverberations of childhood traumas and lingering emotional ghosts from violent homes or a neglectful foster care system.

"In here, you *have* to quiet your mind," he tells us. "Otherwise, you'll go crazy."

When he first entered his cell in 1981, at the age of nineteen, he reached above his head and easily placed his palm flat on the ceiling. He remembers thinking, "It's like I'm being buried alive." The cell felt like a coffin. He knew this was the expressway to crazy—if he took it.

When we spoke over the phone recently, a bewildering nonstop mix of angry and exuberant hollering provided our auditory backdrop.

"The guys in the block used to always get loud *right when I'd meditate*," Jarvis jokes. "I thought there was some kind of grand conspiracy." He laughs now, because he couldn't figure out how they always seemed to know *exactly* when he was meditating. In time, he grew to understand the primary source of noise was his own inner chatter. "It was just me being loud in my mind," he says. "My *responses* to the noise were probably the loudest." Comprehending this reality is one thing; charting a different course is another. But Jarvis knew he had to find a way to meet this challenge in order to survive on the East Block. "I started quieting the noise by *quieting my responses to the noise*," he tells us.

These days, even the wildest noise on the East Block doesn't rattle him. He's found ways to work with it. Jarvis has practices for finding quiet that go beyond his regular sitting meditation. For example, he wrote most of his book *Finding Freedom* during big games—like when the Raiders play the 49ers—when no one calls out his name or cares what he's up to. He finds quiet in moments of doing jumping jacks and yoga in his cell. He finds it when he studies astronomy and plans out when the next solar eclipse will be visible during his time out on the yard. His circumstances require a moment-to-moment discipline to manage his own perceptions and reactions. That's how he stays above the noise.

Jarvis remembers when his friend and investigator Melody

introduced him to meditation a few decades ago. "Are you crazy?" he asked her. "Are you trying to get me killed?" He explained that the last thing you do in prison is close your eyes. It took years of personal setbacks and serendipitous events to bring him to contemplative practice.

"The word 'meditate' is not the word most of the guys here can identify with," he tells us. For the most part, they aren't thinking, "Wow, this is cool right here," he says with a laugh. "They always gonna think 'you're faking it' at first, right? Because they don't think that it's possible for you to be quiet like that . . . They're waiting for you to make a mistake."

Jarvis isn't trying to persuade anybody at San Quentin to do just what he does, but there are occasions when people turn to him for guidance. "From my experience, you have to get in trouble before you do anything." Typically, it's after the trouble that Jarvis finds an opening to introduce silence to a fellow inmate. He described a typical scenario: a man with a hair-trigger temper on the brink of being thrown "in the hole" for cursing out the guards. Jarvis acknowledges that he was once that man. Another scenario that can provoke change is when an inmate loses a loved one. Grief is the great equalizer. They'll ask, "How do you do this, man? I got a lot of stuff going on right now." He doesn't get them reading sutras or studying mantras; he counsels them on how to find a little quiet for themselves in the pain and chaos. A real milestone, he tells us, is when they realize the limits of talking and complaining and blaming and perseverating. The insight is usually expressed in an aspiration like "I'm gonna keep my mouth shut, man." Which, Jarvis says, is a really good start. He adds that we all have to get to the point where "we don't want to create no more bad intentions."

○

As Jarvis thinks about his practice of navigating the noise of San Quentin, he finds that it has cultivated one surprisingly important resource in him: compassion.

Through the quiet he's found in his consciousness over the years, he's started paying more attention to what's really happening around him. He hadn't previously thought much about the backstories of the guys he spent time with in the yard playing basketball or lifting weights. But as the noise in his mind receded, he started to notice faint scars on their hands or faces. He intuited that each one of those scars had its own story, and he carefully and respectfully started asking questions. Though some of the guys demurred, others opened up to him, often about being beaten and neglected as kids. Jarvis started seeing that silence had a moral dimension. Through it, he could get beyond his own trip and cultivate some empathy.

Early on, when all the commotion on the block hampered his fledgling meditation practice, he'd get caught up in judgmental thoughts. "I'd be thinking, 'These guys are crazy.'" But then, over time, he'd come to remember that "they're stuck in a four-by-nine cell, they're on death row." He'd see that "with the screaming and yelling, these people are just dealing with some part of their nature, letting it out." He realized that under these circumstances their behavior was probably pretty normal.

One day, Jarvis stopped and asked himself, "What are these guys suffering from?" He considered the specifics of each man, and then he zoomed out to the bigger picture. He soon realized his question was about the origin of all suffering. "What's *really* going on here?" he wondered. "When and where did their wounding begin?" Then his mind zoomed back in on his own reality: "What am *I* suffering from?" At that point, he saw that he and they were not so different. He resolved to listen more.

"You have to quiet your mind so you can *really* hear," he tells us.

After a few years of practice, Jarvis realized that he had been letting the noise harden him. He was trying to pretend he was at some monastery and working to keep the soundscape of San Quentin out of his awareness. He concluded that he had to stop resisting reality. He had to let his life in. He had to let other people into his heart. He started allowing all that "screaming and yelling" on the block to shift his own inner orientation toward sound and stimulus. "I started feeling things in a more gentle way," he says.

Jarvis pauses and reflects: "I started inviting the noise to quiet the noise."

O

When we first spoke with Jarvis in late 2020, he told us how, earlier that year, he had experienced the deepest silence he'd ever known. He was sick with COVID-19—*very* sick. After a couple of fortunate months with no cases of the virus, San Quentin had been overrun. He'd been reassuring his neighbor, a diabetic, in the cell next door for the first few days. But then "I watched him get sick and die," he says. "It scared the hell out of me because I got sick at the same time." The situation at San Quentin was dire. The *New York Times* reported on the outbreak:

> A number of older prisoners have hung handwritten signs outside their cells that read "Immune Compromised" so that guards will wear masks around them. Other inmates refuse to leave their cells out of fear of catching the virus, according to an inmate, and in recent days, guards have been heard screaming over their radios, "Man down!" after sickened inmates were unable to stand up.

Jarvis had high fevers and debilitating migraines. It was just three months after COVID first hit the United States, and all treatments were still in the preliminary phase. Jarvis remembers a doctor coming to his cell and handing him a bottle of prescription meds with their side effects listed on the back. "I glanced at it, and it just felt like, 'This pill's gonna *kill* me!' . . . Beware of liver pains, headaches, heart aches, high blood pressure, risk of heart attacks, numbness in the feet and legs . . . I mean, it was like, 'What *is* this stuff, man?'" In his dreamlike state of exhaustion, illness, and grief, he just kept staring at the label on the bottle, reading and rereading the list of painful side effects as his mind turned toward all the people suffering in the world from the very same illness.

Then the words came to him: "It's not about you right now."

In that instant, Jarvis's awareness expanded to all the people with preexisting conditions, like his neighbor, who was the very first prisoner to die of COVID in San Quentin. "There's a lot more people sicker than you right now," he realized.

He thought about the "people with weak hearts who were having heart attacks at that very moment." He thought of "all the mothers who would lose their children—who might be losing a child at that very moment." His heart broke open. He joined them in their suffering, and he felt included in something far bigger than himself. In his words:

> It was like giving condolences to so many people that're suffering, and it went from there to constantly telling me, "You're not alone. You're not alone . . . you can get through this."
>
> And it just silenced me.
>
> I didn't even know if I was awake or asleep. I was that quiet.
>
> I needed to feel that way to get out of that sickness.

We spent a lot of time with Jarvis talking through the meaning of this experience—a strange, unexpected, healing encounter with silence. "I don't call those kinds of things miracles," he said, describing the flash of insight that came to him. "But it was a gift to me: that I was in a position to perceive it, to receive it."

THE SPHERE OF CONTROL

How do we find silence in a world of noise?

The answer is different for everyone.

Sometimes it's spontaneous. But usually it's the result of a conscious effort.

As human beings, we all have different means of finding quiet.

Even Jarvis, a meditation teacher, will tell you that sitting alone in meditation isn't the only way.

We all have different degrees of autonomy over how we can choose to spend our days and organize our lives. A single parent working full-time at a minimum-wage job has a different capacity to structure his or her day from the retiree, the college student, or the small-business owner. These differing degrees of autonomy influence how and when we can find silence in our daily lives.

Jarvis is on one far end of this range of autonomy. He spends twenty-three hours of every day in his cell. The prison administration controls nearly every aspect of his life, including whether he can shower. He has virtually no control over the levels of noise and distraction that surround him. And yet Jarvis has become adept at managing the noise in his life. He's able to curate periods of silence. He modulates those buzzing vibrations of anxiety and fear. Although the moments of quiet serenity are scarce, he's able to enter into those moments with a depth of attention. Perhaps most important, he's able to be present for a merciful silence when it graces his life—as it did as he read the label on the medication bottle and heard the words "It's not about you right now." As he says, with thankfulness, he was able to "perceive it" and "receive it."

The obvious place to look for an "expert" on silence is among cloistered monks or cabin-dwelling hermits. But that would miss the point. We're looking to Jarvis precisely because he lives in a high-volume hellscape. It's one thing to find silence in a remote Himalayan hermitage, but it's another to find it amidst anxiety, polluted soundscapes, fear, and trauma. This is what's relevant to most people alive right now.

For Jarvis, the key to finding silence was determining his *sphere of control*. When he first thought to himself "I'm being buried alive," he knew, instinctively, that this line of thinking was catastrophic—even if it seemed to contain a kernel of truth. He'd have to take control, to find the willpower to eradicate that thought. And he did. While Jarvis wouldn't start formal mind training through Buddhist practice until years later, he did, at that time, have a personal guiding motto he learned from the song by Funkadelic's front man, George Clinton— "Free Your Mind and Your Ass Will Follow." He took this to mean he'd need to find some point of leverage to manage his thoughts. Only then could he work toward some semblance of control over his circumstances. Only then could he find some freedom.

We're usually skeptical of the word "control."

We live in a probabilistic world where billions of seen and unseen forces shape everything around us—from the microscopic critters in our guts to Federal Reserve interest rate policies to the configurations of planets and stars in the heavens. Nevertheless, this concept of a *sphere of control* can still be very helpful when we're working to navigate a noisy world.

Leigh once offered this *sphere of control* concept to Justin to help him out of a bind. Justin was in a professional relationship with an active volcano of a man—an influential but highly volatile player in politics. The work was in support of a positive social cause that Justin believed in, and it was a good financial opportunity for his growing family. But the noise it created in his world was unrelenting.

Some of the noise was the usual stuff: an inordinate number of emails, texts, phone check-ins, and videoconferences. But there was subtler stuff, too, like an unhealthy expectation of round-the-clock availability and a tendency to turn ordinary interactions into tense, even outright hostile, arguments. To stave off conflict, Justin kept his phone close and his ringer on. He began compulsively checking it in hopes that an obsequious attitude would help ease the tensions. It didn't. As Justin redoubled his efforts, the noise in his consciousness grew. His internal monologue replayed difficult conversations and projected doomsday scenarios. His nerves were buzzing like a high-voltage transmission line.

Justin was no stranger to high-stress work, and he was a longtime student and teacher of meditation. So he had a respectable array of coping mechanisms. Or at least he thought he did.

Every time he'd go away for a short meditation or employ some cognitive reframing strategy, he'd think he was back to smooth sailing. But then he'd return to the client and get washed into another eddy of internal noise. He noticed how these patterns became a self-reinforcing cycle. Unwanted conversations and device checking at all hours would lead to more worry and preoccupation. Frazzled, he'd cover up the mess with more noise, crabbily commiserating with friends on the phone or seeking solace in late-night binges on Netflix of Latin America's most delicious seaside food trucks.

In that whirlpool, Justin noticed something deeply troubling about himself. In those moments, he wouldn't have sought silence *even if he could*. He didn't want to face himself. It felt better to seek distraction than to face reality.

On a check-in call, Leigh asked Justin *what he yearned for* in the situation—what was the best-case scenario he could possibly imagine? Justin paused to take a seat under the high desert sun. He took in a few deep breaths. He wasn't just yearning for a break or some work-life balance. There was a specific feeling, almost an energy, he was yearning for. It came in the form of an image of standing in the early morning before a serene ocean. After he described that yearning, Leigh asked him *what he feared* most. He said that he was afraid of having to continue to endure this same noise and of being kept away from this oceanic feeling of "reset."

Leigh presented Justin with an image: *an archer's bull's-eye*. The inner circle, she told him, was what he could *control*, the middle ring was what he could *influence*, and the outer ring was *everything else*. Focus on the two inner rings, she said.

For Justin, this wasn't a "Take This Job and Shove It" kind of moment. He wasn't in a position to walk away, at least in the short term. So he started looking more systematically at what was in his *sphere of control* and what was in his *sphere of influence*—where he could still exercise autonomy to reclaim the quiet he needed in his life.

Using the *sphere of control* framework, Justin started to pay closer attention to the sensations in his body and the chatter of his mind when the noise was beckoning. Rather than just doing some ad hoc centering practice from time to time, he got more disciplined about employing a diverse set of strategies for finding everyday silence, including breathing exercises he'd learned long ago, brief breaks under the rays of the sun, and regular hikes with no phone. He thought, too, about how he could *influence* the situation by raising concerns about the sustainability of the work arrangement. As he contemplated the effects of the noise on his mind and body, he renegotiated new parameters with the client. The conversation went better than he expected. He reclaimed the possibility of some silence in his life situation.

Most important, Justin discovered that something precious was actually in his *sphere of control*. He could, as Jarvis would say, "quiet the noise by quieting the responses to the noise." He could work more skillfully with his perceptions and reactions. Noise was not the villain per se. Sure, it was irksome—even painful. But the noise was indicating what needed to change in the underlying situation. With some distance, Justin could see that the worst of the noise—the internal noise—was a function of a flawed way of relating to the client and to the work itself. He was too attached to the outcomes. And it was wholly in Justin's power to change that.

O

There's a certain liberation that comes from knowing what we can change and what we can't. Complex systems like stock markets and global cultural preferences generally fall outside the realm of our personal *influence*; they land in the *everything else* ring of the bull's-eye. Questions like local ballot measures and our partner's behaviors often land in the territory of events we can *influence*. But, unless you're Angela Merkel, Warren Buffett, or Beyoncé, the number of factors you *control* is probably small. But that's okay. A tiny space at the center of the bull's-eye is actually all we need, since the most important work happens inside.

Transcending the noise of this world requires more than high-grade custom earplugs or a "digital detox" at a cabin out of cell range. As with Justin's experience, it requires a certain "archery" of the heart and mind. Just as you get better with a bow and arrow with practice, this form of archery improves the more you do it.

The noise of life is, to some degree, inevitable. Yet we can set our aim for a serene internal soundscape, for a quiet consciousness. We can identify what's in our *spheres of control* and *influence* and, accordingly, apply strategies to steer our lives in the direction of what we want while letting go of *everything else*.

We're going to look at specific strategies for finding silence, starting in the next chapter. But before we can apply these strategies, we need to be able to identify when they are needed—in other words, when there is, in fact, too much noise.

SIGNALS OF NOISE

There's no rigid formula to Jarvis's day-to-day practice. As he works to navigate the noise—to figure out when and how to apply his *control* or *influence*—he emphasizes one essential starting point: *paying attention*. He studies the thoughts in his head and the feelings in his body. He emphasizes that we have to look for *signals*, even tiny ones, so that we can continually steer and course correct.

In chapter 4, we introduced the distinction between *signals* and *noise*—between the kinds of sound and stimulus that indicate what's necessary and the kinds that make unwarranted claims on our consciousness. There's a certain kind of important signal that we can look for within ourselves—in our own minds and bodies. These are personal signals that we've let too much noise seep in; that we've become too overstimulated or distracted. It's important to recognize these signals and to be able to act upon them. Jarvis walks us through an example.

"Nowadays, it's the small, itty-bitty things that get me," he tells us. "Like when I get my breakfast and look at my tray, and there's no butter." He paints this picture for us:

> "Where's the butter at?"
> "You didn't get no butter, Jarvis," they say.
> Or worse: "It's right there on your tray"—when it ain't.
> It gets me every time. I get caught off guard. I make something bigger than it could ever be, you know?

For Jarvis, the feeling of "getting hooked by the itty-bitty things" is a primary signal. The good news is that after years of practice he knows how to recalibrate quickly. He's made it a personal mission to understand his thoughts, feelings, and behaviors—to sense the signals that arise to tell him he's "hooked." While this kind of self-awareness isn't common inside San Quentin (or outside, for that matter), Jarvis regards it as a necessity for survival. His cheery tone turns serious as he tells us, "It only takes two seconds for your whole life to change—*especially* in here . . . In two seconds, I can be in a dungeon somewhere."

For Jarvis, another big signal of surplus noise is when he's too "in his head"—when he gets caught up in intellectual justifications for what's right and wrong, who's to blame, or why life is unfolding one way and not another.

"Logic is a trip, you know?" he says with a chuckle.

The problem isn't thinking per se; it's the torment of overthinking. "We know how to agitate ourselves really, really good," Jarvis explains. "We're professionals at it."

Yet, he adds, we often overthink, "because we care about the people around us, because we care about the causes we're standing for." The "signals" are not the problem. They're telling us something—something important. He isn't advising us to suppress the signals. He's advising us to pay close attention and act accordingly to manage our responses.

Like Jarvis, the two of us are studying our own signals. We recognize our telltale signs of too much external stimulus and internal chatter: *irritability and agitation, rigidity in our thinking and behaviors, knee-jerk defensiveness, and an aversion to listening* (as our spouses and loved ones will attest). Often these signals are accompanied by a tightness in the neck, diaphragm, hips, or lower back. Sometimes there's a shallowness in the breath and a sense of being rushed.

These physical sensations are in themselves important signals. At the edges of our awareness live the noisy emotions—the ones we tend to marginalize most, like rage and despair. These emotions can cause Leigh to suffer middle-of-the-night panic attacks. Justin will clench his jaw to the point of chronic pain. Our automatic reaction to any of these signals is to be anywhere but here and anytime but now; yet they are key indicators of a deeper discordance, and if we ignore them, they'll likely keep coming. If there's something in need of change, you can expect those signals to get louder and be more attention grabbing.

We can wait for signals to find us, or we can seek them out proactively. We can "take inventory" of the noise by asking ourselves questions:

What is the noise like right now? Auditorily? Informationally? Internally?

What am I sensing? What signals are arising?

How does the noise feel in my body? How is it manifesting itself in my mood, my outlook, my focus?

How is the noise reflected in my work and my behaviors? In the tone of my relationships?

Once you sense what the noise of your life is actually like, you can apply the agency you have to make a shift, however small. It's an iterative process—wash, rinse, repeat—or, for our purposes: set your aim, assess your *spheres of control* and *influence*, notice the signals, repeat.

O

Jarvis offers us basic principles for finding silence amidst extreme noise. He studies the nature of the noise we experience—auditory, informational, and internal. He shares strategies for accurately sensing the incoming signals and navigating the way through them.

In the coming chapters, we'll build on this foundation and present a field guide to finding silence. We'll get specific about how to take inventory of our internal and external soundscapes and explore practical ideas for applying our *control* or *influence* to rise above the noise—as individuals, families, teams, and whole societies. We'll look to practices for managing the noise *in the moment*, rituals for finding silence *in the course of a day or a week*, and possibilities for encountering the rapturous silence that can bring transformation to our lives *in the course of a year or more*.

CHAPTER 10

THE HEALTHY SUCCESSOR TO THE SMOKE BREAK

Leigh has a confession to make.

She used to smoke.

Actually, the confession isn't so much that she smoked. It's that she *loved* it. She loved the soft kiss of the cigarette as it dangled from her lips. She loved the "sizzle" as she drew in that first drag. She loved the swirl of smoke rising into sunbeams and light shafts. Contrary to the prevailing mythology in her family, it was smoking—not yoga—that taught Leigh to inhale and exhale deeply.

That said, there were ample reasons to quit: the persistent cough, the ever-increasing cost, the smell of smoke in her hair as she curled up in bed at night. And, of course, her overriding desire to live a long and healthy life.

Looking back on why it took so long to quit, Leigh returns to smoking's one big benefit: *the pockets of silence it provided.*

Some cocktail napkin math reveals that those pockets totaled up to two hours and thirty minutes a day. That's more like a sizable hole.

Over recent decades, when most smokers gave up their addiction, they also gave up those socially sanctioned pauses in the day—especially at work.

Scholars at the University of Edinburgh and the Scottish division of the U.K.'s leading center for independent social research, recently published a qualitative study of why young people choose to use cigarettes today. They took the title of their publication from an illustrative quotation offered by one study participant: "Tell them you smoke, you'll get more breaks." The researchers found that in "certain occupational contexts, notably the hospitality industry and continuous demand jobs in call centres, being a smoker carried the significant benefit of short breaks, and in some cases was the only way of getting breaks." The authors elaborate further: "These tend to be in low-paid, low-skilled occupations which generally have poorer rights."

Think about that for a moment. Large numbers of people consciously choose to inhale proven carcinogens because there's simply no other way to get a break from the grind. This speaks volumes about humanity's unfulfilled need for quiet time.

It also raises a question: *What is the healthy successor to the smoke break?*

In other words, when you feel yourself getting overwhelmed with the noise of the workplace, the household, or the worries in your head, what do you do, where do you go, and how do you hit reset?

How can we find the pockets of silence that we need on an everyday basis?

You might have five minutes to step away from the computer. You might have but fifteen seconds when your child is captivated by a toy. Rather than focusing on the quantity of silence, think about the *quality* of silence—however fleeting it might be. How deeply can you dive into the spaces between all the sounds and stimuli?

In this chapter, we will offer you a variety of strategies for finding pockets of silence in your day. These are not meant to be strictly pre-scriptive but rather as guiding ideas and inspirations. Only you know your life circumstances, your preferences, and your needs. Only you know what's within your *spheres of control* and *influence*. While we encourage you to apply what's useful and appealing here, we also ask you to keep in mind that a strong *"No! Not that!"* reaction might be worthy of closer investigation. Anything that solicits a powerful response may have something to teach you. We won't yet get into the work of finding the most profound and transformational silence; that will come in the next chapter. But remember that these moment-to-moment practices—these little pockets of silence—cumulatively build our capacity to recognize and receive the most profound silence when it comes.

Likewise, we won't yet get into the practices of managing noise in relationships, families, and organizations here. All that comes later, too. We're starting with individual practices—those most in our *sphere of control*—in order to lay the foundation for what follows.

Before we start exploring, we want to share a few general recommendations.

First, *keep an open mind.* Remember the guy who finds immersive internal silence through chain-saw carving? Amidst the sputtering motor and flying debris, that guy's inner noise dissolves. "Quiet is whatever someone *thinks* quiet is," Joshua Smyth reminds us. So, as we explore practices for finding silence, remember that one person's noise may be another person's quiet. It's okay if your style is idiosyncratic.

Second, *explore a bunch of practices.* The noise of the world takes many forms and operates on multiple levels. So it's natural to need a wide variety of tools to navigate a wide variety of terrain. You might pull out a different practice based on the kind of noise you're facing, your location, your mood, or what happens to be in your *sphere of control* or *influence* in that particular moment.

Third, *notice all of your signals.* Just as we need to be mindful of the signals in our minds and bodies that indicate too much noise, it's also valuable to pay attention to *positive* internal signals—the indications that we're finding rest, nourishment, and clarity through quiet. Sometimes these pleasant signals are more difficult to detect. Most of us are pros at noticing unwanted or unpleasant stimuli. This is what cognitive scientists call our negativity bias (or our positive-negative asymmetry), and it's often important for our survival. Yet the welcome signals are equally valuable data points. They show us when we're on track, what works in our lives, and how to build on what's effective.

Fourth and finally, *do what brings you joy.* Part of the reason we decided to write this book is that mindfulness practice has, for too many, become a "should," and sometimes even a cudgel for self-loathing. This principle came immediately to mind when Leigh met Zana, a fellow parent on her daughter's volleyball team. They hit it off instantly. Zana recently made partner at a big San Francisco–based law firm. She was working up to seventy hours a week with a daunting commute while raising two daughters on her own. Somehow, she seldom missed a game. Upon hearing that Leigh was writing a book about silence, Zana launched into a self-berating tirade about not having a meditation practice. "I know! I know! I totally need to meditate! I've got to do that. I've been meaning to do that forever. I don't know *why* I don't do that!" This sort of shame spiral is common in our social circles. But it doesn't have to be. Our practices can and should be relaxing, enriching, and—dare we say it—pleasurable. While some discipline is likely required, pick the practices to which you will gladly commit and stop beating yourself up for those you won't.

As you explore the principles and stories of the pages ahead, keep these four tips in mind and consider what you can seamlessly—even blissfully—integrate into your life.

IDEA 1: JUST LISTEN

It was May 2020. The whole world was in lockdown. City streets were all but empty. Skies were silent and airports shuttered. But for many of us, life was noisier than ever.

With mongoose-like reflexes, Justin hit the mute button again and again to hide the untamed soundscape of his household from colleagues on conference calls. There were babies crying, there was oatmeal burning, there was the hum of the robot vacuum cleaner and the din of blaring Disney musicals. Justin's three-year-old daughter had a battery-powered interactive kids' book that played recordings of songs from the movie *Frozen* on a tinny speaker. One day, she played it on loop for what must have been nearly an hour.

Justin was about to lay down the law when, suddenly, he realized that this obnoxious recording contained a meaningful invitation.

"Let it go! Let it go!" Idina Menzel belted out in her soaring mezzo-soprano.

Justin took the advice.

He stepped outside into the rays of the midday sun and forgot about work and household chores for just a moment. In the backyard, he could hear the distant sound of cars rolling by and a gentle sprinkling of birdsong. Mostly, he heard the breeze rustling the nascent spring leaves. He didn't stop to meditate per se. He just listened—*to nothing in particular.*

We've mentioned the millennia-old Indian tradition of Nada yoga, sometimes known as "the yoga of sound." Some teachers describe the practice as tuning in to the "sound of silence." The Theravada Buddhist teacher Ajahn Amaro offers instruction on how to do it: "Turn your attention toward your hearing. If you listen carefully to the sounds around you, you're likely to hear a continuous, high-pitched inner sound like white noise in the background." Amaro adds, "There's no need to theorize about this inner vibration in an effort to figure out exactly what it might be. Just turn your attention to it." He says you can "use the simple act of listening to it as another form of meditation practice . . . Just bring your attention to the inner sound and allow it to fill the whole sphere of your awareness."

This practice of just listening—opening your ears, along with your attention, to what's present in yourself and your immediate surroundings—has a cleansing and awakening effect. It's like what Imke Kirste discovered in her research—that the act of *listening to nothing* accelerates neuron development. When we *just listen,* we don't trouble ourselves over the source of the sound. Instead, we use our entire instrument—ears, attention, body, and being—to tune in to the vibration of life.

There's no one right way to do it.

Jay Newton-Small hadn't heard of Nada yoga. But she discovered a variant of this practice on her own, and it's been helping her for years. Jay was the longtime Washington correspondent for *Time* magazine and a reporter for Bloomberg News. She's now the founder of a company that uses storytelling to improve health care. Over decades of working in high-stress, high-volume settings in New York and D.C., she started noticing how the intensity of life amplified a "static" that she could actually hear if she took the time to listen. So, on a regular basis, she'd get home after a day's work, sit down on the couch, and just listen to the ringing in her ears. For the first minute or two, she usually experienced it like a wall of buzzing sound that she could feel throughout her body. But after about five minutes of just listening, she noticed that the volume of the sound would subside. Then she'd get up off the couch and go cook dinner.

Jay noticed something important: it's the act of listening itself that diminishes the noise. The ringing in her ears at the end of the day was a proxy for the residual tension left over from a frenetic day. By bringing her attention to that energy and just sitting with it, she found it mostly dissolved. Her nervous system got back to its state of equilibrium. The noise of the world got more manageable.

For the vast majority of us in the vast majority of situations, just listening—simply noticing noise and silence—is within our *sphere of control.* Take two or three minutes. Maybe step outside, as Justin did on that spring day of 2020, or sit down on the couch after work as Jay regularly does. Stop and listen to the sounds around you and within you. Pay attention. Let it go.

In the spring, where Leigh lives, the amber leaves of the California live oak fall gently to the ground in preparation for summer growth. Then, like clockwork, a dissonant chorus of miniature combustion engines commences. The leaf blowers in Leigh's neighborhood are more than background noise. They are so notorious that the neighboring city of Berkeley banned them altogether.

Perhaps you have an analogue. In New York, it's often garbage trucks. In New Delhi, honking horns. Most densely populated places have their versions of the omnipresent, human-made sonic headache. Of course, our perceptions of these noises are relative, as the acoustical consultant Arjun Shankar will tell you:

Sound is when you mow your lawn,
   noise is when your neighbor mows their lawn,
   and music is when your neighbor mows your lawn.

For Leigh, the cacophony of other people's leaf blowers is indisputably noise. Every once in a while, though, she gets a respite. Maybe it's a minute. Maybe it's only ten seconds. But the noise all suddenly stops. When Leigh notices that pause, it's a gift. Her amygdala chills out. Her breathing deepens. It's almost like an extremely condensed retreat.

This whole leaf blower drama provides a metaphor for a broader question about the human experience:

How do we savor the moments when the noise ceases?

How do we make the most of these "little gifts" that unexpectedly come to us?

Perhaps most important, how do we recognize and accept these gifts in the first place?

Brigitte van Baren has built her career on getting executives of large multinational corporations to overcome their type A tendencies and honor little unexpected moments of silence when they arrive. In

1992, her Netherlands-based consultancy became one of the first organizations to overtly incorporate Zen practice into corporate culture. A key element of her work is teaching her clients to accept and even appreciate when their plans—great and small—are thwarted. Almost everyone she works with despises "wasted time." They tend to detest delayed planes and trains, people who are late for appointments, waiting in lines, being put "on hold," and all other unplanned silences. "They *think* they are in control, and they *want* to be in control, but in fact they are not in control," Brigitte tells us. She explains to her clients that when they think their time is being wasted, they have two choices: (1) be frustrated and emotional, and lose energy, or (2) take this time as an opportunity to find clarity and renewal in silence.

"Silence is always with you," she reminds them. These apparent delays are gifts—if they only view them as such. She believes that one of our greatest assets is the ability to access silence, especially when something unforeseen has happened. To cultivate this skill, Brigitte offers simple instructions when plans get waylaid:

- Take this event as a gentle reminder that you are not in complete control of everything.

- Instead of becoming frustrated, reframe the delay as an opportunity to savor an unstructured moment. Avoid the temptation to fill it.

- Ask yourself, "How can I use this moment to recharge?" If we receive these moments as little gifts, she tells us, we may soon look forward to them rather than meeting them with dread.

Justin was in the car recently, immersed in listening to a podcast episode, when the sound of the recording inexplicably stopped. "Is someone calling?" he wondered. "Is the Bluetooth broken?" He felt the physiological and psychological *contraction* that Judson Brewer speaks about as a proxy for internal noise. When the podcast came back on after about three seconds, he felt his body get back toward equilibrium. But looking back, Justin wondered, *why couldn't he just relax into that unexpected gap?* Could he train himself to enter into a feeling of expansion rather than contraction in a moment when the sounds and stimulation give way?

Pema Chödrön, the Buddhist teacher and author whom Jarvis calls Mama, writes about cultivating our capacity to rest in the open space, even "when things fall apart." With this phrase, she's generally referring to the bigger situations in life, where our reality maps fall away and we lose our bearings—like the loss of a job or the unexpected dissolution of a relationship. What we're talking about here is an infinitesimal microcosm of such a serious event. And yet the fundamental mechanism of response is similar. When we lose our reference points, can we avoid the impulse to seek to fill the space? Can we open up? Can we surrender into the silence?

From the trivial moments—like the break in leaf blowers—to the bigger moments—like when we stop to consider our own mortality—a strangely similar line of inquiry applies: *How do we become more perceptive and receptive to the silences that find us?* As with the practice of just listening, the most important first element here is *noticing*. It's paying attention to when these unexpected openings arise. When we really notice, we can start appreciating. We can shift our attitudes to these open spaces, honoring the gaps as gifts.

IDEA 3: WHAT YOU'RE ALREADY DOING—BUT DEEPER

"Where do I find my silence? I find it *in between*—in the breath," says Pir Shabda Kahn, the Sufi teacher.

According to his spiritual lineage, the breath tells you everything you need to know about your internal state. "If you study the mysticism of breath, you will see that every disturbing emotion—if you'd like to call it that—interrupts the rhythm of the breath." He explains further,

"If you're lonely, you will be stuck on the out breath. If you're angry, you will be stuck on the in breath, and so on."

When Pir Shabda speaks of the "in between—in the breath," he's referring to the moment between the in breath and the out breath, the "swing" from one to the other. "No matter where I am—in a busy airport, a busy anything—I can, even in the moment, enter the consciousness through the breath and find my way to silence." He adds, "Making a habit of a rhythmic breath, long-term, is the panacea for everything." The quality of the breath's "swing" is both the diagnostic and the remedy.

This "swing" in the breath happens every few seconds. And if we can enter deeply enough into it, in any given moment, we can encounter an expansive silence. Pir Shabda reckons we should at least give it a little bit of attention.

In 1999, Stephen DeBerry didn't have time for silence. He didn't even have time to think about breathing. "I'm just so busy. And I'm so important. I'm, like, CEO guy," he says, laughing heartily at himself.

Stephen is an anthropologist by training, a dad, an elite athlete, and a pioneer of social impact investment in the tech space. Not long ago, he was named one of the hundred most powerful African Americans in the United States by *Ebony* magazine and *The Root/Washington Post*. Stephen—then, as now—was busy, engaged, and important.

At that demanding time in 1999, Stephen was working with an executive assistant who was also a yoga teacher. He recounts the moment when she made a gentle intervention: "She's like, 'Okay, important guy, here's a hack for you: throughout your day, when you can remember to do it, just take *three breaths*. You're doing it anyway. But just *pay attention*," she emphasized. "'Just three. You have time for that, busy guy, right?'" She was speaking the language of Silicon Valley with its obsession with "hacks" and efficiency, so he had no choice but to listen.

Stephen thought about it and realized, "Yeah, I *am* doing it anyway. I can just pay attention to that," he tells us. "And it changed me." He knows he probably wouldn't have been able to healthily sustain the intensity were it not for this shift in his consciousness.

Since then, Stephen has been working with moment-to-moment breath attention as his ever-accessible gateway to internal silence. He's been following the advice: Three breaths in a row. Pay attention. That's it. He does it in meetings, he does it on commutes, he did it while he was talking to us. He finds silence in this space in the midst of the intensity of his day-to-day life. "It's been over two decades," he marvels, "and I'm pretty much doing the same thing." We love the simplicity of Stephen's approach: just give more attention to some of the breaths that you're already taking.

Bringing your awareness to the movement of the inhale and exhale—and especially to the space between the two—generates quiet in the consciousness. You simply notice what's happening.

And if you can find a few minutes of quiet time and want to exert a little bit of extra effort, you can also go deeper into the breath and encounter a more profound kind of internal silence.

The eccentric and wildly popular Dutch wellness guru Wim Hof (also known as the Iceman for his penchant for bathing in freezing water for hours and climbing Mount Everest shirtless) has popularized a kind of yogic breath exercise that centers on doing a series of about thirty full inhalations and quick exhalations, followed by a pause with empty lungs for as long as you can hold it. When Justin does this kind of breathing practice—oxygenating the body as fully as possible, then surrendering everything for a minute or two—he sometimes reaches a place of unexpectedly rich internal silence. It's like momentarily abdicating the responsibility of having to do anything at all—even respire. To remain in the still space for at least thirty seconds without gasping for air, Justin can't entertain noisy thoughts; he can't let his mind wander into the past or future. He has to stay present. Otherwise, his diaphragmatic reflexes will give him automatic feedback that he's veered back into ruminative thought. Internal silence is a precondition for doing the exercise.

There are dozens of kinds of yogic breathing practices of varying degrees of intensity that train the consciousness for quiet. You might study the traditional disciplines of pranayama with a teacher or simply look up exercises like "box breathing" or "diaphragmatic breathing" to learn techniques to calm the body and quiet the mind. Most of them take less time than the standard workplace cigarette break.

Whether it's integrated moment-to-moment awareness of the breath or a dedicated practice of more intense breathing exercises, it's through the inhale and exhale that we often find the most immediate, direct, readily available encounter with silence. It's a simple path to deeper feeling and bodily awareness, to the inner sensation of expansion. We think of these practices as an extension of what we're always doing anyway—*breathing*. Just deeper.

IDEA 4: SILENCE IN MOTION

Ruth Denison was a trailblazing twentieth-century Vipassana instructor and one of the first Western women to ever become a Buddhist teacher. She studied Zen in Japan in the 1960s and then received transmission from the Burmese Vipassana master U Ba Khin. This means that Ruth came of age at an austere time of meditation practice. It was an era of strict adherence to seated posture. Movement—even stretching between periods of meditation—was largely forbidden. Physical stillness was considered an attribute of Noble Silence.

While Denison was a globally respected teacher who honored the traditions of her lineage, she did break a few long-standing norms. For example, if you went to visit while she was teaching her American students on any given day, you might find her rounding everyone up to go to the local aquatic center for a session of synchronized swimming. On some days, she'd lead her students dancing in formation. Other days, she'd encourage everybody to get on the floor and wiggle around like worms. Denison pioneered many of the diverse mindful movement practices that are more familiar today, like walking, standing, jumping, lying down, yoga asanas, eating with careful attention, and laughing.

If the Buddha had intended for his disciples to practice *solely* by sitting motionlessly, Ruth never got the message.

"I discovered that I had a natural affinity for staying in touch with my body," she told *Insight* magazine in 1997. "Even though I suffered from back problems which made sitting extremely painful, I was able to stay in touch with my bodily sensations and began to enjoy ever deeper levels of concentration."

Ruth believed that deep work in the body was a necessary foundation for mindfulness and a way to honor the essential teachings of the Buddha. When she'd take her students to do synchronized swimming or invite them to crawl around on the floor, she typically asked them to maintain the Noble Silence and to tune in as much as possible to their direct felt experiences.

In chapter 6, we described how states of flow are akin to silence in the mind. When our friend Jamal is "hot on the court," when he "can't miss a shot," he tells us that his "mind is silent." Whether you're involved in a competitive basketball game or synchronized swimming, the eustress created by immersive physical movement demands most of our attention. Because we don't have excess attention to spare, our attentional filters have to bypass the overwhelming majority of gathered information to screen for a minuscule amount of relevant material. As Csikszentmihalyi has argued, these activities leave little capacity for noisy rumination about the past or future.

Justin's friend Clint, who recently started doing jujitsu, put this concept another way: "If I let my mind wander, I'll get my ass kicked." When Clint is caught up in his own noise, he finds himself thrown to the mat. Martial arts, like many kinds of physical practice, train the mind and the nerves to tune in to internal quiet—not just in that one moment, but in life more generally.

"After practicing," Clint says, "I feel this deep silence in my mind and my body for a day or more."

Science is just beginning to recognize the link between physical movement and inner quiet. But the link is intuitive. *Have you ever gone on a walk to clear your head?* Sure, walking is not as intense an activity as Jamal hitting a slam dunk or Clint just barely escaping getting whupped. But the simple and repetitive movement of the feet and the heightened respiratory and heart rates it generates can lead us to fundamental elements of flow. These include what Csikszentmihalyi describes as the "merging of action and awareness" and the tendency toward the "autotelic experience" where activity becomes "intrinsically rewarding." Just as Judson Brewer found substantial reductions in posterior cingulate cortex activity in his study participant who entered a self-reported flow state, physical movement activities that promote present-moment awareness likely dampen activity in the noise centers of the brain, including the regions that make up the default mode network.

Your physical practices don't have to be the epitome of athletic eustress. You might just be rolling around like a worm on the floor of the meditation hall.

What matters is that you're fully into it.

IDEA 5: MOMENTARY MA

Aaron Maniam has prime seating at one of the loudest sporting events on the planet. As a senior public servant in Singapore, he was responsible for organizing some of the programming for the country's world-renowned—and unbelievably high-decibel—Formula 1 championship auto racing competitions. As a widely recognized innovator on e-governance issues and civil service education, an award-winning published poet, and now the country's deputy secretary in the Ministry of Communications and Information, Aaron is as immersed as anyone in the sound and stimuli of the modern world. But spend some time with Aaron, and you'll notice that he radiates the clarity of quiet. It's in his poetry. It's in the feeling and cadence of his speech.

When we ask Aaron how he finds silence amidst all the noise in his world, he describes a simple set of practices. Like that of Pir Shabda Kahn and Stephen DeBerry, Aaron's core approach hinges on breath awareness. But he focuses this awareness specifically on *transitions*. Like the Japanese cultural value of *Ma*, he honors *the spaces in between*.

"I'm a big believer—whenever I can remember—in taking one deep breath before I do anything," he says. "Whether that's opening the door, standing up to leave the room, turning on the tap for some water, or turning on or off the lights—just one deep breath." He adds, "And it takes nothing—like two or three seconds." He applies the practice in his workday. "Before I start a new document, before I read a new email—one deep breath—and then I continue." Aaron recalls learning this approach from the author David Steindl-Rast, a Benedictine brother. Aaron, a practicing Muslim, comes from a big and diverse Singaporean family that includes, among other faith traditions, Catholics. He's had some of his deepest encounters with silence on retreat at Benedictine monasteries. Aaron has found that this technique of working with *transitions* offers a way to bring a monastic presence into his anything-but-quiet professional life. "I tend to think in terms of concentric circles of silence, from the very micro to the very macro," he tells us.

Aaron demonstrates how to harness the moments of silence that often go unnoticed, the transitional moments. Brother David's teaching is that we can go deeply into the micro-moment—to the point that we actually *decompress time*. How fully can you enter the plenitude of a moment of silence? Can you concentrate enough to find a bit of eternity in the space of two to three seconds?

In our own lives, we've found that instead of stretching and savoring time, we too often race through it, like aspiring Formula 1 champions. We tend to view transitions and unstructured moments as voids to urgently fill. In a split-second pause, we might succumb to the itch to check email, shoot off texts, or get a "quick hit" of today's news. But—as the wisdom of *Ma* advises—we find connection to eternity in these hidden spaces. Even though Aaron's day job centers on the prose of policy making, he seeks to make his everyday experience more like poetry, where *what is unsaid* is as important as what is said, where *the space between* is as cherished as matter itself.

IDEA 6: DO ONE THING

Schluuup.

"It's a gorgeous sound, isn't it?" Faith Fuller asks upon releasing the seal of an airtight canister.

She's making coffee—a mundane daily task that she finds surprisingly transcendent.

Faith shuffles to the kitchen each morning. She pulls the canisters—one caf and one decaf—from their shelf in her cabinet. She savors the sound as she releases the seal.

"The best part is the sniff," she tells us, as if relaying a secret. "I meet that smell, and it's meeting me. In that moment, I'm in the pleasure of that connection."

With care, she scoops the coffee grounds, rounds off the scoop, and places the contents of it into the basket of her decidedly unglamorous standard drip coffeemaker. She measures six cups of water and prepares to pour it into the back reservoir. "There is a moment of respect and precision there, pouring the water in," she explains.

Faith waxes mystical about the choice we have before us in every mundane task. "Get out of the outcome and into the process," she says. "If I'm focused on the outcome—the completion of the task—then I miss the smell of the coffee being made." She'd also miss the suction sound that she adores, the chocolate hue of the grinds, the sheen on the water, the empowering push of the start button—all of which is to say nothing of the taste of coffee itself.

"Doing one thing isn't that: it's a string of 'one things,'" Faith tells us. "And almost every 'one thing' is a doorway to a moment of satisfaction."

For Faith, the satisfaction is sensory. These are moments of pleasure. And she's not the least bit apologetic about that. "In Buddhism," she explains, the five senses are doorways to enlightenment. They're not a problem in that Puritan way."

For most of us, making coffee is too often just another part of the grind. We speed recklessly through it as another "to do," spilling grounds and splattering water. Running to stop the beeping microwave. Cursing curdled milk.

Faith challenges us to make a ritual out of little everyday chores. Which is to say, she challenges us to find an experience of the sacred in the ordinary.

The etymology of the word "ritual" comes from the Sanskrit root *Ṛta*, meaning "natural order" or "truth." Rituals are not just about enshrining positive daily or weekly habits. They're about connecting to something higher. That which we regularly do with attention and reverence brings us closer to *presence*.

"Rituals stabilize life," the Korean German philosopher Byung-Chul Han writes. "They turn the world into a reliable place. They are to time what a home is to space: they render time habitable." From the everyday "in-between" moments to the more rarefied states of awe to the once-in-a-lifetime mystical experience, our rituals for finding silence—large or small—do stabilize our lives. They make space and time more "reliable" and "habitable."

"Making coffee is an important ritual for me," Faith observes. It's a simple start to her day—before things get complicated. It's a buffer. She adds, "Rituals combine *structure*, or habit, with *heart*. You have to have both. Structure with no heart, and you're not present for it; you're spaced-out. But heart without structure . . . you're not going to get a good cup of coffee."

In chapter 8, we described how we're most prone to *conceptual overlay*—the subtle noise of habitually labeling things rather than using our senses to fully observe and experience them—when we're in the presence of the ordinary and familiar. Cultivating simple daily rituals, moments of careful attention and connection, is a way of enshrining a direct and quiet encounter. It's a way of cultivating what Michael Taft calls "sensory clarity." When Faith is preparing her daily cup of coffee, she's not in the space of verbalization or even thinking. She's in the space of direct feeling. Not the finger, but the moon. Bruce Lee would wholeheartedly approve.

IDEA 7: SILENCE WITHIN THE WORDS

In *The Shallows: What the Internet Is Doing to Our Brains*—a 2010 book that's more relevant than ever today—the journalist and sociologist Nicholas Carr laments that online life is all about interruption. And this changes how we process information in fundamental ways. Even if efficiency is increased when we gather information by reading online, Carr contends that we've lost our capacity to employ a "slower, more contemplative mode of thought." He explains that we've migrated from a kind of cognition that's about making connections toward one that's merely about foraging for factoids. He argues that we've lost the skill of "deep reading."

Given what we've so far explored about how words work, "deep reading" might sound like a paradoxical concept. If language is inherently like the finger pointing at the moon—"Separating that which is named from that which is not"—then how can language be a pathway to the unitive experience of internal silence?

We'll attempt to answer this question with another question: *Have you ever gotten into a kind of reading that feels like a flow state?*

We've often felt it on long airplane flights or other places where there's no distraction—nothing else competing for our attention—for a set period of time. We've felt it when we're totally immersed in a good story. While reading doesn't have the typical physicality of flow that merges action and awareness, it can take us toward self-transcendence. Sure, reading is a form of mental stimulus. And yet, when we're utterly present in it, it can be a vehicle for getting beyond inner and outer distraction. Even if the mind is tracking details and themes, we're nonetheless *in it*. We're not open to external sound and information. We're not entertaining judgments and expectations about our personal past or future.

Nakamura and Csikszentmihalyi have suggested new frontiers of research on what they call "microflow activities," like reading or doodling. They believe these activities "might play an important role in optimizing attentional regulation."

In the Catholic and Anglican traditions, there's a practice called *lectio divina*, translated from Latin as "divine reading." It refers to the cultivation of a purposeful space through contemplation of the written word. In it, you read a passage of a sacred text with the deepest possible focus and then stop to reflect upon its meaning. Like "deep reading," this is about meeting the words as directly as possible. It's bare minimum conceptual overlay.

It's sometimes possible to find a similar experience in the spoken word. Estelle Frankel tells us, "A good prayer leader is weaving silence between every prayer." She describes a chant-based service of her lineage, called Jewish Renewal: "Chanting fully engages the senses. It quiets the mind to be ready to bathe in the silence." Something similar happens, she tells us, in sacred storytelling. "Let's say you tell a Hasidic story and you tell it *well*. There's a moment of silence, like a Zen koan, where the mind tries to understand it and then it kind of gives up." As a prayer leader, she relishes these moments. She adds, "You've got to slow the mind down; a good chant, a good prayer, a good story, puts you in an altered state that prepares you for silence."

So does a good poem.

"Poetry comes out of silence and leads us back to silence," the storytelling poet Marilyn Nelson said in an interview with Krista Tippett. "Silence is the source of so much of what we need to get through our lives." She continues, "Poetry consists of words and phrases and sentences that emerge like something coming out of water. They emerge before us, and they call up something in us." The Pulitzer Prize–winning poet and two-term U.S. poet laureate Tracy K. Smith said in an interview, "Poetry is the language that sits really close to feelings that defy language." It attempts the impossible. She reflects upon how it is poetry that we turn to in life's most ineffably poignant moments: birth, death, spiritual awakening, falling in love.

All poetry—irrespective of rhythm or word count—has silence built into its structure. It's on the page, amidst stanzas, between words. A good poem holds the creative tension between what's said and what's unsaid. It skips across time like a smooth stone, on and off the surface of the water. It leaves space for what arises for *this one* reader, on *this one* day, in *this one* moment.

If you feel as if you've never "gotten" poetry, ask a friend or a loved one who does what their favorite poem is and what they love about it. When you read their favorite poem or have them read it to you, *listen for the silence*. Hear the interface between speech and space. The balance between "silver" and "gold." The poet David Whyte writes, "Poetry is the verbal art-form by which we can actually create silence." The writer and public intellectual Susan Sontag said the highest form of art, prose, or poetry "leaves silence in its wake."

A simple practice of reading a poem or passage each morning can set the tone for the whole day. One read just before bed can seed your dreamland. Even if you're not reading the most highbrow literature, seek to make the reading itself a practice of pristine attention—an effort that "leaves silence in its wake."

IDEA 8: QUICK "HITS" OF NATURE

"What about birdsong?"

Over years of conversation with others about how they find silence, we've heard variants of this question scores of times. Describing the silence of a sunrise or a pristine lake or a remote cabin, people often wax poetic about the birdsong before pausing to ask, "Wait, does that count as silence?" It's true that birdsong isn't auditory quiet. Sometimes, it might even register as downright loud. When it's wooing a potential mate, the male white bellbird of the Amazon region usually calls at up to 125 decibels, somewhere between the level of an emergency vehicle siren and a jet engine.

But there's something about listening to birds that, for many people, generates the felt experience of quiet.

For some, it's the essence of silence.

Across continents and through the ages, human beings have found enchantment and inspiration from the practice of watching and listening to birds. In the past couple years, it's become unexpectedly *en vogue*. While sheltering in place during COVID, many of us urban and suburban dwellers finally heard the songbirds in our yards. A flurry of articles in 2020 actually questioned if birds had suddenly gotten louder. Scientists responded. No, it's not them. It's us. We've finally gotten quieter.

In the spring of 2020, you likely heard the news story about the writer, Marvel Comics editor, and avid birder Christian Cooper. He's the Black man who, while birding in New York City's Central Park, encountered a white woman with an off-leash dog. He requested that she leash her dog, per park regulations, and instead she called 911 and falsely claimed that he was threatening her. Using his cell phone, Cooper calmly recorded the exchange, which was later posted on Twitter. Tens of millions of people viewed it in a matter of days. When the *New York Times* interviewed Cooper, he spoke about both the real challenges of systemic racism and the grace of second chances as he and the reporter walked through Central Park. "If we are going to make progress, we've got to address these things, and if this painful process is going to help us address this"—he interrupted himself—"There's the yellow warbler!" He paused the interview to look through his binoculars. What struck us about the many interviews that Cooper granted is that in the space of minutes he was able to speak to the white woman's individual responsibility and to the complexity of systemic racism, all while highlighting one of his personal missions—to promote birding, especially for people of color. His quiet—birding—had been intruded upon, but his quiet clarity remained.

The incident—which happened in the midst of COVID lockdowns—coincided with a spike in downloads of birding apps and unprecedented numbers of public submissions of photographic and audio recordings documenting birds near their homes.

The actress Lili Taylor recently echoed Christian Cooper's description of bird-watching as a far-reaching social remedy. "It's not easy to take that time to meditate . . . But you sure as hell can just take a minute—even if you're in your window at work and you're on your internet. You can look out the window and there can be some bird action," she said. "You can just look—a few minutes—and your brain has taken a little rest there."

As the novelist Jonathan Franzen puts it, "Birds are our last, readily available connection to the wildness around us. You see a breeding bird in the summer in your backyard, you know there's got to be a whole ecosystem supporting that." Franzen summarizes, "If the bird is there, there is wildness there." It wasn't that long ago that our day-to-day survival depended upon birds. Their behaviors and language told us about shifting weather patterns and the locales of predators.

Even if we don't need all this information for basic survival, we still need birds. We still need the whole ecosystems they represent. We still need connection to wildness.

While the word "wildness" implies deep immersion, we can often find it through a "quick hit," like a moment simply listening to birdsong. This connection—even momentarily—is one of the most direct ways to find silence in the consciousness. Thankfully, there are so many paths to it.

Joan Blades, the co-founder of MoveOn, MomsRising, and, most recently, Living Room Conversations, tells us that her preferred path to silence is "deadheading." While Leigh first got a mental image of Joan holding a handmade "I Need a Miracle" sign on the way to a Grateful Dead show, she was, in fact, referring to the process of snipping dying flowers off perennial plants in an effort to promote additional bloom. "There's nothing more relaxing," Joan told Leigh.

According to horticultural experts, the use of gardens "to calm the senses" dates back to at least 2000 BCE in Mesopotamia. Beyond the calming effects of gardens, there's also the healing effects, which were widely recognized during Florence Nightingale's era. Nightingale had a lifelong interest in botany—in part due to the medicinal properties of plants, though she also enjoyed collecting and pressing flowers (foxgloves were her favorite). In 1860, she wrote the following of the healing properties of gardens and greenery:

> People say the effect is only on the mind. It is no such thing. The effect is on the body, too.

Nightingale had seen the benefits in her medical patients firsthand—a hundred years before Roger Ulrich's study demonstrated that patients with views of nature recovered from surgery more speedily than those without. Once again, we should have listened to Florence.

There are now numerous best-selling books on how forest bathing or the oils, called phytoncides, of trees can counter modern afflictions, or how "nature deficit disorder" is a real and pressing challenge in both children and adults. Studies in both the U.K. and the Netherlands found that neighborhood pharmacies in communities with more green space filled fewer prescriptions for anxiety and depression, while, in 2018, Scotland became one of the first governments in the world to *prescribe nature* for those same conditions.

According to Ming Kuo, associate professor of natural resources and environmental sciences at the University of Illinois, "Just playing with soil for five minutes, we can actually see your parasympathetic nervous activation change—from 'fight or flight' moving towards 'tend and befriend.'" Kuo's initial interest was in noise and overcrowding; the data, however, kept directing her to the effects of nature on humans. She admits that when she began her work, nature struck her as a "nice amenity." But dozens of landmark studies and thirty years later, she's now a leading voice on the psychological, social, and physical benefits of urban green space and nature experiences, especially among vulnerable populations. Kuo says that research shows your heart rate drops "when you look out at a green landscape, even from indoors." In other words, even a quick "hit" of nature will do.

For Justin, one quick "hit" of nature is taking off his shoes and socks and simply feeling his bare feet on the grass or dirt. It's an opportunity to get in sync with the earth. When he really feels the ground, he can unload the stressful vibrations of the workday into the expanse of rock and soil. While this might sound like a fluffy New Age health fad, there's growing empirical evidence behind this practice of "grounding." In a 2019 randomized controlled trial, a group of study participants who spent significant time in "body contact with the ground, such as walking barefoot on humid soil or on grass," experienced a range of self-reported benefits, including "significant increases in physical function and energy and significant decreases in fatigue, depressed mood, tiredness and pain while grounded as compared to not being grounded."

Connecting to nature quiets the mind. It helps us dislodge the noisy delusion that life is just the mental stuff of a human-centered society. By taking a silent pause to really notice the dusty blue chicory growing through the tiny crack in the sidewalk, we can remember that life is a miracle. It's worthy of our awe.

Your "hits" of nature might be quick, but as research underscores, they're not trivial. Try to do these two things at least once a day:

1. Connect with something *bigger than yourself*, like a towering tree or the stars in the night sky.

2. Connect with something *smaller than yourself*, like a new blossom, a trail of ants, or a sparrow.

Reconnecting to nature helps us to "right size"—to diminish the egoic self as we simultaneously connect with the vastness of life.

IDEA 9: SANCTUARIES IN SPACE AND TIME

When Michelle Millben served as a White House adviser and congressional liaison for President Obama, the idea of finding time for silence and quiet reflection often seemed impossible. But as a practicing minister and a professional musician, Michelle recognized silence as a spiritual necessity. Through her work in Washington managing the relationships between the president and lawmakers in the final years of the administration, she had to consciously arrange her days to safeguard empty spaces. In some cases, she literally had to *schedule* tiny increments of quiet time. These moments of silence, however transitory, were essential. They became a primary way of staying true to her ethics in decision making—a way of staying positive and authentic in her relationships with other people. Michelle pauses, takes a deep breath, and closes her eyes. "It's my own little force field," she says. Today, as the founder and CEO of Explanation Kids—a start-up that provides age-appropriate answers to big questions children have about world events and issues that pop up in the news—she continues to work to consciously guard her sanctuaries.

Since college, Michelle has used a spreadsheet as a "reality check" to see when she might find time for quiet in her day. Each cell generally represents a fifteen-minute increment that occurs somewhere between 5:00 a.m. and 10:00 p.m. She lists first what she *has* to do—the primary responsibilities of her role, regular calls with her mom, and meals—then a bit of what she *wants* to do as well, including self-care. She sits back, examines her schedule, and invariably finds that she does, in fact, have "pockets of time" available.

Those "pockets of time" are easiest to safeguard from her home turf. So, each morning, she reserves a little time for reading scriptures and inspirational quotations. She follows that with quiet contemplation so, as she put it, "God can minister to my mind." Then she sets about her day.

Excel spreadsheets don't usually evoke feelings of quiet. But for Michelle—especially since her time at the White House—they have been a tool to demarcate her sanctuaries. We can safeguard silent time on the calendar like any other important appointment. The former U.S. secretary of state George Shultz, while in office, used to block off one hour per week for absolutely no meetings or commitments—a time to just sit and think about whatever would come to him, with nothing but a pen and paper. He'd tell his secretary to hold all his calls, "unless it's my wife or the president."

Over the course of dozens of interviews, we heard about the importance of sanctuaries—in both space and time. Many seek to guard the "morning mindset," to keep a space of pure attention before sunrise, free from the inputs of other minds. Some emphasize the importance of enshrining quiet time at the end of the day, a way of emptying the mind and cleansing the residual noise in the consciousness. Cyrus Habib, who you met in chapter 2, tells us about the Jesuit practice of the Examen prayer, where you take time in the evening to revisit everything that happened in the course of the preceding day, thinking back on where you've felt grace and connection. Justin has sometimes done a variant of the practice, thinking about where he's felt peaceful quiet in the course of the day, studying the shifting qualities of consciousness.

Sanctuaries ought to be simple. Create a physical space for stretching, bathing, reading, journaling, sitting on a patio, lying on the floor, or finding some other relaxed and quiet way of being. Make space in the calendar. See if you can wake up a little earlier or preserve the evening for intentional "emptying" time. Keep the appointment with yourself. Honor it as though you were meeting an important colleague or a beloved friend.

We usually think of early birds and night owls as opposites. But they share an appreciation for the still hours in the day, the ones that are free from external demands. Poets and seekers have long praised the liminal qualities of the "4:00 a.m. quiet." For Michelle, these sanctuaries in time and space, especially those preserved morning hours, were decisive for her effectiveness in the White House and currently as she's building a start-up. It's how she checks in on her principles. "Experiencing stillness and practicing silence has been essential to sharpening my ability to call upon wisdom in tough circumstances," she tells us, "and to create strategies to make a difference—especially in those times when the odds seem to be against the good you are trying to create in the world."

IDEA 10: MAKE FRIENDS WITH NOISE

In the early pages of this book, we defined noise as "unwanted distraction." We described the auditory, informational, and internal interference that diverts our attention away from that which we truly want. While there are myriad ways to evade and overcome the interference, we think it's also important to reckon with a simple fact: *noise is inevitable.*

Jarvis knows this as well as anybody. There's simply no way around the hollering on the East Block or the blaring of old TVs and radios. Even with decades of meditation practice under his belt, he hasn't totally extinguished the anxiety of never knowing how or when he'll find freedom again.

Yet Jarvis realized that his own "responses to the noise" were, in fact, making things louder. He was getting caught up in the contracted feeling, perseverating on the sound and stimulus that he didn't want.

"I started inviting the noise to *quiet* the noise," Jarvis tells us. In that moment, this shift was all that was within his *sphere of control*. But it made a profound difference.

The Irish poet Pádraig Ó Tuama has a practice of saying hello to whatever shows up in his life. "I think greeting things is an old technology. Certainly Rumi was interested in it," he tells us with a chuckle, referring to Rumi's poem "The Guest House," wherein the great Sufi mystic tells us to "welcome and entertain" the guests who come to the door, no matter how unpleasant. This practice may, Rumi suggests, make room for "some new delight."

As Pádraig puts it, "Finding a way to greet things in our lives can be an important thing, especially the things we don't want to greet." In his book *In the Shelter*, he offers a litany of greetings that give color and texture to the notion of welcoming noise. Pádraig writes,

So, say hello to old wounds, hello to our lack of capacity to control, hello to this circumstance that doesn't seem to be ending quickly, hello to the unexpected phone call, hello to the unexpected sadness, hello to the unexpected happiness and consolation.

And by saying hello to something, you're saying, "You're here," and, "I'm here with you, here."

And what does that mean?

It asks us to do a radical act of naming the simple truth of the present.

When we greet what's present—with respect—we soften its edges. We soften our own edges, too. In observing and recognizing what's present—agreeing to be with the noise that we simply can't avoid—we might even start to befriend it.

When Leigh consults with organizations, she doesn't just ask them what they *want*; she also asks them what they *fear*. She can often see the reaction on their faces: "Why is she stirring up trouble? Shouldn't we focus on the positive?" She emphasizes the work of surfacing and recognizing—of "saying hello"—because it's often counterproductive to attempt to push fears or doubts or disturbances to the margins. Anything hastily banished almost inevitably returns, often amplified in scale.

In conversation, Pádraig emphasizes that saying hello to a difficulty or a disturbance is "not to control it . . . but also not to let it control you. To simply let it be and to speak within that context."

We asked the neuroscientist and longtime meditator Judson Brewer how his research findings inform his own personal practices. He says he now simply pays attention to when he feels *contracted*, as opposed to *expanded*, either mentally or physically. Crucially, he tells us that he doesn't have to do anything when he notices that contracted feeling—the feeling that's associated with internal noise. He doesn't judge it. He doesn't try to force it away. He just pays attention to it. The act of noticing the contraction, of becoming aware of internal noise, is, he notes, sufficient to transform it.

Justin was recently stuck on a customer service line for a total of three and a half hours. Sure, he was multitasking, but he had to keep listening to a cycle of oddly sultry Spanish guitar music and an ingratiating voice saying, "Thank you for holding. We will be right with you." Of course, he went through all the stages: anger, resignation, imagining writing negative online reviews, and simply recognizing the absurdity. But he had to stick it out; there was no other recourse. "Was this some sort of cosmic lesson in patience?" he wondered around the 180-minute mark. He started noticing how the irritating recording was both a signal of inconvenience and a feeling of disrespect—as if nobody cared—and this, too, triggered noisy feelings. So, finally, he took a deep breath and just felt all the bodily and mental contraction. He really paid attention to it. He said a reluctant hello. Did Justin make friends with the noise of the absurdly inconsiderate customer service department? No. And yet, when he greeted the feeling, there was a shift. His edges softened, and he learned something about the sources of internal noise. While we've written this book as a guide to getting beyond the noise of the modern world, we recognize that the only way to get beyond it is, sometimes, to go into it.

HOW TO REMAKE THE SMOKE BREAK

We spoke recently with a smoker who let us in on some bad news. Most people who go on cigarette breaks these days don't actually relish deep inhales or bask in sunlight. They check their smartphones. Our idealized vision of some of the last socially sanctioned "do nothing" time is really just nostalgia.

So, we think it's time to create a new, healthy, socially acceptable, widely recognized category of break in the day. You might call it "quiet time." It could vary according to need on any given day. It might be a pause for deep breathing or focused reading or immersive movement or just listening. But regardless of its format, it ought to be structured into every day.

The Vipassana teacher and author Phillip Moffitt, who once upon a time served as editor in chief of *Esquire* magazine, has a poignant analysis of why we so often fail to afford ourselves quiet time. It's a tendency he notices in some of the CEOs he coaches.

We often mistake the feeling of stress for aliveness.

"We unconsciously begin to believe that our life has meaning only if the mind is receiving an almost constant stream of stimulation," Moffitt tells us. "Even if the stimulation is felt in the mind and body as constant pressure or exhausting stress, we persist in believing unending stimulation means our lives are really happening." He warns, "That interpretation is not true. The mind can be stimulated by anything—wholesome or unwholesome."

The mind, Moffitt emphasizes, tends to "feed upon" self-generated thoughts, regardless of their accuracy or worth. The original thought could be innocuous. But it's soon followed by another and another. Thankfully, he tells us, "the momentum of the mind can be interrupted, and once it's interrupted, the mind feels better." He adds, "Once we step out of the 'flow of stimuli,' our minds and bodies will naturally return to its more quiet state."

Moffitt gives a template for how to think about the healthy successor to the smoke break. He speaks of "the Interrupt," an exercise he uses regularly with his meditation students. The idea is to set a goal for what you want to accomplish for a block of time, say sixty or ninety minutes. Set a timer and, when it goes off, notice the quality of your focus, your mood, and any physical sensations you may be experiencing. If your concentration is strong, simply finish your thought or find an easy place to wrap up what you're doing. If your concentration isn't strong, stop what you're doing immediately. Interrupt yourself. Find something positive for your mind and your body: make a cup of tea, do some breath exercises, stretch or move your body. "I tell people, 'Go for a short walk, stand and stretch, close your eyes for thirty seconds,' and most of all 'deliberately stop paying attention to your thoughts. You may not feel as though you need a break—an interrupt of thoughts piling on more thoughts—but you really do.'" Do something, in short, that brings quiet to your consciousness.

May these ideas spark an assortment of options—possibilities within your *sphere of control* and your *sphere of influence*—for you to find your own healthy successor to the smoke break.

CHAPTER 11

RAPTUROUS SILENCE

Matthew Kiichi Heafy is known for his maximum-volume roar. He's famous for the baroque melodies and impossibly complex time signatures of his lightning-fast guitar solos, the piercing tones of overdrive and wah pedals that resound through massive-wattage amplifiers in packed clubs and sweaty stadiums.

We spoke with Matt—the front man for the Grammy-nominated, multiplatinum, metal band Trivium—about where he finds the most power in his music.

"The heaviest part of the heaviest songs are the breakdowns, the parts where all the noise and intensity are punctuated by moments of silence," he tells us. "It's like you're so *in it* that you wouldn't even know you're in it until the silence."

You have to step outside the sound and stimulus to appreciate its meaning.

Matt—who was born in Japan to a Japanese mother and American father and raised in the United States—gets animated talking about the meaning of the Japanese principle of *Ma*. He tells us how he's always had an overactive mind and how he's had to navigate a fair amount of anxiety. Matt describes the moments of *Ma* in his life as moments of flow. Like the "breakdowns" in his heaviest songs, these are the moments when he steps out of the noise of self-referential awareness so he can really appreciate what's happening. "It's when my brain is quiet, and it's almost like I'm observing myself from outside myself. But if you catch it, and you notice you're in that state, you fall out of it. It just disappears."

Matt mostly seeks this personal state of *Ma* in jujitsu, when he's grappling with a well-matched opponent. It's sometimes in a moment of quiet meditation before playing music. Other times, it's through domestic life, rolling around giggling with his twin toddlers.

On extremely rare occasions, Matt finds his silence—his fullest presence and clarity—when he's actually onstage before an audience of thousands of amped-up metal fans.

"Usually, I walk onstage, and my head is full of thoughts like 'Am I going to hit this note? Do I have this memorized? Am I going to be good tonight? Did I eat too much food before the show?'" But then there are moments when—amidst the cheering crowds, pounding drums, and thrashing guitars—all the internal noise dissolves.

Matt thinks back on a moment more than a decade ago, the first time he played a major festival in the U.K. The band performed two opening songs, and then he approached the microphone to speak to the crowd. The noise lowered to a hush in anticipation of his words. He let the moment stretch on for longer than expected. "I was there onstage, in the middle of this intense show, and it just felt quiet."

This unlikely moment of pristine attention wasn't pure serendipity. It was a result of preparation. "I strive for this kind of silence when I'm playing shows. It only happens when I'm practicing five days a week, up to six hours a day, just rehearsing so much that the music becomes an imprinted muscle memory. *I can just let go.*"

Such a moment, for Matt, isn't just a fleeting experience of clarity. There's something instructive in it. In this deepest silence, the racing clock slows down. Ego loosens its grip. All the everyday worries and what-ifs recede to the distant background.

To Matt, this kind of moment is a lodestar for how to live.

○

The legendary scholar of world religions Huston Smith once wrote that the goal of spiritual practices and rituals is "not altered states but altered traits."

This was a helpful touchstone for the 1960s generation, and it continues to be relevant for anyone prone to pursuing ecstatic experiences. Smith isn't saying that there's anything wrong with chasing glimmering moments of transcendence. He's merely saying that these experiences best serve us when they're integrated into life's larger context: when they serve to help us to better understand reality or how to live with more love and care.

In the last chapter, we explored moment-to-moment and day-to-day practices for working with our "states"—our everyday experiences of noise and quiet in our minds and bodies. These efforts can, cumulatively, help to shape our "traits." When we imbue our ordinary lives with pockets of silence by identifying our *sphere of control* and our *sphere of influence*, we can, over time, increase our attention, empathy, and patience. *These experiences change who we are.*

But the effect of silence on our perceptions and proclivities isn't always just a slow trickle. Just one profound encounter with silence—one mystical experience or moment of awe—can, in and of itself, *change our traits*. It can challenge our assumptions and shift our perspective. It can set us on a new trajectory.

Still—as Matt Heafy's experience attests—finding the deepest silence can require rigorous preparation. It might require some planning and logistics, perhaps taking some time off work or household responsibilities.

Often, finding the deepest silence involves the serious work of facing our fears.

In this chapter, we'll look at principles and practices for finding an uncommon and transformative silence. The same general recommendations we offered in the opening of the last chapter stand here: *keep an open mind, explore multiple practices, notice the signals in your mind and body*, and *do what brings you joy*. As in the last chapter, these ideas are meant less as prescriptive measures and more as examples to help inspire you. While you may be able to work with some of these practices on a weekly or even daily basis, most of what we offer here fits into the longer time horizon—once in a month, once in a year, maybe even once in a lifetime.

There's no one simple definition of "rapturous" silence. It's an experience that's personal and subjective. Like the self-transcendent experiences we discussed in chapter 6, the common denominators include a "decreased self-salience and/or increased feelings of connectedness." You might find it in a remote hermitage, on the top of a mountain, or on the stage at a massive heavy metal concert. It's unmistakable; you know it when you *feel* it. To expand beyond the separate self, while simultaneously connecting to something greater—the natural world, the broader whole of humanity, or the cosmos—is a "rapturous" experience (even though it can be tinged with fear, as we learned in chapter 7). Ultimately, we overcome, however briefly, the delusion of a rigid separate self. This is what we've found in our investigations, both with seasoned spiritual teachers and with leading neuroscientists. It's what we've found in our own lives and the testimonies of others.

We're talking about the kind of silence that elevates our way of perceiving.

While we sometimes tend to associate the deepest silence with "solitude," rapturous silence is something different. If anything, it's transcendence of the ordinary forces that make us feel separate and alone.

IDEA 1: TAKE YOUR TO-DO LIST FOR A HIKE

Gordon Hempton has a simple indicator for determining whether his life is out of control. He checks to see if his to-do list has gotten beyond thirteen single-spaced pages.

When we spoke recently, the acoustic ecologist and cataloger of endangered natural soundscapes had just passed through a busy spell. His list had grown to an unprecedented twenty-three pages.

Thankfully, Gordon already had a protocol in place for such situations. He printed the list, grabbed a pencil, then drove several hours and hiked several miles to a verdant mossy sanctuary in the Hoh Rain Forest of Olympic National Park in Washington State—a spot that's far enough from roadways and flight paths to warrant a designation as "the quietest place in the United States." When he arrived there, Gordon took time to just listen. He got present and connected with this special place—back to "being in my being," he tells us.

Then he pulled out his pencil and his twenty-three pages and, like the hero at the denouement of a violent action movie, he mercilessly obliterated an unbelievable quantity of social and professional commitments. When Gordon folded and tucked his list into his breast pocket to hike out before dusk, he'd removed *four or five months'* worth of obligations from his to-do list. He took off for one day, and it saved him five months.

It's funny how our settings shape our perception. Back on Gordon's home computer, everything on that twenty-three-page list seemed to belong there. But from the vantage point of the remote rain forest, Gordon could connect to what really mattered in his life. He didn't need to attend every conference or take up every online publishing opportunity or agree to every interview.

"The answers are in the silence," Gordon says.

When Justin thinks about the power of silence to transform our lives' mundane obligations and assumptions, he thinks back on a hot summer day in D.C. in 2015. He was eating a Thai rice noodle bowl under the grand marble edifice in Union Station. His friend Elif, who was sitting with him, made a comment that helped him make sense of a lot of what he was experiencing.

"I think you're in your Saturn return," she said. She went on to explain that this could mean he was going through a time of intense change and questioning about life's purpose and direction.

Justin didn't know much about astrology. But her words rang true, nonetheless. He and his wife, Meredy, knew it was time to leave D.C. and head west. It was time to bid farewell to frantic work environments and hard-partying weekends—to start a family, get closer to nature, and become more serious about their spiritual practices. The question was how? What about earning a living? What about being close to the action? What about the community of friends they'd found in D.C.?

Unsure what to do, Justin was feeling a little bit irritable, unusually sensitive to the urban noise, and almost overtaken with distracted thought. He took Elif's astrological observation as a clear guidance: go spend some time in the woods.

Justin went out to a cabin for a few days in the forested hills of northwestern Virginia. There, he spent most of his time lying on the wooden deck, face upward to the canopy of oaks and pines. He listened to the warblers and woodpeckers. He felt the warmth of the sun. No cell signal. No Wi-Fi. No books. Little to no talking. Just a notepad and a pen.

The first thing he noticed was that it was easier to breathe. It wasn't just the fresh air; it was physiological. Tightness started vanishing from his chest, his diaphragm, and his stomach. The air could get to all of his alveoli. After just a day, the volume of his mental chatter turned way down. Justin felt moved to reach for his notebook.

Strangely, without venturing into a deep analysis, Justin jotted down a fairly complete plan for a career transition that allowed for geographic flexibility while still working on the causes he valued. He's been largely working from that plan ever since.

Justin wasn't trimming the to-do list the way Gordon was. He was unwittingly awaiting a cosmic download. Ultimately, he was reinventing the logic underlying what he was supposed to do. This required the kind of spaciousness that can be found only in silence.

When Justin got back to D.C., something had shifted. Maybe Saturn had crossed its celestial trajectory. Just as likely, his encounter with nature allowed him to let go of a ton of old plans and expectations and priorities. His life didn't feel so stuck anymore. It was possible to walk forward.

Take your worries and assumptions to the preferred natural setting of your choosing. If you like, grab your to-do list, your notebook, or maybe just the thoughts that are swirling around in your head. Take some time there. "Absorb the silence," as Pythagoras counseled his students. See what happens.

IDEA 2: TAKE A WORDLESS WEDNESDAY

Earlier, we discussed how Gandhi observed a "day of silence" once a week. He wasn't totally free from external inputs or mental exertion during this time. In addition to meditation and reflection, he sometimes read or even met with people. But he didn't speak. He believed that our ordinary mode of verbalized consciousness—talking, arguing, performing—gets in the way of knowing reality. It conflicts with the most profound kind of service. "It has often occurred to me," Gandhi wrote, "that a seeker after truth has to be silent." For Gandhi, this weekly ritual could be a rapturous event. The people around him could hear the profundity of his "day of silence" practice in the clarity and force of the words he'd deliver the following day.

So, here's a practice that Gandhi inspires: try not talking for a day.

If the responsibilities of work or childcare or eldercare make this impossible, set aside just a few silent hours. In this time, see if you can sense what Gandhi meant about the necessity of silence for the pursuit of truth.

While Gandhi opted for Mondays, we recognize that the first day of the workweek is an especially heavy lift for most of us. We like a "Wordless Wednesday" as a way to find renewal at the midpoint of the week.

Taking your own day of full or partial quiet is, in our understanding, different from an ordinary silent retreat. It's specifically about checking in with yourself. It's about making sure your thoughts, words, and actions are aligned. It's about assessing your relationships and the quality of your listening. And it's a time to see if you're quiet enough inside to tune in to your deepest intuition. "The Divine Radio is always singing if we could only make ourselves ready to listen to it," Gandhi wrote. "But it is impossible to listen without silence."

We think of the silent day as a little vacation from the responsibility of having to think of what to say. It's an opportunity to use all that attention to instead observe your surroundings, notice your authentic feelings and needs, and reflect on how you're treating yourself and others. It's an opportunity to step outside habitual cycles and stuck places in relationships, to get beyond binaries of who's right and who's wrong, to tune in to the true signals of your life.

While Gandhi saw this simple practice as an essential part of his world-changing work, it's a practice that can help any one of us tune in on an ordinary basis.

A few summers ago, Leigh was inspired to try a wordless day while she and her family were on a trip of a lifetime, eleven days of rafting down the Tatshenshini and Alsek Rivers. The rivers run through remote and pristine wilderness in Alaska and Canada's Yukon Territory—the largest block of protected park land in the world.

At about day five, Leigh felt a wave of sadness come over her. The trip was slipping away, and she hadn't yet felt connected to the unique wildlife of the area. At that moment, her human relations didn't need tending. Her family was clearly happy, and the group—consisting of three guides and nine fellow travelers—had bonded. In fact, it was probably their friendly banter that had kept the shier creatures of the land—the golden eagles and moose—miles away. For Leigh, it was her relationship with nature that was calling for her attention.

The next afternoon, when a layover day was announced, Leigh sat facing the Noisy mountain range—named for the clamor of falling rocks and ice that echo through the valley—with the expansive Netland Glacier at her back. She felt sandwiched, literally and metaphorically, between noise and silence.

At dinner, Leigh told everyone about her plan to maintain silence from dessert that evening to dessert the following night. She knew she didn't need "permission" from others, but their support would help to avoid any misunderstandings. Leigh told them just a bit about this book for additional context. Everyone was very supportive, even intrigued. They had questions, like "Will you still eat with us?" "Will you do pantomime instead?" and "Can I join you?" Leigh's answers were "Yes." "No." And "Of course!"

That night, as the euchre game commenced, most of the group set their eyes on the gravel bank across the river in hopes of spotting a fishing grizzly bear. It was certainly the quietest evening they'd spent together as a group. Leigh worried a bit that her request might have dampened the mood. She hadn't intended to change the group's behavior at all. She decided to head to her tent early. En route, she overheard someone say in a hushed voice, "It's probably hardest for her husband," which made Leigh smile. "Hardly!" she thought to herself.

That night, the winds changed direction. Frigid air now blew straight off the Netland Glacier. Leigh was shivering. In her tent, she tossed and turned next to her husband, Michael. Every cell in her very cold body wanted to wake him to say, "It is sooo cold. I am fah-*reeez*-ing!" But then, she'd remember that she was in silence, so she'd have to wait until tomorrow night to tell him. But what good would that do? She'd fall back to sleep, only to wake again with the same insatiable urge, the same internal dialogue, and the same conclusion.

The next day was glorious. The weather warmed up, and the skies cleared. Leigh got her coffee and set up her camping chair overlooking the gravel wash below the Noisy Mountains, an area known for grizzly bear activity. The guides had packed a powerful telescope. So far, they'd spotted only black bears. Everyone was a little disappointed, especially the wildlife photographers. Leigh got what she could only describe as a "tingle." "It feels like bear o'clock," she thought to herself. She picked up her binoculars, and almost instantly a large grizzly emerged from the woods across the river. She jumped up from her chair and began signaling wildly in the direction of the bear. One woman exclaimed, "Leigh found a grizzly!" The group jumped to their feet, and for twenty minutes or so they watched the bear amble around, stop to fish, slowly make its way to the other side of the wash, and return to the dense pine forest.

That day, Leigh and her twelve-year-old daughter, Ava, stayed behind while the group did a day hike. Leigh noticed that in the group's absence, her internal dialogue slowed to a trickle. Leigh and Ava watched puffy white clouds together for hours without saying a word. It was blissful.

This was Leigh's first time among glaciers, the holders of "big time." Tens of thousands of years. In the expanse of not speaking, she felt more connection to the place. She felt gratitude that the park had been created. She longed to know more about the Indigenous people of these lands—how did they travel the rivers and endure the winters?

After the other travelers returned from their hike, a group prepared dinner while the rest set up in hopes of seeing another grizzly. Leigh kept looking up at the sky until she got that "tingle" again. She sat up, picked up her binoculars, and saw that there, again, was a grizzly on the other side of the river. Even with five people on the lookout, they hadn't seen it. "See what happens when you're quiet?" a woman remarked. In the silence, Leigh did feel more tuned in.

The essayist and naturalist Barry Lopez describes the dynamics through which the grizzly bear becomes more visible on a wordless day:

> When an observer doesn't immediately turn what his senses convey to him into language, into the vocabulary and syntactical framework we all employ when trying to define our experiences, there's a much greater opportunity for minor details, which might at first seem unimportant, to remain alive in the foreground of an impression, where, later, they might deepen the meaning of an experience.

Unlike Gandhi, Leigh didn't give any great speeches or make any consequential decisions after twenty-four hours. She just enjoyed the fruit crumble dessert and blended back into the verbal pleasantries of the group. But the day of silence did slightly shift the tone of the trip. It enhanced her ability to observe the details and keep them "alive in the foreground." Leigh felt more grounded and centered. Her day in silence "deepened the meaning" of the experience.

IDEA 3: GO FLOATING IN THE CLOUD OF UNKNOWING

Here's the thing about *apophatic* theology: it ain't so easy to package into everyday life.

The *apophatic* approach to spirituality—wordless dissolution of the separate self into the totality of the cosmic mystery—is typically a lot less accessible than the *kataphatic* approach that centers on verbalized, conceptual practices like reading scripture, listening to sermons, or even most kinds of prayer or guided meditation.

Earlier, we introduced *The Cloud of Unknowing*, the more than five-hundred-year-old spiritual book penned by an anonymous author. Obviously, an ancient Christian mystic text written in inscrutable Old

English is pretty far from the current cultural context in which most of us live. And yet the old tome contains a key to making the *apophatic* way, the theology of silence, practical and accessible.

The key is in the word "forgetting."

We previously shared a core teaching of the text: "The first time you practice contemplation, you'll only experience a darkness, like a cloud of unknowing." Rather than trying to sense or navigate or think your way through things, the instruction is to *forget everything*. The author advises us to tune in to the "gentle stirring of love," to simply let go of any concepts or worries about the material conditions of your life. It's about dropping all our own story lines and narratives about who we are and what's happening in our lives. Just float in the loving essence of life itself.

The teachings of *The Cloud of Unknowing* have inspired practices that can be applied in daily life, including in quick periods of rest. For example, the Christian meditation practice of Centering Prayer is about letting go of all thoughts and simply returning the consciousness to focus again and again on one short, comforting word of your choosing. Of course, within Buddhism and other meditation traditions, you'll find similar instructions about how to drop your own story line and verbal analysis.

We get it: it's *hard* to enter the space of profound contemplation where you can temporarily "forget" all the content of your life and go "floating in the cloud of unknowing." This depth of prayer or meditation requires preparation. We think of how our friend the mythologist Josh Schrei described how the rishis of ancient India lived in nature, chanted, ate a particular diet, and adhered to rigorous ethics so that they could arrive at a place of attunement, where they could *hear* the Vedas. "Ethical practice is necessary for a being to experience harmonious silence," he says. Even if you're not seeking the same rapturous silence as the rishis of ancient India, you might still do some work to prepare yourself.

So, here's a practice to consider: Reserve a few hours to be in silence—in nature or somewhere peaceful by yourself. Safeguard the time. Put it in your calendar. Make whatever arrangements you need in order to be undisturbed, if possible. In this space of intentional silence, you might do breath work or meditation or prayer. If it's in your practice—and you're of the right mind "set" and environmental "setting"—you might choose to consciously work with sacred plants or psychedelics. Or you might just rest and relax. What matters is that you leave all the problems and worries behind. You consecrate the space as a safe container for *forgetting everything*.

As a preparation to enter this space, see if you can first do some practices that help facilitate internal silence. There's no one right way to do it. The way you prepare specifically for finding internal quiet depends on the nature of your own internal noise. For example, in the days or even weeks before you enter this special period of silence, you might think about the important relationships in your life. You might devote some time to thinking about any issues that are lingering and how it might be in your *sphere of control* or your *sphere of influence* to address them. Of course, you're not going to resolve decades-old issues with a parent or partner, but perhaps you make an actionable plan for helping to strengthen an important relationship and take one or two small steps forward on it. Perhaps you clear off some genuinely important items from the to-do list. In the time immediately before you enter your period of silence, maybe you prepare your body and mind by exercising, doing yoga, chanting, journaling, or singing.

Here's a simple pointer: if you know you're not going to be able to let go into the space of internal silence because you haven't sent that email, taken out the trash, or cleaned the fridge, then just do it.

No need to be too ambitious here. Just see what you can do to clear away some of the most immediate contributors to internal noise, at least at the surface level of your consciousness.

The idea here is to actively create the conditions to be able to float in the cloud. It's about "preparing the vessel" for silence.

It's one thing to just take a break from your busy day to try to spontaneously "forget everything" and enter the *apophatic* realm beyond all thoughts or concepts. It's another thing to give it some time and effort: to carefully correct, organize, and align your life as much as possible to be able to confidently—for just a temporary period—say "bon voyage."

IDEA 4: INTO THE DEEP

The word "retreat" has an old military definition: "to give up" or "to stand down." For us, those connotations loom large whenever we think about leaving regular life behind. It's as if we were soldiers leaving our distressed compatriots on the front lines. We feel irresponsible abandoning work and caretaking and citizenship in pursuit of what sometimes feel like quixotic personal interests.

If you look to the etymology of the word "retreat," you'll find that it's derived from the Old French *retret*, a noun from the past participle of *retrere*, "to draw back or withdraw." That definition gets you to the abdication of life's duties. But if you look a little bit deeper, you'll find another perspective. The earlier Latin root of "retreat," *retrahere*, has two parts: *re-* (back or again) and *trahere* (to draw, to have traction). That "traction" has an opposite: "dis-traction." "To retreat," then, is also to recover the capacity to rediscover what's important to us and to pull our lives forward from this fulcrum.

When we think about "retreat" in this sense, new possibilities emerge. Perhaps it's less about what you leave behind and more about *regaining traction to move forward*.

Extended retreats are millennia-honored rituals—sources of illumination for Indigenous rites of passage, Sufi mystics, Vedic masters, Buddhist disciples, and the Desert Fathers and Mothers. They have continued to serve artists, creatives, and professionals of all types in modern times.

Every year, the renowned author, historian, and social theorist Yuval Noah Harari goes on a sixty-day silent retreat. Sometimes he goes for longer. "You don't have any distractions, you don't have television, you don't have emails. No phones, no books. You don't write," he told the journalist Ezra Klein. "You just have every moment to focus on what is really happening right now, on what is reality. You come across the things you don't like about yourself, things that you don't like about the world that you spend so much time ignoring or suppressing."

It's hard to imagine how one of the world's most prominent public intellectuals is able to spend two full months of the year out of contact with the outside world. Yet Harari attests that this time-out isn't at all at odds with his success as a writer; in fact, it is the key to his success.

Despite all the demands on his time, if Harari chooses to prioritize a two-month retreat each year, he has the agency to make it happen. Which is to say, he's determined it's within his *sphere of control*.

So, what about the rest of us?

Sheila Kappeler-Finn is on a mission to democratize personal retreats. Her forthcoming book is a do-it-yourself guide to what she calls "mini-retreats"—retreats that last less than a week and can even be as short as eight hours. Some examples of low-cost options she recommends include the following:

- A week of pet sitting for a neighbor in their house

- A two-day apartment swap with a friend

- A daylong retreat at your public library

- A green-space retreat in a nearby park or university

A change of scenery is always possible. "If you can't go away, rearrange the furniture in your room," Sheila tells us. "Move some pictures around, do something to calm it down or liven it up. Bring in a plant, or buy yourself some flowers," she rattles off an array of options but sticks to her main takeaway: "If the room *feels* different, it will, psychologically, have a big impact. It will *be* a retreat."

Janet Frood wouldn't dare call what she does a "retreat." She's made that mistake before. "If I say, 'I'm taking the month off,' it's like I'm just on vacation," she warns. "People say, 'Oh, you're so lucky!' Whereas when I say, 'I'm taking a *sabbatical*,' it's like, 'Well, *that's* official.'" Now that she's quite deliberate with her wording, people take interest and respect the decision in a whole new way. And besides, why should academics have all the fun?

This is Janet's second time running her own consulting business. The first time—now well over twenty years ago—she got it all wrong. She never took time off. Her credo then had been, "I'm only *viable* if I'm *available*." But when her mother became ill and eventually died of cancer, the fissures in that credo were revealed. She was caring for her mother while raising two young kids and building a business. "I got lost in the equation," she tells us.

In 2000, Janet made the tough decision to close up shop. For the next five years, she made ends meet by working under the banner of another organization. But ultimately Janet was built to lead her own company. So, in 2005, she started anew—only, this time, she incorporated a monthlong sabbatical into her annual calendar. She factors in that month—without income—as the cost of running a sustainable business. It's nonnegotiable. Both new and potential clients are told about it up front. Since making this commitment, she tells us, "I have never wavered."

Janet's DIY sabbaticals have a few key elements to them, including access to a body of water (floating in Lake Huron is an all-time favorite), a place to hang a hammock (being suspended in air is the perfect corollary to floating in water), and time reserved for reading, napping, and cloud watching. Janet floats and soaks and hangs and drifts. That's it. That's enough. She practices the forgotten art of being dormant. In a good year, she may genuinely tire from all the resting.

In her book *Wintering: The Power of Rest and Retreat in Difficult Times*, Katherine May reminds us that we sometimes enter our "retreats" unwillingly. It isn't just that we've had the rug pulled out from under us—like when Janet's mother was diagnosed with cancer. It's that we attempt to defer winter indefinitely. We deny the very ebb and flow of life. May writes, "Plants and animals don't fight the winter; they don't pretend it's not happening and attempt to carry on living the same lives that they lived in the summer."

The Nap Bishop, Tricia Hersey, whom you met in chapter 4, took a three-week impromptu Sabbath in the summer of 2020. "Sabbath" is the root word from which "sabbatical" is derived. A sabbatical, done well, is "worthy" of the Sabbath—the holy day of rest. Hersey was raised in the Black church; her father was a minister and pastor. The weekly Sabbath is baked in her bones, though her first extended Sabbath took place fairly recently.

Before starting it, she'd given everyone around her—including her half a million Instagram followers—a three-month heads-up. She planned for her Sabbath to include "sleeping in, silence, napping daily, lots of detox salt baths, reading books, not speaking about anything related to work/career/Nap Ministry, writing a little, spending time with friends and family and total nesting at the house." To do all this, she forewarned, "I would be off all social media, and there would be no events, no email, no discussing Nap Ministry work details, no bookings, and no traveling." Her only "to-do" was to share a bit about what she learned in the process afterward.

Upon her return, she described her experience in her blog, saying that despite advising her clients that she was going off-line, "I actually received more work-related emails, texts and requests on this Sabbath than when I'm available and working. I found this to be fascinating." She marveled that not only have we convinced ourselves that we don't deserve rest, but we don't know how to support one another as we carve out time either. She wasn't resentful; she was dumbfounded. According to the Nap Bishop, we've all been bamboozled. It's imperative that we "stop saying that rest is a luxury or a privilege. It's not; it's a human right. The more we think of rest as a luxury, the more we buy into these systemic lies." She sees clearly—through her well-rested eyes—the root causes:

> I know that it's not any one person's fault that you're not resting. It's not your fault that you're caught up in grind culture, or that you were born here under a toxic system that sees you as a machine. None of that is your fault. But the good thing is that you can deprogram and decolonize from that.

We deprogram in the silence.

We decolonize when we rest.

Hersey writes, "Rest helps you enjoy silence. Silence and rest removes the veils from our faces so we can truly see what is happening."

So call it what you will—a retreat or a mini-retreat, a forced or a chosen winter, a sabbatical or a Sabbath—it is your birthright. It is what you, and every living creature, deserve.

IDEA 5: FUZZY PUPPIES LICKING YOUR FACE

In the past, Jon Lubecky usually found his flow states in death metal and dirt bikes.

But Iraq changed his relationship to loudness.

In 2005 and 2006, he was a sergeant with an artillery unit in the U.S. Army living on Balad Air Base in the center of the Sunni Triangle—in the middle of some of the most intense sectarian violence of the war. The base was hit with deadly mortar fire so often that the soldiers came to call it "Mortaritaville"—a gallows humor tip of the hat to Jimmy Buffett's breezy drinking song. The jarring sounds of mortars, rockets, and medevac helicopters were constant reminders of their looming mortality. Everyone longed for some semblance of quiet. Everyone was on edge.

One night in April 2006, Jon was exhausted and sitting on a port-a-potty when a mortar landed a short distance away, briefly knocking him unconscious. The shrapnel thankfully missed his body, but he was left with a traumatic brain injury.

Coming home was supposed to be a return to quiet. But it quickly became a barrage of other kinds of noises. His marriage ended. He couldn't focus enough to hold down a job. He was prescribed forty-two pills a day—benzodiazepines, antidepressants, muscle relaxers, you name it. But nothing helped. In his head, there was the relentless chatter of self-criticism and doubt. There was the crushing anxiety of thinking every ordinary guy with a backpack on the sidewalk was a suicide bomber.

"With PTSD, there's no such thing as silence," Jon tells us. "The deeper the trauma, the louder that internal noise—the more you're willing to do anything to make it stop."

On Christmas morning 2006, two months after returning from Iraq, he decided to take his own life. As the hammer of his Beretta 9 mm fell, he felt what he thought might be the deepest silence he'd ever known.

"It was all over. There was no noise. It was just peace."

He thought he was dead for something like thirty seconds.

But the loud sound was only a primer pop. Because of a manufacturing flaw in the ammunition, he lived. He attempted to commit suicide four more times. Each time he survived.

He continued the slog.

One day, at the VA hospital, Jon's usual psychiatrist was out of the office, and he met with an intern fresh out of medical school. She told him she had studied his file. Then she slid a note across the desk and said, "I want you to open that when you leave the VA. I'm not supposed to tell you about it, so just stick it in your pocket." The note read, "Google MDMA PTSD."

Jon followed her advice. He found his way into a legally authorized study of MDMA-assisted psychotherapy for the treatment of people with PTSD. It consisted of three treatments in a comfortable home setting in Charleston, South Carolina, as well as a series of psychotherapy sessions before and after the treatment sessions. What happened in the sessions, he explains, wasn't just "tripping" or "rolling."

Sure, he says, "it felt like being hugged by the person who you know loves you the most on this planet while being buried in fuzzy puppies licking your face." But it was also a process of systematically uncovering and dismantling the sources of debilitating noise in his consciousness.

In the first session, he remembers, "The psychiatrists asked innocuous questions like 'So, what was the weather like in Iraq?'"

"So, you start talking, and you keep talking," he recounts. The drug's physiological mechanism of action, he tells us, is the suppression of the "fight-or-flight response in the amygdala, so you can deal with things that might otherwise make you panic." In other words, MDMA makes it feel safe to access a memory that would otherwise be too painful.

This therapy was far more than a foray in the "altered state" of a serotonin rush, although serotonin release is in large part responsible for the "fuzzy puppy" feeling Jon described and the feelings of safety that allowed him to open up. The MDMA, under the guidance of two trained counselors, helped him to temporarily transcend all the noise so he could consciously go places he wouldn't otherwise go. In those places, he could recode memories and reframe anxieties. He could view his experiences with a healthy distance. This led to a fundamental shift in his overall perspective. It was a lasting change—an "altered trait"—not a temporary state.

He unraveled the sources of his noise.

"I talked about things I hadn't talked about with anyone else before. And it fixed me."

Jon's assessed levels of depression declined steadily over the course of six months. One day, he realized he saw a guy with a backpack on the street and didn't feel scared. He hasn't felt the need to do MDMA again. He's dealt with the worst of the trauma, he tells us. His outlook has changed. He now has the inner resources to guide his continued recovery. And—if needed—he possesses one of the greatest resources of all: the ability to ask for help.

"You can go sit on a mountain and leave your cell phone behind and be in auditory silence. Or, you can go into a sensory deprivation chamber," Jon tells us. "But there's no 'tank' for internal silence," he says. *You have to do the work.*

"The work" we're describing here is identifying and addressing the underlying sources of internal noise.

"The work" looks different for each of us.

Jon's one particular healing practice—MDMA-assisted psychotherapy—allowed him to talk about his feelings in a way that didn't trigger his fight-or-flight response. He felt supported by the team and the carefully curated setting. He felt safe. Calm. Quiet.

For the first time in a very long time, Jon could experience silence. It felt rapturous.

IDEA 6: DEEP PLAY

"There is a way of beholding that is a form of prayer." So says the naturalist and poet Diane Ackerman. "No mind or heart hobbles." She describes this sacred state of perceiving in these words:

> No analyzing or explaining. No questing for logic. No promises. No goals. No relationships. No worry. One is completely open to whatever drama may unfold.
>
> It doesn't matter what prompts the feeling—watching albatrosses court or following the sky-blown oasis of a tumultuous

sunset. When it happens, we experience a sense of revelation and gratitude. Nothing need be thought or said.

These moments of beholding—when "nothing need be thought or said"—aren't always so accessible in our verbally decorated, worry-drenched, grown-up lives.

But we found them on a regular basis when we were kids.

When Leigh was in the third grade, her parents had long been divorced. She and her brother, Roman, and their mother, Rickie, moved to the Carolinas to be near family. They called them "the Carolinas" because their relatives dotted both sides of the border and, unless you were stocking up on fireworks, the North-South distinction was basically meaningless. Leigh was often charged with watching her younger brother while her mom worked the second shift at the gas station half a mile down the rural highway where they lived. The pinnacle of any week was the "road trip" the threesome took. Anywhere would do, like just half an hour's drive to see the construction of the Peachoid, the giant peach water tower off Interstate 85.

As in many single-parent households, the siblings' battle for the passenger's seat was fierce. The front seat was where all the action was—the unobstructed views, the legroom, the radio, the CB, the cassette player, and, most important, the opportunity to do something useful, like uncloud the windshield with an old rag after a downpour.

About half the time, though, Leigh would find herself relegated to the backseat. She might as well have been exiled to a hermetically sealed vault. The Chevy Vega was a notoriously loud rust bucket. The muffler and exhaust were perpetually perforated, so the car roared like a hot rod as the chassis slowly crumbled beneath the floor mats. The mechanical rumble ensured that there'd be no casual communication between the front and the back seats. The odd kid out was sonically sealed in a universe all her own.

And that's where Leigh found quiet—or, more accurately, quiet found Leigh.

When midday heat gave way to rain, Leigh watched the underbellies of droplets as they danced at her side window. She assigned character traits, motivations, even aspirations to each one. She saw firsthand how they shuddered in anticipation. Their goal, she imagined, was to jet across the outer surface of the car window before hurling themselves into the cosmos. The wisest among them would succeed, usually by joining forces with others. Some struggled and stalled. Others vanished entirely.

This was a welcome trance. Unwanted internal chatter about finances and fitting in at school evaporated. Amidst the high-decibel engine noise, Leigh found an exquisite space of silence.

At home, Leigh found this same depth of rapt attention in nature. She often set out for "the swamp" behind their house. A thin path led through the kudzu-enveloped trees. The place reminded her of Yoda's home, Dagobah. From a dry perch, she watched the tiniest creatures move through their fleeting lives. Most traveled by whisper or no sound at all. Their dramas were mesmerizing. The ants were so friendly, always stopping for chitchat. The beetle, so patiently waiting. The water strider was a show-off, but what did you expect from a creature that could walk atop water? Leigh remembers being motionless—in a heightened state of awareness—sometimes for hours.

Once, she witnessed the larvae of a crane fly being eaten by a bullfrog that was then eaten by a copperhead snake—or so she guessed. She ran home to consult the *Encyclopaedia Britannica*, only to learn that the copperhead could just as easily have been eaten by the bullfrog, if the bullfrog hadn't been so preoccupied by the juicy larvae. In the silence of the swamp, Leigh became aware of the precarity of life and how it teetered between the eerie and the wondrous in moments like these.

It's not that the world was totally silent. Sometimes her fearful inner musings would break the drone of crickets. Sometimes she'd bolt back to the house. But most of the time, she'd stay as long as she could, even into the darkness, watching life's mysteries unfurl.

This was a particular childhood way of beholding.

Looking back, it was, indeed, a kind of prayer.

In this chapter and the one that preceded it, we've explored ways for an individual to find silence in both big and small doses, integrated into daily life or dedicated as "special occasions." But some of the deepest silence is the simplest—it's in the moments when, as Diane Ackerman put it, "nothing need be thought or said"—when we reclaim a child's eyes.

In her book *Deep Play*, Ackerman writes of "play" as "a refuge from ordinary life, a sanctuary of the mind, where one is exempt from life's customs, methods, and decrees." And "deep play" is what she calls the ecstatic form of play. It's the kind of experience that brings us into the prayer-like state of beholding.

While Ackerman says that "deep play" is classified more by mood than by activity, there are some kinds of activities that are especially likely to prompt it: "art, religion, risk-taking, and some sports—especially those that take place in relatively remote, silent, and floaty environments, such as scuba diving, parachuting, hang gliding, mountain climbing."

While we might think of ecstatic recreation as the opposite of order, there is often a strong sense of order to deep play. There's the demarcation of a special time or a unique place.

We have to master the rules of a game like music or mountaineering before we lose ourselves in it. It's like how Matt Heafy described practicing so hard that all the music was encoded in muscle memory, making it possible to "let go" into a profound state of quiet on the stage. Or, to paraphrase the late, great saxophonist Charlie Parker: "Learn everything, then forget that shit and play."

The other practices we've described in the preceding pages—for example, short retreats—can facilitate deep play. It's sometimes necessary to cordon off other responsibilities, to make room for forgetting, in order to enter the childlike consciousness with absorbed attention.

Jon Lubecky found a way to make the previously walled-off depths of his psyche accessible. He had to find a means to clear the trauma that was distorting his perception and precluding his presence. While Jon worked with a psychoactive substance under a strict set of medical conditions, the sincere and responsible use of mind- and heart-opening substances can also be a pathway to the rapturous. What makes it sincere? In our experience, it comes back to seeking lasting change in the direction of empathy and ethics. It's distinct from seeking cheap thrills or empty curiosity.

The overarching practice we're describing here is the work of coming into alignment with the pulse of life—as we were before we donned the uniforms and perspectives of "very serious adults."

So, think about how you migrate from the noise of names and distinctions to the silence of pure sensory clarity.

What brings you closest to a childlike way of perceiving the world?

Which activities, people, or frames of mind support you?

How can you carry these ways of beholding into everyday life?

ALTERED TRAITS

Skylar Bixby spent all day in his tent listening to the alternating sounds of rain splatter and snow fall. Close to dusk, the precipitation stopped. He and his tentmates crawled out of their shelter and walked to the top of a nearby hill. The sky cleared and filled with golden light as the sun set over the whitebark pines and granite peaks.

Normally, it would seem strange—even laughable—for a group of twelve teenagers to be standing together without phones in total silence. But here it seemed natural. After the first thirteen days of a three-month wilderness expedition that started in Wyoming's Wind River Range, everyone's senses were attuned to a moment like this one—a moment that summoned respect.

Skylar stayed on the hilltop after sunset, after everybody returned to camp. He kept watching the changing colors of the early-evening sky and listening to the air. In that moment, he noticed something about himself: his mind was nothing like the one he'd known a few weeks prior.

"I had been worrying about school, worrying about which memes to send to friends, worrying about how to be myself," he says, describing his typical high school reality. After months and months of disembodied video classes, college admissions uncertainties, and awkward quarantine-era socializing, this was understandable. But all that anxiety had become a faint memory. The itch to play video games or meet up on Discord was gone. "I noticed how my priorities shifted there. I had a completely different list of priorities from the ones I had in normal life."

Over the course of three months in the backcountry, Skylar first noticed how the auditory and informational noise of everyday life fell away. Next, the subtler internal noise of future projections, worries, and overanalysis receded, too. He faced an all-new set of purposes on which to fix his attention: finding water, counting rations, leading navigation, staying warm, evading bears.

When we spoke with Skylar several weeks after his return from the backcountry, he was grateful and almost surprised that this underlying feeling had stayed with him—in spite of his return to twenty-first-century teenage life. "I can have a quiet moment without needing distraction now," he tells us, adding, "It's a *skill* to be able to do nothing, and I have that skill now."

It wasn't so easy for Skylar to acquire that skill. He had to exchange the ease and familiarity of his daily routine for the physical rigors of months in the mountains. Like Matt Heafy and Jon Lubecky, he discovered that he had to *do the work*. He found that it was worth enduring discomfort and inconvenience for the chance to have an experience like that sunset on the hilltop. In that glowing silence, he realized that he had fundamentally remade his mind. He'd shifted not just his *states* but his *traits*.

Diane Ackerman uses the word "rapturous" to describe such an experience. It's a word, she says, that literally means "seized by force," as if one were being carried away by a powerful bird of prey, a raptor.

It's a funny juxtaposition to the conventional meaning of silence.

But if we accept true silence as a direct encounter with what is *real*, then it's a profound break from ordinary life in the twenty-first century. It's a radical contrast to the artifice of social media and hyper-speed information society.

It's a force for transformation. It's only natural to use the word "rapturous" to describe it.

In the chapters to come, we'll continue to explore silence—both everyday and rarefied—not just on an individual basis, but in settings where the silence is shared.

PART V

QUIET TOGETHER

CHAPTER 12

WORKING QUIET

If you had been walking around Philadelphia in the summer of 1787 and had stumbled upon Independence Hall, you would have encountered something strange. The street in front of the meeting hall—where many of the nation's founders were assembled to draft the U.S. Constitution—was filled with a gigantic mound of dirt. The delegates to the Constitutional Convention had ordered the construction of this earthen noise barrier. They believed the sounds of carriages, street vendors, and conversations outside would disturb their intense deliberation and writing. They weren't going for a monastic silence. As the historical records show, there were plenty of bitter vocal disagreements. Given the social mores of the day, there might have been occasional moments of emotional release through yelling or throwing things—perhaps crumpled paper or pieces of fruit—at one another. Still, there was an underlying recognition of the need for a quiet container in which to do difficult thinking as a group. The big dirt mound was an effort to make this possible.

Fast-forward 235 years, and you'll find a radically different reality for U.S. lawmakers. Throughout his tenure as legislative director for three members of Congress, Justin consistently found that it was too noisy to think on Capitol Hill. With TVs blasting Fox News or MSNBC (depending on the partisan affiliation of the office), ringing alarm bells signaling floor votes, and industry lobbyists schmoozing and backslapping at open-bar receptions, the acoustic environment of today's Congress is wildly different from the one in which the framers of the Constitution functioned. And that's to say nothing of the informational noise modern lawmakers endure: endless time-sensitive emails from advocates, constituent meetings, election strategy discussions, fundraising call sessions, press events, and the pervasive pressures for networking, politicking, and media management. The distraction level in today's Congress is orders of magnitude greater than anything a few eighteenth-century Philly street vendors could have possibly presented. In contrast to the Constitutional Convention, today's Congress does not recognize the necessity of quiet for clear thinking. Making noise is a badge of honor.

Several years ago, Justin took part in a small experiment to help change the culture of Capitol Hill. Through a new mindfulness program that Representative Tim Ryan and a handful of partners had launched, Justin started teaching meditation to policy makers on Capitol Hill. He remembers leading a session for the first time on one particularly tense Monday afternoon in the Rayburn House Office Building, amidst budget battles and a fierce debate over the controversial Trans-Pacific Partnership trade deal. There were about forty policy and communications staffers present. Some were progressive West Coast Democrats with respectable yoga practices, and some were southern and midwestern Republicans who had worked in finance or law and had already come to appreciate the practical necessity of meditation for dealing with workplace stress. In a building that was usually self-segregated by ideological proclivities and social cliques, the space was surprisingly commingled.

As people settled in, Justin could sense the typical Capitol Hill energy in the air—people on edge, heads racing with thoughts about office politics, career jockeying, and the contentious votes to come later in the day. More than a few of them must have been wondering, "What am I *doing* here?"

Meanwhile, Justin welcomed everyone and provided a few minutes of orientation to the practice of meditation. He looked out on a striking scene: in a small meeting room with official-looking blue carpet and dark wood furniture under neon lights and an American flag, an assortment of high-strung government functionaries in formal attire sat cramped together—mostly in chairs, a few with legs crossed on the floor.

As he got them going with a twenty-minute seated meditation, silence enveloped the room, and something shifted. Those turbocharged D.C. amygdalae began to decelerate. In Justin's view, it wasn't the result of any particular mindfulness technique; it was the result of the group just sitting together with nothing to say.

We are not under the impression that nudging one tiny corner of the federal government into twenty fleeting minutes of silence facilitated the kind of clarity necessary to transform "the System." But, for us, the value of this little experiment was that it demonstrated what is possible in the unlikeliest of settings.

We can be *quiet together.*

O

It's understandable to sometimes conflate the words "silence" and "solitude." Sound and stimulus are the ordinary stuff of human relationship. In the presence of other people, we do what we do: banter, chuckle, bicker, commiserate.

That said, some of the most poignant moments of silence that we've ever experienced have been in the presence of other people: *moments of shared grief or breathtaking beauty, moments of shock or wonder.* In these moments, we usually drop our social obligations to verbalize, rationalize, entertain, and analyze.

But the value of shared silence isn't just these rare moments that leave us speechless.

There's a reason why people regularly gather together to meditate in silence, even though it's so much more convenient to just sit by yourself in your own home. Simply put, there's an alchemy to experiencing silence with others. Out of the gray of the mundane, something golden can emerge. When two or more people drop the "conceptual overlay" and enter together into deeper and finer modes of perception, there's a unique feeling of expansion that happens.

The power of silence is magnified when it's shared.

In the previous chapters, we explored strategies that were focused on finding and creating silence as a solitary practice. Here, we'll look at how to navigate noise in groups and how to find shared silence.

As we'll see in the strategies to come, the essential work of finding "quiet together" is about understanding and refining our *norms* and *cultures*. When we use the word "culture," we tend to think of how societies create distinctive art or cuisine or literature. But culture can also refer to our shared, ordinary, day-to-day norms: the spoken and unspoken rules, customs, styles, rituals, rhythms, standards, preferences, and expectations that arise wherever we regularly interact with other people. In the field of organizational development, it's often said that a company's culture is always present and expressing itself, whether its members are intentional about it or oblivious to it. The same can be said of the culture of a friend group, a family, or a couple. Because norms generally emerge and evolve organically and unconsciously, it's valuable to periodically shine light on them and bring more consciousness to their creation and manifestations. It's good to question the default.

Today's U.S. Congress, as a workplace, is clearly governed by norms of noisiness. It's socially acceptable to have the TV on all the time. It's acceptable to talk loudly while someone is writing or to look at a text while someone is telling you something. It's standard operating procedure to send messages after hours with an expectation of an immediate response. People are generally too busy thinking about the moment-to-moment requirements of their causes or careers to step back and consider the distortions and distractions wrought by the sonic and information soundscapes. Justin's experimental session felt so unusual because shared quiet is so far outside the Hill's dominant culture.

The participants in the 1787 Constitutional Convention, in contrast, had norms around quiet deliberation. Facilitating pristine attention was a shared objective. That big mound of dirt reminded them—and the public—that the purpose of the gathering was getting beyond distraction in order to do important work.

Noisy norms like the ones that exist on Capitol Hill are a society-wide default today. Yet cultures of quiet still do exist. Think of a monastery, a library, or a little off-the-grid farm. In these contexts, people adopt clear rules and expectations around noise that reflect the purposes and the values of the specific place. Those norms don't condone blasting cable news commentary or compulsively checking TikTok. To find shared quiet, you don't have to join an austere religious order, hang out among the stacks of books, or move to an isolated rural setting. You can help shape rules and expectations that create elements of quiet in your current life situation—at work, at home, among friends. Doing so takes some creativity, though. Perhaps most important, however, it takes the courage to point out what's not working and to facilitate a constructive conversation about how best to move forward.

HOW TO TALK ABOUT QUIET

They'd been anticipating this move for years. Leigh's mom, Rickie, and her wife, Betty, were relocating from central Ohio to Northern

California. They planned to live with Leigh and her family while searching for affordable senior housing. In the Bay Area, it would take a Christmas miracle to find it, but they figured the rewards—among them, grandchildren—would be worth it.

It didn't take long for everyone to settle into a routine. "My Mom" and "My Betty," as Leigh affectionately calls them, were superb guests. They packed lunches and cleaned house. They volunteered to carpool and help their granddaughter, Ava, with homework. They filled the house with laughter and the sweet aroma of chocolate chip bread. With a four-to-one adult-to-child ratio in the house, Leigh figured she'd finally have that time she needed to work on this book.

Besides Betty's delightful cackle, both she and Rickie fall on the "quiet" side of the personality spectrum. They largely keep to themselves, finding satisfaction in reading, doing puzzles, and playing word games. They don't use speakerphones or auto-dictate texts in the common space. They wouldn't dream of cranking up music without a unanimous vote for a "dance party." Rickie and Betty are very considerate. But their electronic devices are a different story.

From almost anywhere in Leigh's home, she could now hear ringing, pinging, whooshing, and—most maddening of all—keystroke clicking. Leigh knew, for her own sanity, that she needed to say something, but she hesitated to do so. Leigh wanted her guests to feel completely welcome—to extend that southern hospitality she'd been raised to provide. Their two-week cross-country trip had extended to an epic six weeks due to an unexpected pit stop in Arizona for Betty to recover from emergency eye surgery. They deserved to feel at ease. Leigh decided to keep her issues to herself.

But the noise kept getting worse. Leigh had the hardest time with the max-volume customized ringtones—the cringy 1980s hair metal guitar riff (her mom) and the saccharine harp music (her Betty)—playing every thirty minutes or so. The callers were usually telemarketers or robocalls.

Leigh sensed an opening. She knew the ins and outs of do-not-call lists and robocall blocking apps, so she offered to help. But neither minded the interruptions, they told her. "Why all the fuss? Why not just hang up when the telemarketers call?"

Leigh found a peaceful moment. She took a deep breath. She told Rickie and Betty that she recognized that they actually seemed to like the binging, clicking, and whooshing of their devices, and that they didn't even mind the robocalls. She respected their preferences and choices. But, she explained, it was getting hard to concentrate, to work, to have a conversation, or to enjoy a meal in peace.

"Would you be willing to reset the defaults on your devices?" Leigh asked in a loving tone. They stopped and thought for a moment.

"Sure. If it means that much to *you*, dear."

It did.

O

It's a paradox, we know. But the work of finding shared silence often starts with more talking. It sometimes requires a lot of conversation.

Careful communication matters because people can have radically different experiences of noise and needs for silence. Rickie and Betty's norms were working just fine for them. It wasn't until the culture of their relationship met with the existing culture of Leigh's household that any issues surfaced. Ideally, conversations about noise and silence will honor the differences among us and not presume that one way is the only way.

These conversations give us opportunities to bring our respective values to the foreground. In Leigh's little domestic example, Rickie and Betty had never spoken about noise or the need for silence before. There wasn't an established norm in their relationship, because there'd never been a need for one. But since their stay in a different household was indefinite, the conversation became necessary.

For Rickie and Betty, adjusting to a new norm required some small behavior changes that they were gracious enough to agree to. Leigh also felt it was important to check in with them on the impact of her request—to tend the relationship. Leigh made sure they received positive feedback. Their adjustments made a substantial difference for her. She could now focus more on her work. She felt less agitated. In time, everyone could recognize that the quality of their life together, as a family, was just a little bit better.

We know these conversations don't always go as smoothly as Leigh's. Interventions, in some settings, can be awkward or confrontational. They can even put careers at risk. Seeking to change the noisy defaults in an office on Capitol Hill, for example, could be a complex and risky undertaking. It might involve changes to long-standing work processes or prodding sensitive egos. As COVID-19 shelter-in-place orders made our homes double as offices or triple as schoolhouses, many of us had to have these kinds of conversations about norms in the domestic sphere. Even—or, perhaps, especially—among loved ones, these conversations were difficult. But the upshot is that we're now primed to talk about noise—both auditory and informational—in a broader range of settings.

These sometimes-difficult conversations about norms and culture take on different characteristics in different contexts. In our working lives, they often hinge on expectations around topics like constant connectivity, when it's permissible to be off-line, and when it's acceptable to reserve spaces of uninterrupted attention. In our home lives, among family and friends, the issues often revolve around questions like whether it's permissible to have smartphones around or have the TV on in the background during meals. Across contexts, these conversations can get into deeper cultural questions like whether it's possible to be comfortable in silence together rather than always trying to fill the space, or whether it's okay to be multitasking when another person is sharing something with you.

We've found that across settings and situations there are a few general principles to apply when thinking about the work of quiet together.

First, *look inward.*

Starting a conversation about shared quiet doesn't just mean seizing the opportunity to point fingers at other people's noisy habits. The best starting point for a conversation on group norms is a check-in with yourself. How are *you* contributing to the auditory, informational, and even the internal soundscapes of the greater collective? You might consider asking yourself, "In what ways do *I* create noise that negatively impacts others?"

Maybe you unwittingly leave ringers and notifications on full blast as Rickie and Betty did. Maybe you "think out loud" or habitually interrupt others. Perhaps you impulsively post on social media or send excessive texts or emails that require responses. Maybe you play music or podcasts in common spaces without checking in with others or jump on important work calls while your daughter is sitting next to you doing her homework. We've been guilty of these transgressions before. Simply notice how you create noise for yourself and for the people around you. Take some time to question whether any given habit that's generating noise is necessary or if it's really just an unexamined impulse—a default that needs to be reset. If your self-observation doesn't yield clear insights, ask a truth teller in your life for observations about how you could do better.

Second, *identify your "golden rules."*

Think about your own *sphere of control* and how you can leverage it to minimize the noise in your shared surroundings. Start by creating your own personal norms that govern how you generate sound and stimulus in your own home, workplace, or other contexts in your life. One way to think about personal norms is as your own *golden rules* for mitigating noise or bringing in more deliberate quiet. Model what you want to see more of in the world. These might start as small-scale personal experiments. If they work, you can consider making them guiding principles for your day-to-day conduct.

Susan Griffin-Black, the co–chief executive officer of EO Products, a natural personal care product company, tells us that she made a vow years ago to "never be on my phone or computer when someone is talking to me, no multitasking when I'm with someone else." She upholds her golden rule, despite having more than 150 employees, a family, and a lot of social commitments.

So, consider what you value most when it comes to mitigating noise and finding quiet. What personal golden rule reflects that? Or, alternatively, consider what noisy habits bother you most. What golden rule would address those?

Having worked on your personal norms, you'll be in a better position to enter into conversations about group norms. You'll have the credibility to initiate the process of shifting the culture of your household or work team.

Third, *look out for others.*

Where it's appropriate, and where it's within your *sphere of influence,* consider how you can be a champion for quiet—not just in the whole organization, but specifically for the people who lack the power or autonomy to structure their own circumstances. Maybe you're in a position in your company where you can call out the plight of an engineer or copywriter who obviously needs a sanctuary from the workplace din. Maybe you suspect your introverted nephew could use an occasional break from boisterous family events, and you can gently raise the issue with your sibling. Especially when you're in a position of relative privilege—say, a grown-up or a senior member of a professional team—use your influence, when possible and when sensible, to be a guardian of the shared cognitive and emotional space. While you can't set the overall group norms and culture unilaterally on the basis of what you think is right, you can be on the lookout for new ideas to propose or new possibilities for managing the soundscape or enhancing the ambience, especially ones that serve the interests of those who lack influence.

Keep these three guiding principles—look inward, identify your "golden rules," and look out for others—in mind as we explore the process of finding quiet together through a wide range of examples. We'll start off in this chapter by examining our *working lives* with five ideas for navigating collective noise and building a culture of quiet clarity. While no two working environments are the same, consider the strategies employed by these advocates for silence in the workplace, and think about how you might adapt them to fit your specific situation.

IDEA 1: GET EXPERIMENTAL

Michael Barton was present at the creation of the modern open-plan office. As a longtime business executive and consultant focused on optimizing organizational culture and operations, he remembers the dreamy early aspiration that accompanied the concept: fostering collaboration by tearing down walls to promote an "anti-silo mentality." While Michael has seen some of these benefits from time to time, he believes the sound and distraction inherent in the open office is just too costly. "There have been times I've been on the phone with someone who has said, 'Do you want to call me back after your flight and you're not at the airport anymore?' and I'd say, 'Oh no! I'm not at the airport. I'm sitting in my office!'"

Back in the 1990s, as an executive with Citysearch (now a division of Ticketmaster), Michael noticed workers—particularly programmers and developers—struggling with noise and frequent interruptions. He decided to help champion their need for quiet. A young analyst at the company offered an idea: Give each team member a "red sash"—a three-foot-long-three-inch-wide strip of bright red fabric—to wear as a "do not disturb" sign. There would be no stigma involved with wearing it if everyone knew they could simply open their drawer, take out their red sash, put it over their neck, and be considered "out of the office." Michael started a conversation with management, and they agreed to give it a go.

The red sash was not a panacea. It didn't eliminate many of the problems of noise and interruptions. But it was a start. It led to several other experiments, including quiet phone-booth-sized mini-workstations and a hermetic "tech cave" for coding work. More important, however, the red sash intervention raised the issue of noise and distraction and opened an important conversation. Salespeople who had never considered noise problems suddenly noticed the plights of analysts, writers, and engineers. It became clear that the tacit agreement of the open-plan office—that anybody could be interrupted at any time—was not in everyone's best interest. The red sash experiment and the conversations that followed nudged the company out of its problematic norms.

It's hard to imagine it now, but Michael tells us that the open-plan office was once seen as utopian. Proponents made the case that "it improves communication, improves openness, improves transparency; it improves free flow from department to department." People argued that placing the CEO's desk in the center of a sea of desks—or having desk space that is first come, first served—would create a flat organizational structure and an egalitarian culture.

With hindsight, we can see that the 1990s-style techno-utopian vision didn't consider the collateral damage of human concentration. At the time, though, it was hard to go against the grain and advocate for a focus on quiet over priorities like "serendipitous interaction" and "creative collision." To resist this trend was to resist being a team player. As silly as a little piece of red fabric might seem, it took some courage for that young analyst to raise the issue and for Michael to bring it up the chain.

Irrespective of the future of open offices, the takeaway here is simple: Consider what you really want or need. Start a conversation. Envision an experiment. Launch it, refine it, iterate. At some organizations, it's "no email Fridays" or "no meeting Wednesdays." At others, it's eliminating the expectation of being available and on electronic devices during weekends or after 5:00 p.m. For some workplaces, a redesign of the floor plan might help specific kinds of workers get the focus that they need. One solution might be authorizing uninterrupted blocks of time during the workday. Another might be giving up on the open floor plan and moving the whole office to a new building. For others still, it's eliminating email as the primary means of communication and turning instead to twice-daily team update meetings or an electronic system that preserves quiet headspace.

The good news is that with a little creativity and experimentation, seemingly intractable norms of noise can be transformed.

IDEA 2: MA ON THE JOB

Since 1939, when the New York advertising executive Alex F. Osborn first started pioneering group idea-generation meetings, or "brain-storming sessions," people have had their doubts about their efficacy. Decades of academic research now show how social pressures, like fa-voring agreement over dissent and succumbing to the loudest voices or the highest-ranking individuals, kill creativity. High-speed, high-pressure ideation sessions can be good for generating conventional thinking, but they're terrible for generating the kind of novel, emer-gent thinking that's required to address most complex challenges.

In spite of the growing awareness of these issues, most teams are still brainstorming the same way that teams did in Osborn's day. Little room for reflection or introspection. Little time or space.

Earlier, we introduced you to the Japanese cultural value of *Ma*—reverence for the empty spaces "in between." It's a principle and a value that permeates traditional arts and culture, from music to tea ceremo-nies and from theater to flower arranging. The value of *Ma* is percepti-ble as part of the country's professional culture as well. In Japan, you'll often find people leaving moments of silence in meetings and conver-sations and, in the process, leaving space for what's left unsaid.

Imagine for a moment what it would mean to imbue our standard business brainstorming processes with a little bit of *Ma*.

It might mean building in sanctioned time for quiet reflection, even within a group discussion.

It might mean safeguarding the option to "sleep on the question," revisiting an inquiry fresh the next day.

It might mean nonverbal report-outs, including, for example, creating a Post-it note gallery of ideas on the walls so people can silently peruse and vote anonymously.

It almost certainly means *making space* in order to encourage quieter voices and more marginalized perspectives to reach the center. As Gandhi adamantly believed, at least a little bit of silence is necessary for the pursuit of truth.

Of course, this isn't just about brainstorming. Look at most people's weekly calendars or many organizations' penchants for back-to-back meetings. In most professional cultures, there's little regard for the space "in between." Bringing *Ma* to the job means enshrining empty spaces—for *preparation* for what's to come, for *integration* of what's just occurred, and for *reflection* on the present moment.

But, more than any other reason, we need *Ma* on the job so that we have the capacity for listening.

O

The physician Rupa Marya tells us of a study that found that doctors interrupt their patients, on average, within the first eleven seconds of their appointment. "Our training teaches us to *not* be silent," she reflects, "to actually come into the patient encounter with a lot of noise in our heads about what we assume is happening."

She knows this tendency well.

"When I'm interviewing a patient, I notice how many times I feel like interrupting them—to get to the point or to get to what I'm interested in learning," she tells us. "But you can't really hear what's going on for somebody if you are not actively listening in silence."

People of Standing Rock made Rupa aware of the destructiveness of this habit. She had gone to South Dakota to support the health of the Indigenous communities gathered to resist the Dakota Access Pipeline.

In the midst of her work, an Oglala Lakhota grandmother asked Rupa if she might be open to some feedback. The woman explained that the "colonizer's approach" wouldn't work in her community. She described it in this way:

> When you're waiting for that person to be quiet to interject your own thoughts to prove how clever you are or to advance the agenda of the conversation in a certain way, but you're not silent after that person speaks.

The woman's directness at first took Rupa by surprise, but she recognized the weight of her words. "Being silent after someone speaks," the woman continued, "conveys a humility that is essential to respectful communication."

Rupa took this advice to heart, and the Lakhota grandmothers in the camp noticed. They asked her to help set up a clinic with them, and now, four years later, she is still supporting the work.

Rupa began paying close attention to when her Lakhota patients would "shut down" and retreat into themselves. She began to view this break in the bond with her patients as "the antithesis of healing." "I have been humbled and continually 'schooled' when working with Indigenous people because I have to retrain my mind to *not* be so 'clever' in that way, but to be open, receptive, and silent." Rupa shares this insight with us enthusiastically; she's up for the task—or the "unlearning," as she calls it. She recently teamed up with the best-selling author Raj Patel to chronicle the "unlearning" needed in Western medicine in their book *Inflamed: Deep Medicine and the Anatomy of Injustice*. For Rupa, slowing her pace and making space for listening *is* deep medicine. She knows firsthand that it heals.

Rupa's not the only one receiving a wake-up call to incorporate *Ma* into her work through more active listening. Leigh once got a similar message in a radically different context: a pilot program to the climate team of NASA's Goddard Space Flight Center.

Goddard is the operational home of the Hubble Space Telescope and the James Webb Space Telescope. Its scientists and engineers also guide more than fifty lesser-known spacecrafts tasked with the study of our sun, the solar system, the broader universe, and our planet's changing climate. To its credit, NASA is devoted to building the "soft skills" of the highly technical teams that work there.

NASA's workforce is unusual. It consists of *four* working generations. The reason for this is simple: people never retire. The training was intended to address communication issues common to multigenerational teams. In their debut, Leigh and her co-lead threw everything they had at them—a two-week training packed into two days. There was nary a moment to reflect, digest, or even protest. There was no *Ma*. It was a *Ma*-less free-for-all.

This was an enormous opportunity for Leigh. She was equal parts honored and petrified. Unfortunately, it was probably the "petrified" part of Leigh that did most of the agenda planning, and she felt the need to demonstrate her worth, and the value of the content, by way of the proverbial fire hose.

Leigh overlooked the obvious: the room was *filled* with introverts—more than 75 percent, according to NASA's internal tally. By the end of the first day, the participants looked weary and disheveled, as if they'd been hit by a hurricane. Hurricane Leigh—with strong gusts of impostor syndrome, amplified by unbridled extroversion.

With a near-total overhaul, it all worked out. They cut content. They scheduled more breaks. They added intervals for silent observation. In short, they added *Ma*. Leigh went on to deliver the work for years, grateful for the lesson and the patience she was afforded while she learned it—or "unlearned" it, as Rupa would say.

While the word *Ma* is uniquely Japanese, you can find at least some element of this same value in virtually every culture. In Western cultures, the proverb "Silence is golden" is an embodiment of it. Some cultures—including those of many of the world's Indigenous and Aboriginal peoples as well as peoples of Scandinavia and

Southeast Asia—tend to hold the value in a foundational way. Some groups of people, like introverted NASA engineers, just naturally need adequate space and silence. But if you look at the pitfalls of modern protocols and processes—from business brainstorms to meeting schedules to medical appointments—it's evident that virtually everyone needs more *Ma*.

IDEA 3: DEEP WORK, TOGETHER

Marie Skłodowska, known today as Madame Marie Curie, was born into a loving Polish family of educators who quickly recognized her uncommon intellect. After the early death of her mother, Marie vowed to put her older sister, Bronya, through medical school in Paris. She did so by working as a governess, teaching a variety of subjects and languages. In her off-hours, Marie pursued her own studies, conducting chemistry experiments and puzzling over math equations. She was guided by instructions her father provided in letters. When Bronya completed medical school, she returned the favor by offering to house Marie while she attended the Sorbonne.

In addition to all the barriers she faced as one of the few women at a world-leading university, Marie had to catch up on years of scientific study that she had missed. She also needed a greater command of French. She realized she would need to study even more than she'd anticipated. In her words, she needed to "find perfect concentration."

Bronya's home was filled with visitors, music, and patients who would show up at all hours in need of treatment. Marie was unable to "find perfect concentration" there, so she set out in search of a room of her own and found an attic apartment. She nearly starved and froze to death there because she prioritized buying lamp oil to study by over food for sustenance or coal for heat. Still, the sacrifices paid off. She caught up and then surpassed her peers. In the best-selling biography of her mother's life, Ève Curie writes, "She had a passionate love for the atmosphere of attention and silence, the 'climate' of the laboratory, which she was to prefer to any other up to her last day."

At the Sorbonne, Marie met and married Pierre Curie, a professor and physicist. The foundation of their marriage was a shared love of this "climate" of the laboratory—a shared space of "attention and silence" where they conducted groundbreaking research in the field of radio-activity. In 1903, they were awarded a Nobel Prize in Physics. French academics had originally suggested the distinction go to Pierre only. But Pierre insisted that he and Marie be co-laureates. They did all their deeply focused work together.

A few years after the Nobel was awarded, Pierre was tragically struck and killed by a horse-drawn carriage. Marie, while heartbroken, continued the work for more than two decades.

She was appointed to her husband's position, making her the first woman professor of the Sorbonne. Her father-in-law helped raise her daughters, Irène and Ève, allowing Marie to "find perfect concentration" and continue her life's work. Famously, she'd become not only the first woman to receive a Nobel Prize but the first *person* to receive two Nobel Prizes in two scientific categories—physics and chemistry.

The older Curie daughter, Irène, showed promise as a scientist and soon joined her mother in the lab. During World War I, while still a teenager, Irène accompanied her mother as she drove her mobile X-ray units to field surgeons on the front lines who used them to locate bullets, shrapnel, and broken bones. These ambulances became known as Les Petites Curies. It's estimated—with two hundred vehicles secured and 150 women trained—that they examined more than a million wounded soldiers.

Marie later founded the Radium Institute, where Irène trained fellow researchers, including Frédéric Joliot. Irène and Frédéric would fall in love and marry, working side by side—as Marie and Pierre had—in the "climate" of rapt attention in their shared laboratory.

In 1935, Irène and Frédéric Joliot-Curie received a Nobel Prize in

Chemistry—twenty-four years after her mother and thirty-two years after her parents.

The Curie family was awarded five Nobel prizes—more than any other family, even to this day. They faced obstacles, including poverty, war, gender barriers in education, and societal norms around women in the professional sphere. But the Curie family shared a norm around the power of "perfect concentration." Not just alone, but together; not only for men, but for women and girls, too.

It's an example of what a culture of quiet clarity can generate.

O

In his 2016 book, *Deep Work: Rules for Focused Success in a Distracted World*, Cal Newport laments the loss of immersive attention—like the work of the Curie family—and advises readers on how to reclaim it. Newport defines "deep work" as "professional activities performed in a state of distraction-free concentration that push your cognitive capabilities to their limit. These efforts create new value, improve your skill, and are hard to replicate." Looking to this lodestar of "deep work," Newport scrutinizes the true costs of open office floor plans and our expectations of constant connectivity. He turns to historical figures, current thought leaders, creatives, and decision makers for examples of why "deep work" is the essence of meaningful and effective work. Newport emphasizes that the point of "deep work" isn't just productivity hacking. It's about the power of immersive attention as a way to overcome widespread feelings of anxiety and malaise in an increasingly superficial online world.

Newport recently wrote about the story of Tom, an employee at a tech company with a particularly noisy culture. According to Tom, all work emails and IMs seemed to insist upon an immediate reply—even if he was in the middle of something else. "If you didn't respond quick enough, people would assume that you were slacking off," Tom said.

After weeks of doubt, Tom mustered up the courage to talk to his boss. He asked her, "How much time do you expect me to spend each day researching and writing, and how much time do you expect me to spend communicating with team members through email and chat?" For Tom's boss, the answer was obvious. Tom's job was to research and write; that's what he was paid to do. Tom got her blessing to bracket ninety minutes to two hours of uninterrupted research and writing time every morning and afternoon. Others took notice. They asked for the same allowances. Old norms started shifting. As Tom recalls, "The only reason this had become a problem in the first place is that we'd never been deliberate about setting expectations."

Tom's industry, like so many others, is in the midst of a reshuffle. While we don't know what the next workplace will look like, we do know that the ability to "find perfect concentration" and to produce "deep work" will need to be a part of any positive future. Although the term "deep work" evokes solitary pursuits, we believe that it's essential to think about the social dimensions of this kind of pristine attention. The Curies found their most powerful space of silent immersion—of what Cal Newport calls "deep work"—together. The mound of dirt outside the Constitutional Convention indicates that there was at least some degree of deep work happening within that shared work space. Today, the challenge isn't just that many of us, as individuals, lack the discipline or interest in the pure attention of deep work. It's also figuring out how, as teams, organizations, and whole societies, we can formulate shared values and operational systems that enshrine it.

IDEA 4: SITTING IN THE FIRE

For five years, Pádraig Ó Tuama led the historic Corrymeela Community, the oldest peace-building organization in Northern Ireland. The role put Pádraig at the center of the work of healing a multigenerational violent conflict. It was a practical position with serious administrative duties as well as the heavy responsibility of helping to heal his community from decades of wartime trauma.

But Pádraig didn't approach the job as a typical NGO leader, therapist, or mediator.

He approached the job as a poet.

Pádraig worked to find the right words and narratives to get people to open up. And in addition to finding empowering language and stories, Pádraig sought to facilitate spaces of silence, the quiet crevices where people could really hear each other—where they might even reconsider firmly entrenched positions or calcified hatreds.

Pádraig invited people to the "borderland of the self," asking them to probe the stories they tell with questions like "Have I considered it from a different point of view?" He asked them to look more closely at their good intentions: "Have they borne out in terms of good impact?"

"I think we do all need a salting of anarchism to ask, 'Am I *really* doing the good?'" He cracks a slight smile and says, "We might even need to ask, 'What if *we're* the bastards?'"

"Silence," Pádraig says, is an essential element for doing this kind of reconciliation work, with its inner and outer dimensions. "Silence," he says, is "having enough space in yourself to ask yourself strange questions."

As Pádraig writes, "The quality of the telling of a story will be related to the quality of the listening of the people." It's not just about storytelling but also about *story catching*. This is where the transformation happens. It's in the capacity to receive.

In his book *Sorry for Your Troubles*, reflecting on the work with Corrymeela, Pádraig formats his poem titles with spaces between each letter "as a way of indicating the importance of silence, listening, grief and the things beyond words." It's in the little spaces that healing becomes possible.

We're the first to admit it: in times of crisis or moral indignation, our first impulse has often been to *get loud*. To draw attention. To call out the perpetrators. To hard charge for change. This underlying impulse is valid. We do need to make people aware. We often need to act swiftly to address issues of persecution or war or environmental destruction. Likewise, we often need to act quickly and decisively to address the smaller-scale injustices and indignities that happen in a workplace or a community.

And yet, Pádraig indicates, there's a level of resolution and healing that can only happen in the open space—through a depth of attention and listening. Earlier, we shared the story of how Sheena Malhotra, the scholar and feminist activist, sat in silence for nine minutes with thousands of other people at a Black Lives Matter demonstration in Los Angeles in the summer of 2020. In the still space, she went deeper into the pain and indignation that she and others were feeling. "Silence is kind of like an ocean," Sheena tells us. "It can change forms. Silence gives you the space for a shape-shifting of emotions. It gives you the space to absorb the energy of people around you."

Cyrus Habib tells us how the Jesuits' reparations process is unprecedented. A dialogue between the "descendants of the enslaved and descendants of the enslavers" is steering the disbursement of more than $100 million. And it's happening, Cyrus tells us, through "a whole lot of silence." By this, he means space for listening, for shared prayer and contemplation, and for deeply discerning the right course of action. "Restorative justice" practices, like the reconciliation efforts in Northern Ireland and this Jesuit reparations process, are increasingly prevalent in schools, communities, and even formal judicial systems. Often inspired by Indigenous council practices from around the world, the essence of restorative justice is *listening*. Rather than focusing on punishment, it's about ensuring that everyone involved understands the fullest possible causes and impacts of a transgression. Rather than focusing on "sides," it's ultimately about restoring wholeness. A prerequisite of success is the capacity to be together in silence.

Rob Lippincott, the birthright Quaker who you met in chapter 4, describes how silence is the force that equilibrates anger and division in contentious meetings. When it's clear that the participants in a deliberative session are not listening to each other—that people are getting entrenched or agitated—the clerk, the chair in a Quaker proceeding, will ask for a period of silence. As Rob describes it, he finds his own center, takes a few deep breaths, and connects to the higher purpose of the meeting. The silence isn't forcing a resolution before the group is actually ready. It's simply ensuring that people are present and listening. The group silence forces everyone into a place where they have to drop their verbalized positions and arguments and connect to the underlying energy of the shared space. It's like the wisdom of dropping "conceptual overlay" and finding the "sensory clarity," but applied to the work of conversation and deliberation.

While the word "silence" can sometimes imply withdrawal, here it connotes the essence of full engagement. Silence, in this sense, is the courage to face the utmost discomfort. It's sitting in the fire. Whether we're involved in a major conflict or a trivial workplace quarrel, we need to be able to be "quiet together"—to withstand the frightening nakedness of shared silence—in order to find direct and durable resolutions.

IDEA 5: SLOW DOWN, THERE ISN'T MUCH TIME

The coastal redwoods of California are the ideal setting for contemplating an important and perplexing problem. The soft bark and fallen foliage of the gentle giants are like guardians of quiet. It's a place that emanates calm and clarity. You can feel it, even when you're strategizing around one of our most urgent environmental challenges.

Since 2013, the mountaineer and biophysical chemist Arlene Blum has handpicked a small group of scientists, government regulators, NGOs, retailers, and manufacturers to come here to analyze problems and envision solutions to the global crisis of toxic chemicals. Arlene asked Leigh to design and facilitate these annual four-day retreats.

It's worth taking a moment to explain *why* solving the toxic chemical problem can make all of us healthier. In the United States, there are tens of thousands of untested and unregulated chemicals added to everyday products. Water repellents, flame retardants, bisphenols, and other chemicals in consumer products are contributing to cancer, obesity, falling sperm counts, and neurological, reproductive, and immune problems. American children have lost an average of five IQ points from exposure to one flame retardant chemical, costing the United States an estimated $266 billion in annual productivity loss.

The chemical companies do not need to prove the safety of their chemicals before they are used in consumer items. Chemicals are presumed safe until scientists show they are not, and proving harm is time-consuming and expensive.

But the problem remains even when the regulatory system works: scientists collect data, demonstrate harm, and successfully advocate for phasing out a chemical—as was recently the case with BPA (bisphenol A) in water bottles. What then?

Most manufacturers look for a drop-in substitute for that chemical—something similar in its structure and function—as the fastest and least costly solution. However, usually, the substitute chemicals share the original chemicals' harmful qualities. Case in point: BPS (bisphenol S), the replacement for BPA, is just as harmful as its predecessor. Once you phase out one chemical, you get its close cousin. Once you've done the same for the cousin, another replacement, perhaps just as bad or worse, is next in line. The metaphor Arlene uses to describe it is an eternal game of whack-a-mole.

Most conferences on these topics are dominated by cataclysmic data and rising panic. Arlene and Leigh try to set a calm and reasoned tone. Their motto is "Slow down, there isn't much time."

Each retreat has intensely focused morning and afternoon sessions devoted to strategy and problem solving. But each afternoon, Leigh and Arlene bring in some quiet with offerings like scenic hikes and trips to the beach, or there's always the option to nap in the cabin. Work sessions are peppered with three-minute dance parties, poetry readings, creative improv, and time for quiet reflection. These interludes of playful activities and quiet ones are meant to prepare the group for the complex and difficult journey that lies ahead. At first, participants seem surprised by this schedule. Some people have traveled halfway around the world to tackle this global problem—*shouldn't the work be grueling?*

At times, *yes*, it will be.

But the best way to arrive at transformative solutions is to create a general atmosphere of space and silence—an ambience where participants can calm the amygdala and expand beyond the frenetic mindset of the default mode network. It's about being receptive and letting answers emerge, rather than simply "powering through."

On the final morning, Leigh sends the participants out for thirty minutes of solo time in nature. She shares some simple instructions: (1) *remember why you're here*, and (2) *listen*.

Some people struggle with the lack of mental stimulation during even this modest amount of time. But as the minutes progress, most people *tune in*. They reconnect with the "why" that brought them to the work. Many people gain insight into what's within their *spheres of control* and *influence* for making change. One guy, Mike, a decidedly left-brained engineer with no previous interest in mystical experiences or Gaia consciousness, came back and said he was "told by the redwoods" to write a book documenting the history of toxic chemical use in manufacturing. The room erupted in applause and cheers of "Yes! We *need* this book!"

The breakthrough that came out of the first retreat was to sort chemicals into six "families," with similar structure or function, now known as "the Six Classes." One example—the worst of the worst—is PFAS chemicals, which provide products with stain and water repellency. However, they never break down in the environment, and the few that have been studied are toxic. When managing PFAS, you can't just focus on a single chemical, because there are *thousands*. You must consider the whole class. "When we dreamed it up back in 2013, we called it 'the Big Idea'—it was so new. But now the whole class concept is accepted very broadly," Arlene reflects. "For example," she continues, "IKEA learned about the harm of PFAS and decided to remove the whole class of chemicals from all their products worldwide." Nine months later, they called Arlene to say, "We did it!" They had analyzed their supply chains and identified all the products that contained any PFAS. They found nontoxic substitutes for the PFAS to make their shower curtains and umbrellas waterproof. For the grease-resistant tablecloths, they could not find any substitutes, so they told Arlene, "We're just not going to sell tablecloths anymore." And they don't.

For Arlene, who self-identifies as "an off-the-charts extrovert," the quiet built into the retreat was counter-instinctual. But Arlene is also extraordinarily focused on results, and she found that by slowing down and bringing in quiet, the group was achieving outcomes beyond what even she had imagined. The gregarious, results-oriented, skeptical scientist has come to appreciate the power of silence to support novel thinking and breakthrough strategies.

MODERN-DAY DIRT BARRICADES

As Justin continued teaching mindfulness on Capitol Hill, he started noticing the noise of the place in a more intense way. There was precious little deep work happening. There were no red-sash-style interventions to help people who were struggling with the amount of sound and stimulus. The idea of bringing together aggrieved parties to work toward healing and reconciliation in a conscious, silent encounter was outlandish.

But why? If there was, in fact, a tradition of quiet, focused attention going back to the eighteenth century in the American government, how come no one was challenging the modern norms of noisiness?

One day, as Justin led one of the mindfulness sessions in the Rayburn House Office Building, he decided to speak about what might be the "dirtiest word you say on the Hill."

"Surrender."

The point of pretty much everything in Congress is to win: *to win the argument, to prevail with the election, to prove yourself more capable and cunning than your competitors.* Shifting the norms of noisiness will require more than conversations.

But that day, Justin spoke about how the word "surrender" might actually be a remedy for so much of what ailed the people working in America's legislative branch. "Take a moment to surrender worries and what-ifs to the breath and the present moment," he said. "Let's see if we can surrender rigid combative identities and complicated power relations to the simplicity of just being."

In Congress, as in countless other workplaces, the norms and needs haven't yet been systematically examined. It may be a relatively simple matter of surfacing shared values and aligning around a few norms—as was the case with Rickie and Betty, Michael Barton and the young analyst, Rupa and the Lakhota grandmothers, Leigh and the NASA engineers, Tom and his boss, and others.

It may require some time, some sitting in the fire, to find those places of shared concern and the norms and culture that reveal a path forward.

But in some situations, like Capitol Hill, the issues run deeper still.

We're not here to tell you that we have any clear idea about how to shift the hypercompetitive values of an extremely noisy place like the U.S. Congress. But the ideas we've presented in this chapter represent some baby steps.

Come together. Have an honest conversation about noise and quiet. Experiment. Iterate. *Listen.*

CHAPTER 13

LIVING QUIET

Once in a blue moon, Jarvis manages to share some silence with guys on death row in San Quentin. One night, years ago, it was literally *because* of the moon.

Jarvis was in the Adjustment Center when his neighbors started hollering about the sight of a full moon rising. It was the time of year when the moon was low enough to view through the window opposite their cells. "That thing was so close," Jarvis tells us. "I never thought the moon could get that close."

Everybody knew Jarvis loved astronomy. So they started asking him questions: "Why does it look so big? Where's it gonna go next?" Jarvis saw his shot and took it. "I told them, 'Oh yeah, that's the moon, but it's five minutes late,' and I just took off from there." Jarvis pretended to know the exact speed and path it would take. He told them to pay special attention to the shadows on the face of the moon and described, in flowery terms, the features they should watch for. And then he explained the most important aspect of proper moon-watching etiquette: "*You have to be quiet.* Every time you ask me a question, it takes my mind off it!"

The guys fell silent, like a classroom of obedient parochial school students.

It was astonishing, Jarvis remembers. He had the whole tier—fifteen incarcerated men—watching the sky in silence for almost twenty minutes. Typically, he tells us, nobody in San Quentin shuts up for more than ten seconds.

One of the guards, taken with the scene, started gazing upward, too. There they all were: a bunch of guys on death row and an employee of the state prison whose job it was to keep them in line.

Watching the moon.

Together.

In silence.

The trance might have continued, had one guy not decided he'd had enough.

"It's not like the motherfucker can hear!" he exclaimed, referring to the earless moon. He realized he'd been tricked into being quiet for that long. "The jig was up," Jarvis tells us, "but I got twenty minutes out of them!"

O

The ancient Buddhist text called the Lotus Sutra presents a parable of a wealthy man whose house is on fire. In the house are many children who don't realize they're in danger. In fact, they don't know what fire is or even, for that matter, what a house is. The man can't carry all the children out to safety or persuade them to leave on their own, so he tells them that there are three toys outside—a goat cart, a deer cart, and a steer cart. The children rush out of the house. When they get outside, the three carts aren't there. Instead, there's a single jeweled carriage, drawn by a white ox, waiting to bring them to safety.

The point of the story isn't to promote half-truths or child bribery. Rather, the parable is often used to explain that some practices are not illustrations of the ultimate reality but rather expedient means to save a person from suffering and help bring them toward illumination. In Buddhism, this is called *upaya*, or "skillful means." We often think about *upaya* as the importance of respecting where people are in their journey—what they are capable of understanding or willing to hear—and using the language that's appropriate for them.

While we encourage direct conversations about the need for more silence—like the one Leigh had with her mom and her Betty—whenever possible, we recognize that in our own real-life situations with small children, teenagers, our partners, housemates, friends, and relatives, it's not always plausible to take the noisy norms head-on. In a world where most of us are socialized to live in constant conversation and electronic stimulation, we often have to find skillful means to get our friends and loved ones to lower the volume and get comfortable with silence. As we've said before, our *sphere of control* looks a bit different when we are navigating relationships. We usually have more *influence* than control here.

Jarvis used *upaya* with his neighbors in San Quentin. He indulged the notion that something fantastical was happening with the rising moon in order to seize a rare opportunity for silence and appreciation. Neither we nor Jarvis encourages you to make stuff up to win the fleeting attention of your friends, neighbors, or loved ones. But we do encourage you to get creative.

Sometimes, when Justin is walking in the mountains with his five-year-old daughter, he'll say, "There's something special about the wind today. Let's stop and listen to it. Can you hear how it's dancing in the tops of the aspen trees?" They'll stop for a moment and pay attention together. Other times, Justin notices his daughter using the same strategy on him. He'll be talking loudly on a hike, and his daughter will point out a big crevice in the trunk of a cottonwood tree. "There's a fairy house, Daddy. Where fairies live. You need to be quiet to not disturb them." Justin dutifully shuts his mouth.

We often use "skillful means" of finding silence on *ourselves* as well. Sometimes we create ways to lure ourselves away from the gravitational pull of work or nonessential communications. We tell ourselves that this is the one perfect time of year to see the maples turn colors or that the computer must be glitchy for a reason. Perhaps Mercury is in retrograde, making it time to sever our electronic bonds for a spell. Leigh often jokes that her *present-day self* is frequently caught by surprise when she realizes that her *past self* signed up her *future self* for a weekend retreat. So, yes, we do sometimes need to get creative to figure out how to overcome our own noisy tendencies. The smaller parts of ourselves know that the bigger parts of ourselves have our best interest at heart.

O

When we first started asking people about the deepest silence they'd ever known, we were expecting to hear about solitary experiences. We hadn't anticipated that most of the deepest moments would actually be shared ones. We realized over time, too, that most of our personal deepest moments were also shared—like Justin's first time holding his newborn twins skin to skin on his chest. These raw, intimate, and sometimes awe-inspiring encounters are the inspiration for the chapter ahead.

In the pages that follow, we will continue to explore how to turn down the dial of auditory, informational, and internal noise on a collective basis by zooming in on what it means to find shared silence in our homes, in our free time, and in our lives with our families and friends. We'll consider deeper questions of what it means to prepare the soil for quiet together, including how we decide consciously on norms and shared cultures that respect our authentic and evolving needs. We'll investigate seven different ideas for cultivating the space in our lives and our homes that invites rapturous silence.

IDEA 1: PUMPERNICKEL!

Rosin Coven is an "umpteen-piece" musical troupe that defies categorization. When pressed, though, Midnight Rose, their founding front woman, will offer this description: "We are the world's premier pagan lounge ensemble." While their genre classification is questionable, their musicianship is not. Most members are formally trained, and several have played in major orchestras. They command an untold number of instruments including cello, contrabass, trombone, violin, accordion, trumpet, vibraphone, drums, harp, guitar, percussion, vocals, and a few odds and ends you might find in your kitchen or a junkyard. As any ensemble member will tell you, you can't display all that talent at once. In fact, sharing the space is a prerequisite of success. "That's a tremendous part of what makes an ensemble sound good," Midnight Rose tells us. "There's nobody that needs to be front and center all the time."

In their twenty-five years of composing and arranging together, Rosin Coven has come up with a shorthand term for when the sharing goes off the rails and the soundscape gets too crowded. Someone shouts, "*Pumpernickel!*"

A declaration of "Pumpernickel!" is like the pulling of a rip cord. "It means, 'What we really need is a subtractive process right now' in order to create space and silence," Midnight Rose explains. The French composer Claude Debussy once said, "Music is in the silence between the notes." We've heard that the legendary Parliament bassist Bootsy Collins said that this same in-between space is "where the funk is." Both sentiments speak to the underlying premise of the Pumpernickel Mechanism. It's a call to "put on the brakes" when the musicality is lost. It initiates a process of shaving down the excess sound, calming nervous systems, and sharpening perceptions.

After some time thinking about it, the two of us came to realize our purpose in writing this book is to call "Pumpernickel!" on the whole wide world.

This brings us back to the question of norms and culture. "Pumpernickel!" is Rosin Coven's eccentric norm reflective of their eccentric culture. They embraced it to address their shared need to name the obstacles that get in their way.

This leads us to a pertinent question: *How can we call "Pumpernickel!" when the orchestra of our lives becomes discordant and the volume too high?*

In many families, the idea of saying "things are getting too loud in here" is completely taboo. It might be viewed more as a personal attack than as a yearning for quality time. As a result, communicating the need for silence can feel daunting; there's seemingly no way to reel in excessive screen time, overactive calendars, or over-the-top verbal processing. There's no acceptable way to call "Pumpernickel!"

But this is where some red-sash-style experimentation can come in handy. Maybe you and your loved ones launch your own experiment. Maybe you come up with your own silly word, like the German name for the darkest of all whole-grain breads. Whatever you try, an experimental mindset and a bit of playfulness can go a long way toward expanding a group's norms to embrace a full range of possibilities, including shared silence.

IDEA 2: REMEMBER THE SABBATH DAY

Throughout Marilyn Paul's twenties and thirties, she was mired in a debilitating state of urgency, a nagging feeling of always being "behind." By most people's measurements, she was "ahead"; she held advanced degrees from prestigious universities, she had a good job, and she enjoyed a vibrant social life. But as time went on, she became so fatigued that she was physically incapable of getting out of bed. She was eventually diagnosed with an immune deficiency syndrome brought on by her nonstop workaholic pace. Soon after the diagnosis, a friend pleaded with Marilyn to take a night off and join him and some friends for a Shabbat dinner. As a secular Jew, she wasn't that interested. She delayed accepting his invitation for months, but eventually she succumbed. Her decision to attend that dinner was life changing.

Over time, Marilyn took up the weekly practice of observing Shabbat, the Jewish Sabbath, from dusk on Friday to sundown Saturday. Decades later, the practice is a centerpiece of her whole life. Keeping Shabbat is a weekly declaration of "Pumpernickel!"—even if the bread of choice is challah.

"One of the costs of the noise," she tells us, "is that you don't really know what's important in life." Shabbat, she explains, is how she, together with loved ones, gets beyond the noise to connect with what's truly important.

As you may know firsthand, Shabbat is quiet with respect to *certain* things but can be quite spirited with respect to others. Surrounded by friends and family, Marilyn might find herself in hours of boisterous conversation, laughter, even heated debates. Together, around the table, guests often sing songs, recite prayers, and share stories.

But there's very little sense of life's ordinary worldly obligations. Marilyn and her family turn off their cell phones, computers, and televisions. They don't work or even discuss their professional lives. "Talking about work fires up a set of neurons that we do not want to be firing up on Shabbat. It reignites that sense of urgency," she tells us. "We know that work goes on and on and on, without limit . . . of course, we have to partake in the work of the world, but we also have to *stop* because if we don't stop, we *can't* go on."

Done well, Shabbat acts like a force field. "When you reconnect with what's important," Marilyn tells us, "a lot of hecticness just dies down. To me, Shabbat practice, though it may not be 'quiet' in the external sense, generates so much internal equanimity and joy." Because Shabbat is so countercultural, often people resist the idea. They might say, "I need eight days a week to get everything done, not six." Marilyn reminds them that good rest puts things in perspective, enhances joy, and deepens creativity; these are good ways to cut back on the ever-present to-do list.

She's a best-selling author who found so much value in Shabbat that she wrote a second book, *An Oasis in Time*, which helps anyone who's interested, Jew or gentile, observant or secular, bring a little Shabbat into their week.

IDEA 3: INTENTION AND ATTENTION

Zach Taylor had big plans for the summer.

His wife, Mara, would be teaching, and he planned to be home from his own teaching job, taking care of their five-year-old and six-month-old daughters while, at the same time, taking on an impressive list of home improvement projects. As summer began, Zach was playing soccer. He got side tackled and fractured his ankle. "Life," as John Lennon sang, "is what happens when you're busy making other plans." Zach had to abandon all his home improvement ambitions. He was stuck on crutches. All he could do for the summer was sit on the floor with his girls and play.

One day, they were all lying around having fun with blocks. There was music on softly in the background, but it "was so quiet," he remembers. Just focused attention on the colorful blocks. Zach was reflecting on what a sweet moment they were having when, serendipitously, the John Mayer song "Daughters," about the importance of relationships between fathers and daughters, shuffled on the stereo. "This is a beautiful song," his five-year-old said. They sat in silence and listened. Then she exclaimed, spontaneously, "Daddy, I want to show you all the beauty in the world! Let's get up." After he managed to get himself up off the floor, she took him out to the yard, where she proceeded to show him the spiral shapes of plants and the ways that ants walked in zigzag patterns and how the pine needles shimmered in the light.

"It was a moment that marked me," Zach says. "And it wouldn't have happened if I hadn't fractured my ankle. It wouldn't have happened if I had been busy with house projects, if I weren't present."

Today, Zach is a recognized leader in the field of social and emotional learning, which endeavors to introduce mindfulness to schools. He studies how young people reach states of inner quiet and deep engagement, and he advises school districts and administrators on how to facilitate the right conditions to enable these modes of attention.

We asked Zach about the deepest silence he's experienced among kids. He took us into the scene of a classroom of fifteen kindergartners that he visited one day. "When you walk in, you see all these bright colors, and you expect the audible decibels to match the visual scene. But there's this atmosphere of quiet." The kids were rotating through various stations, painting pictures of nature scenes at one, doing counting exercises with beads at another, and working with 3-D objects at yet another. "It wasn't 100 percent silent, because there were some instructions and discussions happening, but there was this internal quiet. There was deep learning happening.

"What I've most noticed in my work with silence and mindfulness," Zach says, "is that kids are most engaged when they have something to create. The quiet that comes in a focused state of creation—when they have the right materials, the right atmosphere, the right container for parallel play—that's a marvel." Today, Zach underscores, there's growing society-wide recognition of the pitfalls of engaging kids through too much intense entertainment—overstimulation with lots of screens and bells and whistles. The deepest engagement is when there's *presence*, like what happened that summer day when he was on crutches. Or the kind of present-moment immersion of painting a beautiful picture or building a castle with blocks. While the growing movement for mindfulness meditation in schools is a positive development, Zach emphasizes that it has to go "with the grain" of kids' nature. You can't always ask kids to close their eyes and sit still. Some kids just aren't able to be still. Some kids, owing to traumas from challenging situations at home, aren't able to close their eyes and feel safe. So, the work is to help cultivate awareness and presence in what they're already doing: moving, doodling, breathing. It's about cultivating a basic appreciation for silence.

Addressing silence in our home lives, Zach tells us about the importance of both "intention and attention." It's one thing if you turn off the devices and create a quiet auditory and informational soundscape, but it's another thing if you're able to do all that and then also stop doing your chores and multitasking and give your kids some focused attention.

Zach describes the opportunity he takes every night at the dinner table. As they eat, he likes to present his kids with questions like "What are we grateful for? What's a choice we've made recently that's led to a good outcome? How have we failed recently? What have we given to others recently?" It's about asking the question and then allowing silence, working through the awkwardness of not speaking and allowing the time that's needed to process. "If there's silence after a question is posed, the tendency is to often think, 'Oh, they don't understand. Let me give a hint.' But you have to let the silence be." In that space, Zach says, kids can "listen for the small voice." For the youngest among us, he says, "the small voice is much more on the surface. Their spontaneity is really connected to intuition. If you allow for silence, then the quiet kid at the back of the room or the quieter child at the dinner table can find the space to speak. And when this happens," he continues, "it feels like something important has happened—like a transmission of something that needed to come into the room, something profound that was just waiting for the right time and the right space to surface."

IDEA 4: SMALL IS BEAUTIFUL

Here's an important disclosure. While we've waxed poetic about the experiences of shared silence with friends and loved ones, we're not actually very graceful when it comes to facilitating these moments. Unless you're a Buddhist nun or a Benedictine monk, you're probably not used to social time in total silence. Just proposing the idea of a wordless walk or meal with someone else is typically clumsy and awkward.

The poignancy of a shared silence is usually a function of its spontaneity. You're silent together because something profound happened that rendered speech inadequate. You're in wonder or grief or awe. You can't always just engineer it.

And yet, based on our experience, there is one simple recommendation that we can offer for cultivating spaces of meaningful shared silence with friends and loved ones.

Keep it small. Snack-sized, in fact.

When Justin and his wife, Meredy, go hiking in the mountains near their home, it's typically a special opportunity to really catch up, with no attention turned to work or the demands of parenting three kids or the distractions of electronic devices. They exchange lots of words, sharing stories, trading perspectives, and working out life's details. But, when it's possible, they'll often take some time at the highest elevation or the best vista to just sit on a comfortable rock and be quiet together. They'll listen to the birds and the atmospheric churning of the air. It might just be five minutes. Maybe only three. But it's the centerpiece of the whole sojourn.

In high school, Justin and his friend Rob had a tradition of lying out on the driveway in front of his house watching the night sky. They'd get into all sorts of surreal jokes and storytelling as well as reflections on what had happened in the past week at school. But there was an understanding that for at least a few minutes they would just be silent. It was a shared norm they didn't really need to talk about. It was the space in which their friendship most flourished.

Sometimes this practice of sharing a brief silence amidst speech can be part of a collective creative process. When the two of us met up in the Bay Area several years ago to get started on this book, we took a short jaunt into the eucalyptus-lined hills and gulches just to the east of Berkeley. We spent half of the time planning and the other half just quiet. It was only about twenty minutes of not speaking, but it was a time when some of the shared vision for this project really started to crystallize.

Whether it's verbally planned or simply emergent, a brief period of silence with another person can add depth and texture to a connection or to a shared effort. In these small spaces, the silence isn't just an interlude between speech. It's a balance. A symbiosis. Like silver and gold. The content of the conversation and the tone of the speech feed the quality of the silence. Likewise, the clarity of the silence can enhance the quality of the surrounding conversation. Holding space for *both* silence and speech makes the intentional practice of shared quiet manageable and accessible.

IDEA 5: COLLECTIVE EFFERVESCENCE

A few years ago, we took a drive up through Northern California to speak with Bob Jesse outside his one-room cabin in the towering redwoods. Bob is the kind of man whose time horizon runs roughly twenty to thirty years ahead of convention. Bob, who trained in engineering, was a Silicon Valley pioneer. Decades ago, as a senior executive at Oracle, he persuaded the software giant to lead Fortune 500 companies in offering benefits to same-sex partners—something almost unheard of at the time. In the early 1990s, he convened the Council on Spiritual Practices (CSP), whose mission is to make "direct experience of the sacred more available to more people." Through CSP, it was Bob who, in the late 1990s, approached the psychopharmacologist Roland Griffiths of Johns Hopkins University with the idea of studying mystical experiences like the ones discussed in chapter 6.

Bob has also played an important role in the formation and development of an innovative experiment in shared silence: a dance-based church in the Bay Area.

"I'm not fond of the word 'founder' for various reasons—it carries too much gravitas and authority with it—but we were the first to the table, you could say." That table was set in 1996, when a church in San Francisco agreed to let Bob and the church's musician, Charles Rus, use its sanctuary, library, and garden for an all-night, curated ecstatic dance event—provided the venue was put back together the next day. Bob and Charles gathered ten more friends to conceive the first of what became many dance celebrations, to which they would invite other friends. A community was born.

While the venue has changed and the community has organized as an independent church, the seasonal gatherings—held near each solstice and equinox—remain constant. "We haven't missed a quarterly celebration in our twenty-five years," Bob tells us.

The group's roots can be traced to the electronic dance music that originated in England in the 1980s. If you've ever been to an underground rave or large festival, you've surely noticed some of their signature sonic elements, like stacks of speakers and a thumping *unnn-cha, unnn-cha* beat. That scene is louder than loud, and this church's celebrations are, too. However, this spiritual community is unique in the many precautions they take to lessen other types of "noise" at their celebrations. The group has spent more than two decades honing an ever-evolving set of agreements that participants must be "on board with" in order to attend. These guidelines promote "a safe environment for the exploration of spirit in all its forms" in ways that don't impinge upon the experience of others.

For example, the community's all-night celebrations are alcohol-free and refreshingly "quiet" of the noise associated with drunkenness. The lack of inebriation fortifies other agreements, such as "Consent is critical . . . be respectful of each other's boundaries." The extravagantly decorated venue, light shows, and art installations are a feast for the eyes; yet, another agreement dictates that the only pictures that can be taken are those that linger in the mind.

As an occasional beneficiary of the church, Leigh has been the direct recipient of these thoughtfully curated agreements. She's found that they drastically reduce the external sources of noise and, with it, her own internal sources. She can go with a crowd or arrive alone, in yoga pants or a lavish costume. Most important, her experience is unencumbered by the "sleaze factor." She trusts there will be no ogling, no fear of harassment, and no threats or concerns of violence—all of which have impeded her ability to dance freely in the past. Leigh revels in such freedom. In fact, "Leigh" usually disappears. She transcends the self that's preoccupied with these everyday concerns, and in the most extraordinary of moments she merges with the whole, in a state of group flow—what the French sociologist Émile Durkheim called "collective effervescence." It's an experience also encapsulated in the group's motto, you could even say its sole dogma: "We are one in the dance."

The whole point of this booming, carefully orchestrated sonic ritual is to facilitate maximum internal silence.

Early in the formation of what developed into a community, Bob looked to an unlikely source of guidance: Quakerism, the religion of silence. He wanted the group's decision making to be collaborative and its decisions to be wise and durable. Bob was also interested in breaking a few personal patterns. In the past, he tells us, before presenting a proposal at a meeting, he'd run it by a few friends and colleagues—taking his idea for a "test-drive." He'd think to himself, "I've probably worked this through more than anyone else coming to the meeting. I've deeply examined the pitfalls and possibilities. And my job is to convince people." Now he jests, "That's *extremely* un-Quaker-like! That's not collaborative; it's presumptuous. And if you're a pragmatist, above all, you may forfeit a better solution."

So, on Bob's advice, the nascent group baked in some Quaker-inspired principles. Still today, with a community of five hundred, they refer to each other as "Friends"—in Quaker fashion—and they take turns speaking, listening, and holding silence to surface ideas, concerns, and resolutions. Crucially, they seek their version of what Rob Lippincott describes as "unity."

"We use a phrase, 'reasonable community concord.'" Bob explains, "'Concord' is a contrast term to 'discord.' 'Community' means community-wide . . . and 'reasonable' means asking, are we *reasonably* close to full concord? This allows decisions to be reached in the face of a few dissents, if necessary." When a proposal is presented to the community, Friends may comment and the proposal may be revised, iteratively. When a small oversight group, the council, concludes that reasonable community concord has been achieved, the proposal is ratified. The process can be time-consuming—you might not run an agile business that way—yet it appears to have served this church community quite well.

"I'm getting chills now as I think about it . . . This is what I've come to *relish*," Bob tells us. "When a decision has been reached in this way, I very often leave having [been] disabused that my terrific idea was the best one. And I now see that not only has a much better idea emerged, but there's a quiet form of collective effervescence that people feel. When it goes well, it's uniting and profound."

Perhaps it's the Quaker-inspired governing practices that preserve the group's custom that each event—as high decibel as it may be—includes sanctuary spaces and moments of quiet. At every event, there is an altar that is usually visited in silence. Most venues include a tranquil healing space as well as at least one down-tempo "chill space" for resting and quiet conversation. And just before midnight all music and dancing stops as everyone gathers in a single designated place for shared silence. After an opening ritual, the participants disperse throughout the venue until daybreak, a closing ceremony and the need for cleanup bring the celebration to its close. Like Debussy's notion of music living between the notes or Bootsy Collins's Zen-like assertion about the fundamental formlessness of funk, these boisterous yet intentional celebrations arise from silence and return to silence.

IDEA 6: TUNING IN, TOGETHER

In chapter 11, we described some rarefied moments when we find ourselves in spaces of utterly profound quiet—moments of awe, when we're "floating in the cloud of unknowing."

While these moments are often unplanned, many of the people we spoke with emphasized the importance of *preparation* for encountering these rapturous heights. Preparation can mean adhering to some previously set guidelines and thresholds for when to enter silence, like Gordon Hempton's thirteen-page limit for his to-do list or Tricia Hersey's signals of exhaustion and need for rest. But even more crucially, preparation means practices and rituals to "prepare the vessel," as the rishis of ancient India did through chants, dietary commitments, and strict codes of ethics.

When we "prepare the vessel," we ready ourselves to become like the tuning fork—enabling the mind and body to perceive the finest vibration. We can do this individually, as we've emphasized in previous chapters, but it's often most powerful to engage in *preparation* and, once ready, to engage in a type of *synchronization*—together.

For nearly six decades, Ralph Metzner, the German-born, Harvard-trained psychologist, traveled the world exploring, researching, and guiding groups of people through expanded states of consciousness. In a 2015 interview, Metzner demystified the meaning of the phrase "expanded states of consciousness." As he put it, "Your consciousness expands every morning when you wake up." Describing his own morning landscape, he elaborates, "'Oh, here's my room, my bed, my wife, my family, my dog, my job.' That's a series of consciousness expansions. And every night when you go to sleep, you kind of close in." He adds, "And that's a perfectly normal thing."

Until his death in 2019 at the age of eighty-two, Metzner studied, practiced, and taught diverse modes of both expanding and focusing consciousness; however, his greatest contribution was in what he called entheogenic psychotherapy: the use of psychoactive substances in psycho-spiritual contexts for the benefit of personal, collective, and planetary transformation.

Metzner believed that to do this responsibly, it was up to each participant to "prepare the vessel": their personal vessel. He saw it as his role, as the conductor, to prepare the larger, collective vessel: *the ceremonial container.*

To begin, Metzner screened participants for contraindicated medical and psychological issues. Then he required each applicant to write a "spiritual autobiography" detailing their religious and spiritual backgrounds and past experiences with entheogens, including any negative experiences. In some cases, he worked one-on-one with people for years before clearing them for group work. Metzner limited a lot of "noise" with his clear expectations and parameters, which were similar to the formalized agreements among participants in the dance-based church.

People signed up months, sometimes years, ahead of time for the hundred or so spots available each year across Europe and North America where he ran his entheogenic circles. Once together, the group of twelve to twenty participants would adhere to monastic-like behaviors and uncompromising confidentiality.

The group kept a surprisingly demanding six-day schedule— preparatory workshops for learning, meditation, and exercises by day; ritualized ceremonies by night; and integration sessions each following morning.

Metzner further helped people prepare their individual "vessels" through personal reflective activities like journaling, drawing, and time on the land. Participants shared their artwork and synthesized their thoughts by way of small and large group report-outs that focused on the day's theme. They might explore psychological frameworks such as life phases, Jungian archetypes, or family constellations. The themes covered by day would be revisited in that evening's ceremony with the added layer of entheogens, music, and Metzner's verbal guidance.

As his students would have you know, Metzner was a real talker. He was a professor, a lecturer, a man of many words. He wrote more than twenty books in his lifetime. He relied heavily upon verbal instruction, especially early in the week, before he'd relax into the ceremonial field that he and the group co-created.

Still, the point of everything was to prepare to enter the rapturous silence *together*. You can't count on such an experience to happen spontaneously. You have to put in the work.

Metzner's preparation extended to the physical space of the ceremony. As one of his longtime students, Carla Detchon, put it, "He was *very* par-tic-u-lar." As he set up the room for the ceremony each night, he needed things "just so." "He deeply cared about that energetic alignment of the container," she tells us. "And so that showed up in the way he set up the altar; it showed up in the way we had to round out the circle where we gathered." A good deal of his refinements came by way of his very clear "no." She ribbed, "No, the cloth on the altar isn't completely lined up and smooth. No, I don't like those branches or flowers there. No, you can't have your feet pointing toward the altar." But Ralph was particular for a reason. As Carla puts it, "He understood that when everything lines up, the energies can flow better. And when Ralph and the group were fully prepared, aligned, and in flow, the resulting work was absolutely transcendent."

"He had a beautiful sense of music," Carla tells us. He particularly enjoyed beats that promoted *entrainment*, which, in Metzner's words, is when "all the rhythms come to be harmonic to each other." This term, "entrainment," in physics, means "the process whereby two interacting oscillating systems assume the same period." And that's a metaphor for what can happen among humans who, with adequate preparation, enter a state of *synchronization*.

In the film *Entheogen: Awakening the Divine Within*, Metzner describes how entrainment happens in groups of people through drumbeats, singing, and dance. It's how choral groups work. The point isn't to sing the exact same note, Metzner explains. "They're harmonic and therefore resonant with one another." He loved to bring this ancient technology into his entheogenic circles. "They may be thinking different thoughts and having different pictures in their mind," he says, but when the group enters a collective state of entrainment, "There's a tremendous feeling of oneness and bonding."

That synchronicity is the "We are one in the dance" feeling Leigh gets at the all-night dance celebration. It's what Justin experienced when he felt his heartbeat link with his newborn twins as they rested together for the first time, skin to skin, on his chest.

As with several other events we've highlighted, auditory quiet isn't the goal here. For hours, Metzner gave elaborate invocations, guided visualizations, and told mythical Norse stories from his ancestral homelands—like the one about the three Norns who create and determine one's destiny and the one about Mimir, the disembodied head that grants wisdom. Through rigorous preparation, the use of music, and mythic storytelling, Metzner guided groups past internal noise, toward synchronization, toward entrainment—the experience of self-transcendence, *together.*

IDEA 7: HEALING PRESENCE

"Presence," says Don St. John, "is having all your energy and attention at your disposal and not inaccessible because of worry, distraction, anxiety, or chronic tension." Growing up, he never thought this state of consciousness was actually attainable. "I can't remember when the beatings became a daily occurrence," he says, recalling the abuse he received at the hands of his fire-eyed and resentful mother. "If I attempted to block her blows, she became even angrier, screamed louder, and continued her attack until she knew she had landed some solid hits."

Don, now a psychotherapist in his seventies, has been on a multi-decade journey of overcoming early childhood trauma. When we spoke with Don, he pointed out the silences of childhood are often "loud silences." They might include the thunderous rage of stonewalling, the ache of never feeling heard, and the sting of neglect. Don pointed out that, typically, a loving home for a child is loud; it's one where you hear laughter and conversation. It's filled with warmth and the presence of others and the child's own unquestionable sense of belonging.

And yet silence—of a shared sort—has, for him, been a crucial pathway for healing from those childhood wounds. In particular, it's been the space of affectionate silence with his life partner that has enabled the richest healing.

The word "silence" evokes complicated feelings with regard to romantic relationships. As with the silences of childhood, we often think of silences in partnerships as signs of inattention or rejection. Nobody wants to get "the silent treatment." Stonewalling is an age-old expression of emotional overwhelm to describe throwing up an invisible wall to withdraw behind. We may shut down, busy ourselves, or flat out refuse to respond. The relationship gurus Drs. John and Julie Gottman describe it as one of the four toxic behaviors common in relationships. The remaining three—blame, defensiveness, and contempt—may be equally familiar. While ostensibly quiet, stonewalling is born of the world of noise.

But intentional silence can be a tool for profound bonding in a partnership. Don tells us about a unique practice that he and his wife, Diane—who's a counselor—have cultivated. While we said earlier that it's best to keep planned silence "snack-sized" so as to not be too ambitious, Don and Diane point to the possibility of something like a shared "Wordless Wednesday."

"One of the things we've done over the last ten years or so is to designate a weekend to simply be silent," Don tells us. They cook food ahead of time and avoid using their phones, sending emails, or doing anything else that might distract from resting in pure presence. They spend the days reflecting, doing movement practices, reading books, and taking walks in the mountains near their home in Salt Lake City.

Soon after starting this practice, they realized that carrying a little sign might be helpful for their occasional encounters with other people. They have a pad of paper that says, "We're in Silence. If you have to tell us something, write it here." But very rarely does anyone bother to write on the notepad. It turns out that when you ask people to limit their communications to only what's important, very little is. That's what Leigh discovered on her "Wordless Wednesday" on the Tatshenshini as well.

In the chapter on rapturous silence, we explored the essential elements of a personal retreat. As Sheila explained, a simple practice like rearranging your furniture at home can create a container for the sacred—one of many ways that you can establish a "temple." In a shared retreat with a partner or friend, the silence itself can be a pillar of the temple. When two people are together observing a commitment to silence, she explains, a rare ambience emerges. This is an age-old technology that we can feel on a cellular level. "Silence alters what the space feels like between two people," Sheila says. "It builds the tensile strength."

For Don, cutting off the everyday barrage of stimuli allows for emotional rest. It is, in itself, an aid for the lifelong work of metabolizing trauma—both the trauma he personally endured and the trauma he helps his clients work through. Yet the shared silence with Diane is about even more than that. It's about deepening their domestic sanctuary and the bonds of their marriage. Because they set their "operating agreements" ahead of time, they can cross the threshold to where all of the energy and attention is present.

QUIET TRUST

There are forms of shared silence about which there's nothing much we can say. We can't tell you, for instance, about the silence shared in the deepest of all intimacy. We can't tell you about the silence two people encounter together in a moment of unthinkable grief. These experiences are, by their nature, profoundly personal. There are just two words we would dare offer as a recommendation for being in these kinds of spaces: "Pay attention." Notice how meaning arises as much in the silence as in the words.

We're only beginners at the work of sharing silence with loved ones. It's a lifetime process of continual improvement. For us, it's still mostly about the work of *upaya*, finding the "expedient means" of cultivating small experiences of silent togetherness, like Jarvis sharing that unthinkable moment gazing at the moon with his block mates in the Adjustment Center.

In introducing this part of the book, "Quiet Together," we offered an observation: *the power of silence is magnified when it's shared.*

Throughout this chapter, we've also explored a corollary: *silence amplifies the power of human connection.* It expands our shared awareness. It empowers us to feel more deeply together. It ultimately imbues our relationships with more and more gentleness and care.

Shared silence is a counterintuitive idea in a culture that associates silence with solitude and human connection with the content of conversation. Yet, at least at some level, we all know that we have to drop the chatter and transcend the noise in order to be truly present with another person—to be able to fully *trust.*

In an age of rising isolation and eroding social trust, reclaiming genuine silence ought to be a priority—not only for individuals or families or workplaces or groups of friends, but also for society as a whole. We agree with Blaise Pascal's basic premise that humanity's problems stem from our "inability to sit quietly in a room alone." But we'd add that the problems worsen when there's an inability to sit quietly in a room *with another person.*

Next, we will zoom out to bigger groups of people, examining how the power of silence in politics, policy, culture, and global society can be a force for far-reaching transformation.

PART VI

A SOCIETY THAT HONORS SILENCE

CHAPTER 14

MA GOES TO WASHINGTON

Richard Nixon was a terrible Quaker. As scores of leaked White House tapes document, he cursed like a sailor. While his Quaker faith's requirement for pacifism made him eligible to avoid direct combat service during World War II, he later, as the thirty-seventh president of the United States, escalated the Vietnam War and undertook the devastating and illegal bombing of Cambodia. The Watergate investigation revealed that Nixon kept meticulous track of political adversaries and the dirt that could be used against them. The man appeared to have little interest in a defining ethical tenet of the religion of his upbringing: "Love your enemies."

Still, as one of two Quaker presidents in American

history (Herbert Hoover was the other), Richard Nixon did one thing befitting an adherent to a religion that reveres silence.

He launched the nation's first policy regime devoted to managing noise.

The Noise Control Act of 1972 sought to give Americans the right to a reasonably quiet environment.

The act created the new federal Office of Noise Abatement and Control (ONAC), which had a mandate to coordinate research on noise control, promulgate federal auditory emission standards for products, and provide both grants and technical assistance to state and local governments—particularly in urban centers—to reduce noise pollution. While the office didn't have the authority to regulate noise from aircraft or rail, it did lead a public education campaign that built awareness of these challenges, eventually prompting airports, airlines, and freight companies to take noise more seriously.

In the 1970s, there was still some dispute about the health impacts of noise. Interest groups, including manufacturing industries and public transit authorities, opposed binding noise regulations, and yet the government forged ahead with regulations. Speaking in support of the movement for noise abatement in 1968, Surgeon General William H. Stewart asked, "Must we wait until we prove every link in the chain of causation?" He continued, "In protecting health, absolute proof comes late. To wait for it is to invite disaster or to prolong suffering unnecessarily."

Ronald Reagan's administration defunded and dismantled the federal noise control programs as part of its anti-regulation agenda in 1982. Nevertheless, ONAC remains an admirable example of precautionary public policy that prioritizes genuine human well-being.

The Nixon-era noise management regime was predicated on a notion that's still largely unheard of in the U.S. government—or in most governments for that matter: *there's inherent value in pristine human attention, and society has a compelling interest in upholding and defending this value.*

The story of Nixon's noise reforms is deeply relevant right now.

As online platforms and their proprietary algorithms assume an ever-greater role in our economy and public discourse, debates are raging over the politics of human attention. In particular, policy makers are struggling to decide how to defend privacy, ensure free speech, combat disinformation, and address rising Big Tech monopoly power.

These are critical questions. But we believe there's a bigger, over-arching question that we should be addressing as well: *How can we structure our society to preserve pristine human attention?*

It was around the time of Nixon's noise reforms that the Nobel laureate Herbert Simon wrote the words we quoted at the beginning of this book: "A wealth of information creates a poverty of attention." In the pages to come, we'll look at what it means to build our economic and political architectures around the objective of minimizing, or at least managing, the auditory, informational, and internal noise of the modern world through laws, regulations, public investments, business transparency, and the mobilization of social movements. We'll examine how whole societies can prioritize the cultivation of focused attention as a key element of the common good.

Of course, it's not possible to regulate or legislate the entirety of the problem of noise. So, in this chapter and the one that follows, we'll imagine something broader and deeper: *a society that honors silence.*

We'll imagine what it would be like, for example, to have a public discourse that follows the logic of a Quaker Friends meeting: where it's prudent to speak if the words are believed to improve the silence.

We'll explore a range of possibilities: What if legislatures and boardrooms appreciated the importance of preserving pristine attention? What if our society recognized that solving complex and daunting problems—like climate change and inequality—required not only engineering and analysis and debate but also the space for contemplative visioning about the future that we really want?

What if the principle of *Ma*—the Japanese word that signifies the power of the silent spaces "in between"—had a place in the public discourse?

While all of this might sound fantastical, there are some plausible changes to our existing systems—including how we calculate our economic "externalities," how we assess the costs and benefits of new regulations, how we identify prudent public investment, and how we deliberate over difficult public challenges—that could help awaken this kind of transformation.

The five ideas presented below are based on a U.S. public policy context; however, these principles are relevant to—and can be adapted for—a wide variety of countries and political realities. Noise—auditory, informational, and internal—is a global problem. Every nation has to imagine and experiment with its own means of addressing it.

IDEA 1: INVEST IN PUBLIC SANCTUARIES

Many years ago, the New York–based writer George Prochnik was on a silent meditation retreat. He was "gazing at a group of people scattered across a grassy hillside like roosting birds—all of them concentrated on doing nothing but being still and listening to the natural world." In his 2010 book, *In Pursuit of Silence*, he writes about how much he cherished this moment.

Yet, as he continued to look out at the silent crowd of meditators that day, Prochnik had a troubling thought. He recalls, "Like me, they had the money, the time, or simply the social context that enabled them to wake up one day and say to themselves, 'You know what? I'm going on a silent retreat.'" He continues, "I'm worried about all the people who, for one reason or another, lack the resources to discover what silence can bring."

Prochnik is right to be concerned. Much of humanity today seems to lack the opportunity—or what he called the "social context"—for seeking silence. In dense urban areas, or among people who have to work multiple jobs to make ends meet, silence can feel unattainable. In a world of fewer and fewer wild places and almost ubiquitous internet and smartphone connections, the most rapturous silence is, for most people, out of reach.

So, how can we expand and democratize access to silence?

Throughout this book, we've underscored the importance of cultivating our personal appreciation for silence and making the choices within our own *spheres of control* and *influence* to find it. Yet broader society, including the public sector, has a role to play. One of the most important things we can do as a society is invest in public spaces of quiet sanctuary—places that invite us into silence. As Prochnik writes, "We must encourage the kinds of urban-design projects that nurture appreciation of silence. We need more pocket parks"—tiny green spaces, often between skyscrapers in a dense metropolis. "And bigger parks when the money can be found."

Some societies do find the money and the commitment to invest in these spaces. As of 2018, the densely populated city-state of Singapore had met its goal of ensuring that 80 percent of households would be within four hundred meters of a park. Singapore first set its sights on its "garden city" vision in the late 1960s. By the 1980s, the city-state's green cover was estimated at 36 percent, and today it's at 47 percent and trending upward. For comparison, green cover in Rio de Janeiro is 29 percent, and New York City comes in at 14 percent. The government of Singapore set and implemented a long-term strategic plan to invest in green space fifty years ago. Today, the country is getting creative in continuing this mission—investing in vertical living walls and forested rooftops, thick tree-lined boulevards and walking corridors, as well as more traditional parks and nature reserves.

During a trip to Singapore, the journalist Florence Williams decided to tour a community hospital that Florence Nightingale would have appreciated. In it, Williams writes, "many rooms face the inner, luxuriant garden courtyard, dense with trees and shrubs specifically selected to attract birds and butterflies." She was taken through the ICU, where "every patient has a view of trees out six-foot windows." Williams found, "at many points, corridors and landings open up to the outdoors," as well as an "organic vegetable garden on the roof." Williams doesn't suggest that green urban spaces are any sort of substitute for natural wilderness. But with urban density on the rise, green space solutions like these do promote the felt experience of quiet and, along with it, better sleep, less anxiety and depression, and more pro-social behaviors.

"The quiet spaces we make shouldn't be limited to outdoors," Prochnik writes. He asks, "Why not take some of the money seized from drug dealers, gun runners, and financial crooks and use those funds to buy up a few dozen fast-food franchise [buildings] that can be turned into contemporary quiet houses?" His question got us thinking. What about all the abandoned shopping and strip malls—could they be repurposed for quiet commons? Could more empty lots be turned into neighborhood or school gardens? And what about community centers, senior centers, and places of worship? Could they be incentivized to provide weekly scheduled quiet time for people who need it? Prochnik suggests filling some public spaces with comfy chairs and free pens and pads of paper and simply letting people relax, journal, read, doodle, reflect. As we've explored at length, the quiet doesn't always need to be auditory. People might come together to play board games or do crafts; the important element is being able to get away from smartphones and computers—informational noise—for a little while.

Tricia Hersey, the Nap Bishop of the Nap Ministry whom you met earlier, has hosted more than fifty pop-up "public napping events" to encourage rest as a revolutionary act. That's right; she creates inviting spaces filled with comfy pillows to woo people out of "the grind." While this is valuable insofar as it provides people with a needed break, it also helps to *normalize the activity of just resting in silence.* We imagine local governments and community organizations supporting creative ways like this to bring people together for shared silence. By curating beautiful, art-filled pop-up spaces, communities can invite their citizens to relax and do nothing. Maybe nap. Be in the unprogrammed space with other people from different walks of life. Enjoy the novelty of silence.

IDEA 2: INNOVATE LIKE THE AMISH

In his 2010 book, *What Technology Wants*, Kevin Kelly describes the personal journey of his young adult years: dropping out of college, wandering through Asia, and then returning to the United States for a five-thousand-mile cross-country bike trip. Of all the surprises he encountered on this multiyear, multi-continent voyage through hundreds of different communities, Kelly was perhaps most struck by what he found on the farmlands of eastern Pennsylvania.

Pretty much everything he thought he knew about the Amish was wrong.

Contrary to the popular belief that adherents of this wagon-riding, butter-churning religious group oppose all industrial technologies, Kelly finds that "Amish lives are anything but antitechnological." For example, he tells of meeting a family who operate a $400,000 computer-controlled milling machine that serves the community. Yes, Amish women cover their heads with bonnets, and Amish families employ many labor-intensive, centuries-old farming techniques. But Kelly describes the people he met as "ingenious hackers and tinkerers, the ultimate makers and do-it-yourselfers," who are "often, surprisingly, protechnology."

As Kelly studied the Amish approach to technology, he found that they have an unusually thoughtful method to assess whether to adopt a new innovation. It usually goes something like this: Someone in the community will ask the elders (the "bishops") in an area for permission to try out a new technology, such as a personal device or an agricultural tool. This first adopter will typically receive that permission. Then the whole community pays close attention to how the new technology is affecting the first adopter's life. Is it making their work more efficient? Is it healthy? Is it making them self-centered? Is it negatively impacting their personality or work ethic? After the community has contributed their thoughts, the bishops will make a final assessment.

In short, the Amish generally *start with their own values as a culture*, including values like community cohesion, humility, a strong work ethic, and, yes, quiet. Then they consciously *assess whether a new technology can produce benefits for the community without undermining these values*.

If the answer is yes, they'll adopt the new technology for use.

We first learned about Kelly's work and the Amish model of technology assessment through the writings of Cal Newport, who suggested that we can all apply elements of the Amish approach in our own individual lives. As part of his philosophy of "digital minimalism," Newport wisely suggests that we each identify our own personal values and work backward to ensure that any technology we adopt in our lives really improves our well-being and honors these values. We love this recommendation. And we can also bring the same logic to a societal level.

We believe that our governments can take a cue from the Amish approach to regulation and start to place priorities like physical and psychological well-being over blanket deference to whatever is "shiny and new." In some spheres of science and technology policy, we already have processes for formally assessing new innovations. For example, the Food and Drug Administration (FDA) requires clinical trials of drugs to assess not only their effectiveness but also their wide-ranging side effects. Drug regulators do their own far-reaching cost-benefit analysis and make determinations about approval.

But we don't do anything of the sort for the most consequential tech decisions. There was no rigorous clinical trial or independent cost-benefit assessment before Facebook inaugurated the "like" button. There were no required studies of its potential impacts on working memory, its possible effects on teenage anxiety, its potential for misinformation campaigns by foreign governments, or an increase in mortalities resulting from attempts to take the "perfect selfie" (there were 259 recorded between 2011 and 2017).

We need a tech-oriented version of the FDA to monitor and potentially regulate technologies that significantly impact our social, emotional, and intellectual health. We're not asking for a cloistered group like the Amish bishops to make decisions about what is good for us. But, rather, a technically capable, well-funded body of experts to ensure that policy makers and the public can understand and act upon true costs and benefits.

This isn't a totally new idea. The U.S. government once had the Office of Technology Assessment (OTA)—a team of about 140 mostly PhD analysts used to educate lawmakers and do deep-dive research on legislation related to tech. In the mid-1990s, this office was dissolved to save taxpayers a measly $20 million. Today, the legislative branch research agencies that are supposed to assess the implications of tech and other big societal trends have an estimated 20 percent less staff than they did in 1979. As Justin and his colleague Sridhar Kota explored in an article for *Wired* in 2017, the loss of the OTA was a contributing factor to unworkable cybersecurity bills and inept oversight of National Security Agency surveillance programs. It has also contributed to the government's inability to meaningfully track and understand technology trends and to defend the public interest accordingly. Without an apparatus to assess the impacts of technologies, there's no way to assess whether the choices we're making about technology reflect our true values.

The case for an Amish approach to tech governance is getting stronger every year. The growth of AI, the expansion of the Internet of Things, and the emergence of wearable (and even implantable) informational technologies are likely to shift our internal and external soundscapes in ways that are hard to forecast. There's nothing particularly radical or excessively interventionist about subjecting our most consequential technology decisions to rigorous review. We should assess these decisions not only on the basis of their impacts on economic growth or job creation, but also on the basis of their impacts on what most of us value—like being able to hold an uninterrupted conversation with a loved one or savor a simple moment of peace and quiet.

IDEA 3: MEASURE WHAT MATTERS

In 1930, the legendary economist John Maynard Keynes published a short essay called "Economic Possibilities for Our Grandchildren." In the piece, Keynes imagined that by the year 2030, because of technology and productivity improvements, nobody would have to work more than fifteen hours a week. We would be able to devote the remainder of our time to leisure and culture. In a sense, Keynes's optimistic vision was of "a world beyond the noise," where advances in laborsaving technology would enable us all to transcend distractions big and small, empowering us to focus on the activities that promote our highest flourishing. We could, in Keynes's vision, spend most of our time with our loved ones, appreciating nature, creating art and music, perhaps finding our way into the internal silence of the flow state—immersion in doing what we love.

About a hundred years after Keynes's writing, pretty much the opposite has happened.

Most of us are working—or at least thinking about work—more than ever. "Leisure and culture"—in the sense of the pursuit of deep fulfillment that's not necessarily economically productive—doesn't seem to be happening. Technology isn't freeing us from noise. It's creating more of it.

So, why are we so far off from Keynes's 2030 vision?

One answer is that we've been measuring the wrong things. We've been steering our economy according to objectives of quantity rather than quality, maximum output rather than optimal well-being.

In the opening pages of this book, we explored how gross domestic product has become the dominant benchmark by which nations measure their success. While it's really just an indicator of raw industrial output—the monetary value of the finished goods and services produced in a given time period—GDP has become the single most important numerical yardstick for public policy and business decision making in most countries. Yet, as we described in chapter 2, rising GDP often runs counter to what's good for us. GDP often goes up as natural disasters, environmental degradation, crime, and hospital stays increase. It goes up when an algorithm seizes on your quiet time, boosting usage statistics, or when your employer figures out how to get more work out of you by sending a late-night email request (and getting your response). The number says strikingly little about real human well-being.

If we "manage what we measure"—as the common business axiom goes—then we're currently managing our economies and societies to maximize production of both mental and material stuff. We're measuring "success" by the roar of industrial machines, the number of hours that managers can keep employees glued to their computers, and the effectiveness of advertisements and algorithms in diverting our attention away from what we intend to be doing in order to steer us toward buying products and services.

So, here's an idea: *improve our measurements to better reflect what makes us flourish.*

This is one systemic shift that could help bring us closer to John Maynard Keynes's optimistic dream. It could help dismantle the "altar of noise."

Over recent years, there's been some movement in this direction. Esther Duflo and Abhijit Banerjee, 2019 Nobel laureates in economics, recently wrote that it may be "time to abandon [their] profession's obsession with growth." A number of countries, including Germany, France, and the U.K., have started working on broader national progress indicators. Meanwhile, researchers in Vermont, Oregon, Maryland, and Utah have experimented with new indicators that account for costs like traffic and benefits like family time. Famously, the Himalayan

Kingdom of Bhutan has spent decades developing measures of what it calls "gross national happiness." While the work on these kinds of indicators isn't yet complete, advances in statistics and computing make alternative approaches to economic measurement increasingly viable.

For about a decade, Justin and his colleague Ben Beachy, director of the Living Economy Program at the Sierra Club, have been thinking about the kinds of practical policy changes that could transform GDP. In early 2021, Justin and Ben published a piece in *Harvard Business Review* describing how the U.S. government might remake national indicators.

Here's how it would work: Given that the standard measure of GDP still has its practical uses, we shouldn't totally abandon it. Rather, governments should transform economic measurement from reliance upon one single indicator (GDP) to a *series of indicators*. Similar systems are already in place for measuring unemployment (which is calculated as U1 through U6), the consumer price index, and the money supply.

Under this approach, the series might look as follows:

- G1 would be traditional GDP—a standard measure of national income.

- G2 would build on the GDP formula as a base, but offer a broader snapshot of the economy, revealing, for example, how equitably income is distributed while also reflecting the value of unpaid services like childcare that are currently ignored.

- G3 would focus on the longer-term future and account for the costs associated, for example, with pollution or the depletion of resources while also considering the benefits of longer-term investments in education and conservation.

- G4 would measure something like Bhutan-style gross national happiness, integrating broader indicators of human well-being, such as public health and social connection statistics.

The goal of moving away from a single crude number (GDP) to a series of adjusted indicators (G1–G4) is not to put a spotlight on problems like pollution and inequality, although it would help shine a light on these issues. The aim would also be to emphasize important aspects of progress that don't typically get represented in statements of economic output—aspects like environmental preservation, innovation, and educational outcomes, all of which require looking at longer time horizons.

By turning GDP into a series of indicators—incorporating broader and deeper underpinnings of real human wellness—we could start to measure, and therefore manage, the costs of noise and the positive value of undivided attention. We could, for example, estimate and assign costs to the "economic externalities" of distraction and denied concentration—the harms of pop-up ads, blaring TVs in public spaces, and requirements for round-the-clock availability. If we account for how noisy practices undermine our well-being and long-term productivity, then we'll no longer value them as pure positives from an economic standpoint.

More refined GDP indicators could even assign value to factors like rest, access to nature, and positive mental health outcomes like the absence of anxiety.

In short, we could structure our economy to finally recognize that unmonetized human attention is something more than mere "uselessness." We could make our success metrics reflect the fact that auditory, informational, and internal silence matters for our health, cognition, and happiness.

Of course, this raises a big question: *How do we assign a quantitative value to something as personal and subjective as quiet time?*

For decades, economists and environmentalists have been debating the question of whether it's even desirable to assign a monetary value to, say, a redwood forest like the one Robert F. Kennedy lamented the loss of in his visionary speech on the problems of national economic accounting. Many would say that the redwoods are priceless. We're inclined to agree. Yet the fact is that under the current economic paradigm of GDP, the value of the forest that's not exploited for any monetary purpose is implicitly set at *zero*. In fact, the value of anything or any activity that is not contributing to economic output in an obvious and easily measured way is zero. So, in a political and economic system that's organized for the purpose of managing growth, there's no structural incentive to defend these resources or activities.

Part of the necessary work of building a more refined system of measurement is the imperfect work of putting a price on the values that our economic system currently deems valueless. Today, a variety of intergovernmental organizations, academic institutions, and businesses are developing models of "true cost" or "full cost" accounting— assigning quantitative values to negative externalities like pollution and the positive benefits of environmental and social assets in order to enact better benchmarks of progress. As part of this effort, researchers and practitioners should consider how to account for the costs of noise and distraction as well as how to assign value to pristine human attention and even to quiet time. As countries pass legislation to modernize GDP, it will be essential to create new deliberative panels to agree upon these accounting values. While these are technical questions, they're ultimately vital for integrating our values into our measurements of progress. These decisions are necessary for setting more humane priorities and benchmarks.

IDEA 4: ENSHRINE THE RIGHT TO ATTENTION

At the start of his presidency in 1981, Ronald Reagan signed an executive order to empower a little-known government office to assess potential new regulations based on a process called a cost-benefit analysis.

This was established as a method of determining whether "the potential benefits to society from the regulation outweigh the potential costs to society."

This seemed like a sensible approach. But in practice it became an embodiment of pretty much everything that's wrong with the noisy paradigm of GDP growth.

It quickly became clear that big companies could win these regulatory battles by hiring lawyers to show how burdensome regulations would be to their clients. Noise abatement expenses, like insulating buildings or conducting research into quieter internal combustion engines, were immediate and easily quantifiable. Meanwhile, the "benefits" of noise legislation—like the emotional value of *not* seeing a loved one sicken and die due to toxic pollution or the long-term effects of a reasonable soundscape to a New York City elementary school classroom—are harder to put on paper.

As a result, the Reagan-era antiregulatory crusaders had a straightforward job axing the budgets for Nixon-era noise mitigation initiatives, among other programs.

A true accounting of costs and benefits would almost certainly justify the existence of Nixon's Office of Noise Abatement and Control. The concrete steps that government took in the 1970s to reduce auditory noise—research into quieter industrial technologies, product standards, and grants to local and regional governments to enforce standards—are still needed today.

But we also need to look beyond just the auditory noise. We need to reckon with the vastly increased intensity and complexity of all kinds of noise these days.

With that in mind, we wondered what it would look like to have an Office of Noise Abatement and Control that's focused on addressing not just the auditory noise but the informational and internal noise, too.

On the campaign trail for the 2020 Democratic presidential nomination, Andrew Yang proposed creating a new cabinet-level "Department of the Attention Economy." While it sounded kind of like a gimmicky campaign tagline at first, his idea raised an important point. If most people spend something like a majority of their waking lives on computers or phones or TVs (or on other media on which advertisers and data miners compete to capture their consciousness), why wouldn't a policy apparatus regulating attention—on par with matters like defense, foreign affairs, and transportation—be warranted?

Herbert Simon—of "poverty of attention" fame—also coined the term "attention economy." Simon regarded multitasking as a myth, calling our attention to the "bottleneck of human thought." Decades ago, he recognized that our scarce attention could be commoditized, manipulated, and traded. And he recognized that when it came to attention, there was no effective regulatory apparatus to keep markets functioning fairly or defend the public interest, like the ones that exist to regulate other resources like water and timber. There's still no such apparatus today.

Over recent years, a vanguard of former Silicon Valley engineers and designers, including the team at the Center for Humane Technology (CHT), have been taking stock of the consequences of the poverty of attention that their erstwhile industry has wrought. The CHT's "Ledger of Harms" is an effort to do some of the true cost accounting that our governance systems currently neglect. The center catalogs evidence of what it calls "online harms." One harm, for example, is the fact that digital media has been designed to encourage most people to switch between visual content every nineteen seconds. This attention switching produces a demonstrably addictive "neurological high" that is detrimental to our ability to focus. Another is the evidence that even the simple presence of their smartphone in a room drains a person's attentional resources.

Many of us as individuals are increasingly aware of harms like these. So, how do we collectively deal with them as a matter of policy?

We spoke recently with Nicole Wong, who served as general counsel for Google from 2004 to 2011 and as deputy chief technology officer in the White House during the Obama administration. She's now an advocate for privacy rights and the preservation of human attention. In our conversation with Wong, we floated a few relatively straightforward ideas, such as banning features like infinite scroll and autoplay videos that are designed explicitly to maximize screen time. "I generally dislike regulations geared toward technical design," she tells us. "Technologists create work-arounds faster than legislation will ever come into being." In other words, banning specific technologies can turn into another game of "whack-a-mole."

Wong advocates looking at what harm is being done, especially when it's the "purposeful creation of harms." She describes an example of this: "'I'm building autoplay because I know it will increase engagement, particularly between those of the age thirteen to eighteen.' That's the thing we can go enforce." For her, this sparks another idea: "I could imagine siccing the Federal Trade Commission [FTC] on practices that are unhealthy," she tells us. In the United States, the FTC's areas of influence include consumer protection, cybersecurity, and privacy, especially as it relates to children. The regulator is mandated to defend us from "deceptive practices or any unfair practices." Wong offers "attention theft"—an admittedly provocative term—as a means of giving the FTC authority to investigate harms caused by technologies designed to capture and monetize human attention. "By investigating [them]," she says, the FTC "will send a signal to the rest of the community."

David Jay, the chief mobilization officer at the Center for Humane Technology, puts the herculean task of managing these harms in clear and simple terms: "Articulate what is off-limits." Identify and seek to manage the kinds of practices and algorithms that are designed to deliberately extract attention and, especially, he says, the features that send people "down rabbit holes"—like endless news-feed scrolling or binge-watching into the wee hours on a school night. An important objective of any policy-making effort in this space, he says, should be "to give users more agency over how the algorithms are operating." Still, Jay contends that formal government regulation is only a limited part of the solution. "Tech will advance faster than regulation can keep up." Ultimately, he points out, we need "accountable public discourse about what algorithms *should* be doing."

In a recent conversation, CHT's co-founder and executive director Randima Fernando described the fundamental challenge: "The whole system is built on incentives to *not* be quiet. If you're quiet in the attention economy, you lose." The fact is that the defense of human attention runs up against the core moneymaking propositions of some of the most powerful corporations on the planet. Design features for social validation—like the "like" button on Facebook—are critical to companies' business models precisely because they're particularly effective at hijacking our dopamine receptors and, therefore, our conscious attention. One of the reasons that a nearby smartphone is so damaging to our attention is that our brains start longing for the biochemical hit that comes with social validation. No matter how egregious these kinds of neurobiological manipulations may be, it's still difficult to imagine how to disassemble a whole market built on this powerful profit motive.

In a world where platforms have strong incentives to extract attention as well as the capability to adapt quickly to the strictures of regulations, it stands to reason that any new public policies to address the harms of the attention economy should focus heavily on building public awareness and changing consumer behavior. That means emphasizing transparency. Think back to cigarettes for a moment. The massive decline in smoking rates over the past several decades didn't happen because governments banned tobacco products. Imagine a "Surgeon General's Warning"—like on a pack of Marlboros—on the Facebook log-in page describing how the product uses sophisticated tools to intentionally manipulate your brain chemistry for the purpose of selling advertisements. Governments could take a first step toward real transparency by requiring that Big Tech firms publicly disclose their own research findings regarding the impacts of design features on human attention. They'd have to present their own, honest "ledger of harms" so that we in the public could better grasp what's happening to our brains. The right transparency and pressure could shift consumer preference and ultimately force companies' behaviors to change.

Wong thinks this is possible. "The tech community is sort of starting to wake up and, more importantly, their user base is starting to wake up," she told us. It was negative publicity—and all the accompanying economic consequences—that recently drove some platforms to experiment, on a limited basis, with hiding social validation features like the "like" button or letting users know that they're "all caught up" on posts from their friends, rather than filling the feed with limitless scrolling suggestions. These are very small steps, but they're evidence that change is possible.

A Los Angeles–based attorney, Jasper Tran, recently published a law review article proposing the "right to attention" as a statutory right that should exist through legislation or common law. This "right," according to Tran, is really a "bundle of rights" that includes, for example, "the right to deny attention when demanded, the right to be left alone, the right to not be spammed and the right to not receive ads when such advertisement is unwanted or uninvited, . . . and the right to not be required to receive information against one's will."

When we think of what it would mean to actually realize a right to attention, we think about safeguarding human consciousness from the unrelenting noise of the information age. We think about the complex questions of tech regulation, like the rules and transparency requirements we just described.

But some of the most important ways of defending human attention come down to old-fashioned questions of political power. They're less about hi-tech "whack-a-mole" than classic organizing and collective bargaining.

In *How to Do Nothing*, Jenny Odell tells how, in 1886, the U.S. labor movement launched a multi-decade campaign for an eight-hour workday. The Federation of Organized Trades and Labor Unions championed a now famous motto: "Eight hours for work, eight hours for rest, and eight hours for what we will." The union created a graphic that visually depicted the three sections of the day. It showed a garment worker at her station, a person sleeping with feet sticking out of a blanket, and a couple sitting together on a boat on water, reading the union's newspaper. This period of "eight hours for what we will" wasn't defined as "leisure time" or time for "household responsibilities" or anything else. As Odell puts it, "The most humane way to describe that period is to refuse to define it." It's a chunk of time when people can be free from employer-imposed mental stimuli—the noise of someone occupying your attention against your will.

Today, 135 years after the inauguration of that labor motto and more than a century after the establishment of the eight-hour workday, we need a renewal of this original movement for human attention. The noise of excessive work obligations is a serious problem for most people today. Online connectivity has allowed work to creep into personal time and space, eroding the "eight hours for what we will" and, for that matter, often eroding the "eight hours for rest," too. The work-from-home revolution has only accelerated this erosion.

Thankfully, there are policy options for dealing with this aspect of human attention theft. In 2017, France enacted a law that gives workers the "right to disconnect" from email, laptops, phones, and other "electronic leashes" after the workday has ended. For years, French unions had lamented an "explosion of undeclared labor," with often-unspoken requirements for workers to be online after hours. This recent regulation requires firms with fifty or more employees to negotiate out-of-office communications guidelines with their staff, ensuring that employees get a break. As France's Ministry of Labor said, "These measures are designed to ensure respect for rest periods and . . . balance between work and family and personal life."

The "right to attention" harkens back to what the twentieth-century French philosopher Gilles Deleuze called the "right to say nothing"—the notion that we are all entitled to our own unperturbed "interiority" and the accompanying notion, that society should honor this fundamental aspect of being human. While this is a sweeping idea that has implications for politics, law, economics, culture, psychology, and even spirituality, the basic premise is simple: *no one should have to submit to an unsustainable burden of noise.*

IDEA 5: DELIBERATE LIKE THE QUAKERS

Michael J. Sheeran is both a Jesuit priest and a political scientist. When he was doing his doctoral work at Princeton in the 1970s, he became fascinated with a topic that had important implications for both religious organizations and secular political institutions: *consensus-based decision making.*

Sheeran notes that some of the most famous deliberative bodies in the world employ consensus as a way of doing business. The U.S. Senate, for example, typically proceeds through much of its agenda under "unanimous consent." According to the rules, just a single senator has the power to block a good portion of the body's proceeding if she or he denies consent. The UN General Assembly also operates by consensus in many situations. And many corporate boards make decisions primarily on a unanimous basis.

Yet, as Sheeran points out, there's something missing from the spirit of true consensus in these examples. In the Senate, for example, unanimous consent might be the standard operating rule, but it's only used these days to efficiently manage the most routine, uncontroversial matters. Serious stuff is subject to filibuster battles and contentious votes. At the UN, the norm of unanimity is typically a way for countries to avoid going on record on any given issue, allowing them to eschew controversy while going behind the scenes to do real negotiations. In corporate boards, unanimity often reflects blanket approval of decisions made by upper managers that the board has put in place. Examples like these are, in large part, why consensus building has such a miserable reputation.

Sheeran did study one organization that practiced deep consensus-based decision making—the real kind that doesn't just avoid or gloss over dissent but rather incorporates it in order to craft more enduring solutions. It was the Quakers. Sheeran attended the Philadelphia Yearly Meeting, a major deliberative gathering in the City of Brotherly Love. He then spent two years conducting hundreds of interviews with active Quakers to better understand how they do business.

In his 1983 book, *Beyond Majority Rule*, Sheeran describes how the Quaker "Meeting for Business" operates on unanimous decisions, with no voting. Yet, in these meetings, Quakers often take on very contentious issues. He discusses an example: a community's deliberation over whether to expand a burial ground. On one side, proponents of the expansion were adamant that everyone deserved burial plots near their loved ones, their ancestors, and the rest of the community. On the other side, opponents argued that the expansion would decrease the size of the area where the children could play. Emotions ran high at the meeting. Because it was clear that unanimity wasn't possible, the clerk, or chair, of the meeting took no minutes. He decided that the problem should be allowed to "rest" for a month. The community members went home and "put the issue on the shelf" for a later date. Ultimately, over the course of six months of alternating deliberation and "rest," emotions cooled, and new solutions started to emerge. The group found a way to allow a limited expansion of the burial ground that wouldn't interfere with the children's playground. In the silence and time and space, previously unrecognized possibilities emerged. Everyone agreed to the new solution. Even in the welcoming space of the Friends meeting—a safe space for dissent—Sheeran notes that no one in the proceedings registered regret about the compromise.

In the 1951 book *Roads to Agreement*, Stuart Chase identifies several characteristics of the Quaker approach to deliberation, including unanimous decisions and no voting, participation by all with ideas, the absence of leaders, a focus on facts, and the principle that no one outranks anyone else. While you can find elements of this kind of "orderly anarchism" in some other kinds of organizations, there are three other characteristics that Chase identifies that are especially unique to the

Quakers: silence at the beginning of all meetings, a temporary morato-rium when agreement can't yet be reached, and the primacy of learning how to listen, including the injunction to never attend a meeting with your mind already made up. These structures are formal encapsulations of the Quaker values.

Earlier, we discussed how Rob Lippincott, the nonprofit leader, educator, and birthright Quaker, described the purpose of the Business Meeting as not "debate" per se, but rather to do what's often called threshing. It's an exercise in *discerning*. It requires a commitment to avoid seeking to defend your position, affirming your ego, and proving you're correct. It's a model for a group deliberation that's about deter-mining not *who is right* but *what is true*. "A seeker of truth," Gandhi emphasized, "requires silence." A shared enterprise of discovering truth requires mechanisms of silence and rest as means of overcoming the noise of distraction and animosity. It requires a shared commitment to nonjudgmental listening.

The Quaker approach isn't the only model of true consensus-based group decision making that's grounded in contemplative silence. The Iroquois Confederacy—which is known as the oldest participatory de-mocracy on Earth—built a diverse and highly egalitarian society on the basis of consensus deliberation at multiple levels. Many scholars be-lieve that the Great Law of Peace, the oral constitution of the Iroquois Confederacy—with its emphasis on checks and balances and separation of powers—was a direct inspiration for the U.S. Constitution. But the U.S. Constitution centers on majority rule, whereas the Great Law of Peace centers on consensus.

The capacity for consensus in the Iroquois model is directly related to the capacity for shared contemplative silence. If you attend an Iroquois decision-making meeting, you'll likely hear a recitation of the Haudeno-saunee Thanksgiving Address. It's a statement of gratitude to the waters, the plants, the animals, and all the forces of nature. After each part of the statement is a moment of shared reverential attention and a transcendent phrasing that repeats itself: "Now our minds are one."

Try to imagine an institution like the modern U.S. Senate, the UN General Assembly, or a Fortune 500 board finding consensus through practices of union brought about by shared contemplative quiet. Imagine the participants in one of these gatherings seeking to *make their minds one*. The idea is pretty implausible. And there's a reason for this. As Sheeran observed forty years ago, consensus practice is possible in a Quaker meeting because the meeting members hold common values. The Quaker approach—and the Iroquois approach—are possible because, in Sheeran's words, "the participants are in community." They're part of an "organic group whose good and goals would be the initial point of reference." Members of the Senate and the UN General Assembly are not "in community." Most members of modern Western society participate in what he calls an "individualized, atomic" culture that is "incapable of community because of the inability to surrender the individual-focused starting point." The United States is, of course, the epitome of such a culture.

In order to work toward consensus-based decision making, we have to learn to transcend our hyper-individual perspectives. We must learn to step outside the default mode network—"The me network"—of the brain. We have to be able to get beyond the noise of the separate self.

Of course, there's no easy answer for how to make this shift in values and communal orientation. Yet practices of silence—like the "rest" mechanisms of the Quaker meeting or the unifying ritual of the Haudenosaunee Thanksgiving Address—are a starting point. Building a society that honors silence requires shifts in both official rules and small-scale norms; it requires both top-down and bottom-up change.

R-E-S-P-E-C-T

In chapter 5, we mentioned the environmental psychologist Arline Bronzaft's pioneering work in the 1970s. She's the one who examined the cognitive impacts of noise pollution on elementary school students in Manhattan whose classroom was adjacent to a screeching elevated subway track. Since her landmark study, she's spent nearly fifty years thinking about how to help societies turn down the volume of auditory distraction. She's been a counselor to five New York City mayors on questions of noise pollution, a technical adviser to the federal government on national policy, and an advocate for the reestablishment of a serious regulatory apparatus like the Office of Noise Abatement and Control.

In late 2020, reflecting on these decades of efforts, Bronzaft spoke of one essential key to the management of the noise of the modern world.

"One word could really cut back on noise intrusion," she said in an interview.

"Respect."

This word, respect, gets used a lot these days, and yet it conveys something profound: the recognition of another person's dignity and the commitment to preserving others' prerogative to find their own meaning and well-being. The word "respect" comes from the Latin *respectus*, which means "to regard." It's literally "the act of looking back," as if to give someone the deeper consideration that they are due.

The simplicity of Bronzaft's point gets to the essence of the work before us. We have to honor every person's right to experience their own "interiority," their own clarity, and even their own wonder. This kind of deep respect gets lost in our modern modes of communication. This loss contributes to both our rising levels of global noise and our dwindling ability to find consensus.

Fifty years after the enactment of the Noise Control Act, the nature of noise has changed dramatically. In the face of a massive onslaught of informational noise, the work of regulatory policy has become a whole lot more complicated. Still, Bronzaft's point about respect is relevant not only for the auditory but also for the informational and even the internal noise. There's work happening now to imbue our social, economic, and technological systems with the value of respect. We think, for example, about how the advocates at the Center for Humane Technology speak of a "switch from tech that creates value by extracting attention to a tech that creates value by promoting presence."

While we believe formal structures of government have an important role to play in these transitions—setting shared rules and expectations to counter the forces of noise—we know the most important work is in changing culture. It's in cultivating respect writ large.

CHAPTER 15

A CULTURE OF GOLDEN SILENCE

"House open!" a voice calls out.

Joyce DiDonato is already onstage, sitting in meditation.

Or something like it.

She's motionless, like a sculpture, in a full-length metallic-gray gown. She's lightly veiled behind smoke screens and ornate lighting in the baroque cavern of the Kennedy Center's grand concert hall. While she's keenly focused on her breath, the situation isn't exactly conducive to deep introspection.

"There's a lot going on," she recalls.

Even though Joyce has performed hundreds and hundreds of times, on the great stages of the world, garnering almost every high accolade in opera, the relics of rookie feelings—"The nerves and excitement and adrenaline"—never totally go away. "The heart is beating," she tells us. "The palms are sweating."

There's a seemingly supernatural clarity in her voice and a calmness in her presence on the stage. Yet Joyce explains that she's doing a whole lot of inner work to navigate noise. "My goal as a performer is to eliminate the things that inhibit me so that the music can arrive unobstructed to the listener; it's getting past the internal noise, the internal doubts." It's odd to think of singing boldly on a stage in front of thousands of people as the work of silence. But that's how she describes it. "I have to find a kind of silence, to actually give voice to the music, with honesty and integrity. I have to work toward inner silence. It took me—*it's taking me*—a long time," she adds. "I was unaware of how loud it was inside my head."

For twenty-five or thirty minutes, people file into the concert hall. As they settle into their seats, they're surprised to find the curtain up and the celebrated mezzo-soprano already sitting onstage. "The noise rises, the energy, the frenetic sense of anticipation starts to build," she tells us. "Then the lights dim. It's as though somebody just dropped the volume lever." There's a crackle of alertness in the air.

And then a single pluck of a low note on the lute.

"The lute is this very soft-grained instrument; it doesn't make a lot of sound, so it's a surprising call to attention. We then settle in for another twenty seconds or so of silence before I then finally move, and the music begins." Joyce tells us that she grew quite fond of this gradual and unconventional beginning: "It just feels full of a lot more—consciousness."

The concert she describes took place in Washington, D.C., in November 2019. It was the closing event of a three-year world tour of forty-four cities in twenty-three countries, called *In War and Peace: Harmony Through Music*. The idea came to Joyce by way of a "lightning bolt," she tells us. At the time, she was poised to do a very different tour. "It was going to promote a disc of rare Neapolitan arias," she says. The tour was scheduled—all the arrangements had been made—but when the tragic terrorist attacks happened in Paris, "something shook deep inside of me," she says. Her internal voice was resounding: "I cannot do a niche recording for the five hundred people that are going to find this academically interesting . . . *The world needs something else.*" Shaken by the violence in France as well as the rancor of American politics, Joyce wanted to explore—through music and art—how people, in times of noisy upheaval, find solace.

As she toured, she asked scores of people, "In the midst of chaos, how do you find peace?" She published the answers in *Playbill*— opening a dialogue and ensuring that her tour wouldn't be another "ninety-minute, drive-by musical experience," as she put it. The inquiry and the audiences' responses sparked a broader conversation that became the backdrop for the tour.

Joyce reflects on her own answer to the question: How, in the midst of chaos, does she find peace? While the concerts have this contemporary mission, she performs centuries-old pieces of music. She tells us how she feels a bond with the people who have performed the songs over the centuries as well as the audiences who've listened over those hundreds of years. "It lines you up on a kind of thread that goes back in time," she tells us. Joyce transcends time as we know it—especially within the silences. "The silence is amplified by and builds on all of those silences that have come before."

As the concert concludes, she tells us, "the voice finishes by handing the melody over to the solo violin, which then slowly gives way to the final elongated chord of the orchestra. Imperceptibly, it simply dissipates—seeming to last forever."

Then the grandest silence.

"There are two thousand people in the audience," she tells us, "two thousand experiences happening at the same time. It's as if there's this unspoken, collective agreement—this *silent collective agreement*—not to move, not even to breathe." She continues, "The audience is setting this atmosphere of electricity. It's not anticipation at this point—like the silence at the beginning. And it's not nervousness," she adds, parsing the varieties of silence she's come to know so well. "They're just *in* the silence. They're fully trusting the experience—bathing in it."

Time feels "suspended," she says. "This kind of silence feels sacred."

Just blocks from the White House—in the twilight of the Trump years, at a time of so much uncertainty and uproar—there's a momentary culture of presence and peace. The performance leaves a rapturous silence in its wake. And, ever so slowly, it dissipates.

A roaring applause comes. Then, after the jubilant cries of "Brava!" subside, the audience settles into collective silence once again.

Joyce then speaks to the audience. First, she acknowledges what's palpable: the pain and turmoil that's out there. As she continues, she builds up to what feels like an operatic crescendo, saying, "Our world doesn't have to be this way." She tells of how life can and should "overflow with immense possibility, improbable beauty, and relentless truth."

Then she stops and stands motionless, once again, onstage. She allows the words some space to resonate through the hall.

When we asked Joyce about the words she spoke, she seemed to barely remember them. It wasn't that she hadn't spoken them. It wasn't that they weren't consequential. It's more as though *they'd spoken her.* It was as if the entire tour had been orchestrated to deliver those words and that silence—on that day, at that location, to that particular audience.

Justin remembers her words vividly. He was there. In the shadow of Joyce's words about struggle and hope, he felt some of the deepest silence he'd encountered in such a large crowd. He felt the collective agreement Joyce spoke of; he had entered that collective agreement.

The late justice Ruth Bader Ginsburg was also in the audience for the performance. It would be less than a year before she'd pass away. It was an intense time for the Supreme Court, and she faced many contentious cases. "There were big decisions on her desk," Joyce recalls. "The morning after the performance, she expressed to me how grateful she was; for those two hours, she stopped thinking about the briefs. There was a space that allowed her to breathe, to restore herself, to replenish herself, and return to a fresh perspective."

We reflect with Joyce upon just how much Justice Ginsburg was holding—for herself and for the country—in that moment. We reflect upon how rare it is to find a *container* to allow this kind of renewal. A public space, a secular space, a space of silent collective agreement.

"Because so much of our society is structured on production: staying up, being ahead of the curve, getting on top of things—going, doing—our intellects trick ourselves into believing this is the only way," Joyce says. "But then here's an invitation to stop and experience something spacious and true." She continues, "I think this is the power in culture, art, performance. It doesn't always happen. But when it *does* happen, it's a chance to climb out of your head and dive into your center."

In meditation or quiet contemplation, Joyce has only rarely experienced a kind of silence she would call "rapturous." But, she tells us, "I've had multiple times, *plentiful* times, when it's come from the collective . . . There's an attunement that comes in, and it is gloriously amplified."

THE DAY OF SILENCE

Dewa Putu Berata grew up playing games and music with friends under the shade of five giant banyan trees in his village, Pengosekan, near Ubud. "In Bali, we have *many* ceremonies," he said, grinning. This is a charming understatement. Offerings and rituals are the centerpiece of Balinese life.

As a boy, Dewa's favorite ceremony was the one that took place the evening before the New Year, called the Ngrupuk Parade. It was chaos, by design. Villagers pour out of their compounds and into the streets carrying giant effigies of monsters and demons. They'd bang on drums and make loud noises to scare away the evil spirits. The music is "loud and serious," Dewa tells us, dropping his tone considerably.

"It's like—*Tata! Tata! Dum! Tata! Dum! Ta Dum!*"

He'd stay close to his father, a renowned drummer, who played that driving beat for hours to exorcise the bad and ready the people for purification that takes place the following morning on Nyepi—the Day of Silence, the first day of the New Year and the most important ceremonial day of the Balinese lunar calendar.

Nyepi forbids the ordinary activities of daily life. For twenty-four hours, very different rules apply: there can be no fire, including cooking and use of lights; no activity, including work; no leaving your home; and—last but not least—no eating food or partaking in entertainment. "You have to be quiet, stay at home, and think," Dewa tells us. "You let nature take a break for one day, and you let yourself take a break for one day."

Dewa describes his village as being impossibly loud nowadays. You can barely hear the birds over the traffic of diesel trucks and motorbikes, the constant honking of horns. But during Nyepi, no one is allowed to drive, the international airport is closed, even cellular data is shut down.

"It's silent in our world," Dewa says. "But there's a lot in our heads and in our hearts."

On this day of purification, people are expected to appreciate all they have rather than grumble about what's prohibited. Dewa and his family ask themselves, "What if I *didn't* have a job? What if I *didn't* have food? What if I *didn't* have a home or the ability to afford electricity?" These questions prompt their practice of gratitude.

Dewa says that for "regular people" like him, those who "are not strong in meditation," it's okay to spend Nyepi in quiet conversation with loved ones—as long as they make sure to not disturb the neighbors. In Dewa's family, they use the time to tend their relationships. They talk about how well they've been communicating and getting along. They revisit and refresh their commitments to one another. They envision how they want to be—as a family. For Dewa and his family, these quiet conversations set the tone for the coming year.

Dewa's favorite part of Nyepi today is when he, his wife, and his kids pull a few mattresses into the courtyard of their compound. They recline with their heads close together, just listening to the birdsong and gazing into an expansive sky.

We half expected Dewa to tell us that Nyepi was a disappearing tradition. But he tells us that the opposite is true: people are more observant than ever. When he was a child, Dewa says, "Nyepi was not a big deal." Back in the day, the government asked the Pecalang, the traditional guards who maintain village security in daily life, to enforce the rules of Nyepi. Today, they still roam the streets, but Dewa says they're hardly needed. "I think people understand what Nyepi is," he told us. "Today it's so crowded, we're so stressed out, a lot of work, a lot of activity . . . I think we really *need* Nyepi."

Dewa says that he and his fellow citizens welcome the ritual.

"We say, 'Thank you, Nyepi. *Thank you.*'"

REMEMBERING

In the preceding chapters, we've explored what it means to find silence in our individual lives as well as among friends, colleagues, and loved ones. We've imagined public policies that respect our internal worlds and honor what is unspoken.

But what does it mean to live in a whole society that honors silence?

What if the collective agreement at Joyce's performance or the annual day of reflection in Dewa's observation of Nyepi wasn't a rare occurrence but, instead, an element of ordinary life?

Where can we look for a culture that cherishes clarity and wonder?

We recently explored this line of inquiry with Tyson Yunkaporta, the author of the book *Sand Talk: How Indigenous Thinking Can Save the World*.

Tyson's answer was unequivocal: "It doesn't exist."

"There's no Indigenous culture on the planet that is not infected with the same noise," he tells us. "There are people who are still living in the same patterns," he says, speaking of traditional knowledge and modes of connection with nature. "But those are also falling apart."

"The noise is everywhere. In the same way as every mother on the planet has dioxin in her breast milk—even in the middle of the Amazon, *especially* in the middle of the Amazon—there is no perfect place, it's all polluted," he says.

"There's so much noise you can't have an unpolluted relation with a person. Our relationships are infected with the noise, and there are a thousand layers of abstraction between any two people."

Tyson pauses and acknowledges that this sounds negative, and then he says exactly the opposite of what we expect him to say.

"I'm really excited about being alive right now."

"All this sounds hopeless, but—*no*—it's a gift," he says. "Our job is to actualize the systems our descendants will inhabit. I'm talking about a *remembrance* of connection."

He concludes, "There's this massive, dysfunctional juggernaut that's covered the planet, and our responses to that are informing the amazing regenerative culture that's coming."

O

In the age of auditory, informational, and internal noise—when at least a third of the world's natural "aural ecosystems" have gone extinct, when every square inch of Earth has some form of digital connectivity, when the welfare of a society is judged by the raw quantity of sound and stimulus and stuff it produces, and when the "success" of a human life is sized up according to one's personal brand on the digital platform du jour—Tyson is probably right. There is a degree of pristine attention that is, today, unattainable.

But Tyson contends that there is something important and wonderful that we *can* do, even in this world of noise.

"Recall the memory," he says.

We can "recall the memory" to *preserve* the memory. Even if there's no perfect golden silence in this world of noise, we can connect with silence across time. We can tend to the remaining roots and limbs in hopes that they will flower again in the future.

Throughout this book, we've explored what it means to "recall the memory," in ways both big and small. We've explored what it means to awaken a quiet and connected presence that feels utterly outside the noisy and isolated times in which we live. The grand opera house in a global political power center and the little village shrouded in motorbike smoke among rice paddies are, literally and metaphorically, a world apart. But these are two examples of what it means to "recall the memory" of silence.

THE SIGNAL

We ask Tyson to tell us about the deepest silence he's ever known.

He answers with a friendly challenge to the premise of our question.

In his Indigenous language, Wik Mungkan, he tells us, there is no word that even approximates the ordinary idea of silence.

"A vacuum is just a theoretical concept," Tyson explains. Most of the modern "quest for silence"—the notion that we can transcend all the relationships and vibrations and patterns of our world—is a delusion.

But he says there *is* a concept in his traditional language that relates directly to the deeper idea of silence as presence, as something more than the absence of noise.

He calls this concept "the ability to perceive a signal."

"It gets subjective," Tyson cautions, because we think "one person's signal is another person's noise."

But he says there is a true signal that runs deeper than all our individual stories and opinions. "At the foundation, at the bottom of the stack," he says, "there is the law of the land, the law that is *in* the land, the forces and patterns of creation that provide for the growth and the limits to growth of all things."

"And that," he says, "is *the* signal."

He reflects for a few moments and then gets to the heart of what he means when he talks about perceiving the signal: "tuning in to what is *really* true."

In our conversation, Tyson emphasizes that this true signal isn't only in the land.

It's within us, too.

"Whales have a genetic signal that tells them what their migration routes are, and birds, too, have these signals, and our biologists say humans don't have that memory. But we *do* have a signal that tells us how to organize in groups."

Tyson's words take us all the way back to the original intuition that led us to write this book.

Beyond all the noise of the world and all the interference in our own heads, there is this presence—this true signal—to which we can attune.

When we "recall the memory" of this presence and align our lives to it, we can find something more than personal calmness or enhanced productivity or some other form of what Tyson derisively calls "self-actualization." We can find guidance on how to live well with one another. We can find orientation on how to heal our cultures and how to organize our societies. We can find guidance on how to live in harmony with nature, too. Tyson reminds us, "The law of the land lives *slowly*." It tends to operate over the course of centuries and millennia rather than the pace of cable news cycles and social media "hot takes." We can't discern the signal when we're running at breakneck speed. We can't hear when we're all caught up in stories of the self.

EXPANSION

There are a thousand ways to describe the power of silence—what Tyson calls the ability "to perceive a signal" or to "tune in to what's *really* true." We've named many in this book.

For example, you can describe it in neurobiological terms as getting beyond the default mode network of the brain.

Or paint the picture in religious terms as the *apophatic* essence of reality—beyond concepts and beyond that which can be named.

Or look to the poetic, like how Cyrus Habib talks about being a "connoisseur of creation."

Or turn to how it feels in your own direct experience—like the sensory clarity of watching the ocean churn or feeling the cool breeze on our skin, unmediated by narration or analysis.

One of the most potent ways of describing the dynamic essence of silence is through the word "expansion." It's the unfolding of the attentional space and the easing of the strictures of the separate self. The word "expansion" is a key to understanding why silence is so rare in our world, why we live today with what Tyson calls the "dysfunctional juggernaut" of noise.

In conversation, the neuroscientist Judson Brewer describes to us how virtually all of his academic research studies—his decades of explorations of the interplay of thoughts and behaviors with the biological mechanism of the brain—point to a spectrum of human experience between *contraction* and *expansion*. In states of contraction, he says, we are immersed in labeling things, fixated on past and future, caught up in the noise of individualized identity. In states of expansion, we are present in the internal silence, where we can transcend those rigid boundaries of self and other.

Brewer points out that our societies actually tend to *celebrate* the contracted states. Or, as Joyce DiDonato said, "so much of our society is structured on production: staying up, being ahead of the curve, getting on top of things—going, doing." Brewer points out that we tend to seek and glorify emotions of "excitement." While there's nothing wrong with being excited, it's a contracted state. "Excitement," he says, "does not equal happiness."

There exists a deeper and more sustainable kind of joy that's grounded in something beyond the fleeting rush. Aristotle spoke of a kind of happiness called *eudaimonia*—the experience of human flourishing that's rooted in virtue and truth. It's the goodness we feel when we're expanding beyond the limited interests of the individualized self. It's a vast and penetrating happiness—full of clarity and calm. Gandhi spoke of this more expansive kind of fulfillment as the alignment between *manasa*, *vāchā*, and *kārmana*, the Sanskrit words for mind, speech, and action, respectively. He's quoted as saying, "Happiness is when what you think, what you say, and what you do are in harmony." In this light, it makes sense that Gandhi, even as one of the world's most engaged and prominent political leaders, spent so much time in silence. His notion of well-being *required* it.

Every culture has its vision of what constitutes a good life. Every society has its answer to the question of what makes for human flourishing. The intuition that inspired this book—about the power of silence to help us transcend tired old opposites and to get beyond a point-and-counterpoint culture—is about shifting our North Star from contraction to expansion. It's about moving from a fixation on speed, entertainment, competition, and the maximum accumulation of mental and material stuff toward an appreciation of presence, of clarity, of the golden spaces between and beyond all speech and thought.

We've explored a wide range of ideas for making this shift—for recalling the memory of silence in a world of noise. We started with personal practices, like the ones that Jarvis describes, of finding your *sphere of control* and *sphere of influence*. We then looked at ways we can honor pristine attention in our workplaces and share quiet moments with our friends and family. Finally, we examined opportunities for cultivating silence at the society-wide level.

But, really, all of these strategies come down to the very simple idea that we introduced in the opening pages of this book:

Notice noise.

Tune in to silence.

Go as deeply into the silence as you possibly can, even when it's only present for a few seconds.

Cultivate spaces of profound silence—even rapturous silence—from time to time.

This is how we can start to listen for the true signal. It's the essence of remembering. It's the clearest path to the expansion of our awareness—both personal and shared.

O

In the opening pages of this book, we expressed our sense that the most intractable problems won't be solved with more talking or thinking. With due respect to the voice and the intellect and the buzzing machinery of material progress, we asked you to consider the possibility that the solutions to the most serious personal, communal, and even global challenges could be found somewhere else: *in this place of expansion, in the open space between the mental stuff.*

We don't want to imply that through silence the solutions will emerge automatically. We still have to challenge oppressive social systems, to radically reduce greenhouse gas emissions, and to build equitable economies. All these shifts are necessary. It's just that they're not, on their own, sufficient. We also need to address the underlying agitation in our collective human consciousness. *To repair our world, we need to reclaim our capacities to cultivate silence, to be in silence, to perceive the signal.* We need to find our way to humility, renewal, and respect for life. These are prerequisites of solving the challenges we face.

Don't take our word for it.

Take a moment to return to the feeling of the deepest silence you've ever known. Come back to where you are, whom you're with, and what's happening around you. Remember what this deepest silence is like in your body. Maybe it's active, like a state of flow. Perhaps it's passive, like a state of rest.

Take your time here. Breathe.

See if you can recall the felt sense of the memory.

Now, imagine your loved ones feel this presence, too. And your neighbors, and the people in your workplace. Imagine the top political decision makers and cultural influencers in your country feel it. Imagine everyone, for at least a moment, feels this resonance, this spaciousness.

Imagine we all stop and appreciate it.

How might this experience change the way we deal with conflict? When we sit in this silence, do we hold on to the hardening impulse to win the argument, or do we expand into listening and understanding?

How does this presence shift our sense of what constitutes progress? Do we keep clinging to an idea of the "good life" as the endless accumulation of more and more mental and material stuff? Or do we ease, open, and slow ourselves—aspiring to harmonize more with nature and with one another?

How does this presence of silence change the way we make decisions, how we hold ourselves accountable, how we spend our time? How might this presence of silence change what we hold in our hearts?

Imagine if all of humanity could absorb this golden silence.

What's possible when we remember?

What happens when we all tune in?

THIRTY-THREE WAYS TO FIND SILENCE

On the pages to come, you'll find quick summaries of some of the key practices and strategies that we've laid out in this book. These ideas range from small personal ways of finding pockets of quiet time, all the way up to big shifts in our societies. Next to each entry, we've included a page number where you can find a more detailed description of each practice.

EVERYDAY PRACTICES FOR INDIVIDUALS

Just Listen, Page 165

Step into a quiet place. Turn your full attention to your hearing. No need to think about *what* you're hearing—just listen to the soundscape around you. If it's silent enough in your surroundings, see if you notice any sensation of an "inner sound," like a vibration or ringing in your ears. *Just listen*, without labeling or judging. Remember how Pythagoras advised his students to "let your quiet mind listen and absorb the silence." Recall how Duke University Medical School researchers found evidence that "trying to hear in silence activates the auditory cortex," stimulating brain cell development. When you anchor your awareness in simply listening, *how do your thoughts and feelings shift?*

Little Gifts of Silence, Page 168

The next time you face an unforeseen break in what you're doing or an interruption of the ordinary sound and stimuli of your day—say, the podcast you're enjoying unexpectedly stops streaming in your headphones or you're stuck in a ridiculously long line at the post office—*see if you can receive this gap as a gift.* Rather than getting frustrated, can you take a tiny vacation from having to fill the space? How deeply can you immerse yourself in an unanticipated moment of quiet?

What You're Already Doing—but Deeper, Page 170

Throughout your day, whenever you remember, *take three breaths.* You're doing it anyway. But, as you take these three particular breaths, *pay close attention.* You can use these breaths as a "diagnostic" to sense where there's noise in your body and mind. And you can use these breaths as a way back to internal quiet. Can you find the silence between the in breath and the out breath, in the "swing" from one to the other? As you take your three breaths, can you tune your body and mind to this silence? See how even thirty seconds of conscious respiration can shift your emotions and perspective.

Silence in Motion, Page 173

While it's understandable to conflate silence with stillness, silence also lives *in motion*. As you walk, run, dance, swim, do yoga, or shoot hoops, can you bring the most *exquisite attention to your body in motion?*

Experiment to see if you can find a "merger of action and awareness" where there's no more mental chatter. See if you can get so immersed in what you're physically doing that you have no excess attention to devote to self-conscious rumination. In a true state of physical flow, the mind is silent.

Momentary Ma, Page 175

Take a cue from the Japanese cultural value of *Ma*. Seek clarity and renewal in *the spaces in between*. In conversation, sense how the pauses in words and sentences contribute to the meaning of the exchange and the connection that's generated. As you go throughout your day, stop to pause in moments of transition. When you're opening a door, turning on the tap for some water, or turning on the lights, take a quiet conscious breath to mark the transition. By appreciating the silence and space in a micro-moment, we can *decompress time*.

Do One Thing, Page 177

Think of a daily "to-do" that you usually just speed through on the way to doing something else. See if you can—like Faith Fuller's simple, yet elegant, practice of making a pot of coffee—"Get out of the outcome and into the process." Can you slow your daily activity down by just 10 percent? Can you bring a sense of appreciation, even ritual, to it? Experiment with turning an ordinary part of your daily grind into an opportunity for sensory clarity. Find internal silence through the simple pleasure of doing *just one thing*.

Silence Within the Words, Page 179

Read a book with your fullest attention—no phone nearby, no intermittent side conversation, no distracted thought about what you're going to do next. Make time for "deep reading" with the explicit intention of bringing silence to your mind. Some kinds of reading are especially conducive to this kind of quiet, like, for example, reading on airplanes or in remote cabins with no cell signal. One of the best ways to engage in this kind of reading is through poetry. Place a favorite volume of poems by your bedside. Seed your dreamland by reading (and rereading) a poem before you drift into sleep. Notice how good writing—to quote Susan Sontag—"Leaves silence in its wake."

Quick "Hits" of Nature, Page 181

While a rushing river or a flock of trilling birds might register as high decibel, these sounds of nature don't make claims on our consciousness. They generate the felt experience of quiet. Seek to encounter nature in two simple ways every day to help put life in perspective: (1) connect with *something bigger than yourself*, like a towering tree or the stars in the night sky; (2) connect with *something smaller than yourself*, like a new blossom, a trail of ants, or a sparrow. Connecting to nature—big and small—helps us dislodge the noisy delusion that life is just the mental stuff of a human-centered existence.

Sanctuaries in Space and Time, Page 186

Think about all your responsibilities in life and the commitments on your schedule. What are the *pockets of time and space you can preserve* to be in silence? It can be a few moments alone in the washroom (no phones allowed) or luxuriating in the gap between your morning alarm and a snooze cycle. Perhaps it's late night or early morning, when you can make time for stretching, bathing, journaling, sitting on a patio, lying on the floor, or finding some other relaxed and quiet way of being. Make space in the calendar. Keep the appointment with yourself. Honor it as though you were meeting an important colleague or a beloved friend.

Make Friends with Noise, Page 188

Sometimes the noise is inevitable. The Irish poet Pádraig Ó Tuama counsels us to say hello to what's unwanted but inevitable in our lives.

So, find ways to say hello to the noise. Investigate it. Notice your responses to it. *Is there anything helpful that the noise might be signaling for you?* Is there a need you've been neglecting? Is there a request to be made? Is there something you're being called to accept or to let go?

PRACTICES FOR FINDING DEEPER SILENCE

Take Your To-Do List for a Hike, Page 197

Print out your to-do list and go to the most remote place in nature that you can reasonably access—like, say, a pond in a forest or a mountain overlook. When you get there, take an hour or more to center yourself and recalibrate your senses. When you feel as though your nerves have settled and you've absorbed some of the silence, take out your to-do list and *cross out everything that's not really necessary.* Notice how some of the things you thought were important in your ordinary state of mind at home or at your office might not actually be important from this vantage point. As Gordon Hempton says, "The answers are in the silence."

Take a Wordless Wednesday, Page 199

Try not speaking for a day. Gandhi had a "day of silence" once a week. Beyond meditation and reflection, he sometimes read or even spent time with others. But he didn't say a word. If the responsibilities of work or childcare or eldercare make a wordless day impossible, set aside just a few hours. The key to getting started is simple: Check in with the people around you who will be most affected. Tell them why a silent day is important to you. Describe your plan. See if they have any questions, and find agreement on the ground rules—like, for example, under what circumstances colleagues or loved ones should interrupt you. Ask for their full support (they might even ask to join you). Once you've prepared yourself, your environment, and those around you, *pay attention to what's different for you when you're not engaged in speech.* What comes into the foreground and what falls away? How might these observations inform your everyday life?

Go Floating in the Cloud of Unknowing, Page 203

Plan and prepare so you can enter profound quiet. As *The Cloud of Unknowing* explains, it's important to temporarily *forget* all the challenging circumstances of life in order to engage in the deepest prayer or contemplation. But *how* do we let go? Reserve a few hours or a full day to be in silent contemplation—in nature or somewhere peaceful by yourself. As a preparation, do what you can to *set the stage for inner quiet.* Clear off some genuinely important items from the to-do list. If you know you're not going to be able to let go into the space of internal silence because you haven't sent that email, made that phone call, taken out the trash, or cleaned the fridge, then just do it. In the time immediately before you enter your period of silence, do what you need to prepare your body and mind—like exercising or journaling. No need to be too ambitious here. Just see what you can do to clear away some of the simple contributors to internal noise. This will make it easier to *go floating.*

Into the Deep, Page 206

Create a DIY silent retreat. It doesn't need to be lengthy or pricey or far from home to be substantive. You can organize it for yourself and "create the container" according to your own circumstances. For example, rearrange the furniture in your room. Or pet sit for a neighbor. Or swap apartments with a friend. Arranging a new setting or ambience can enable a psychological shift. While a simple DIY retreat might not be as immersive as something long and remote, even a short time in silence can shift your perspective and amplify your clarity.

Fuzzy Puppies Licking Your Face, Page 210

Consider what it means to identify and address your deepest sources of internal noise. The Iraq War veteran and PTSD survivor Jon Lubecky says,

"The deeper the trauma, the louder the internal noise." He adds that, unlike for auditory silence, there's no "sensory deprivation tank" for finding internal silence. *We have to do the work.* For Jon, this work first came through an MDMA-assisted psychotherapy session that felt, in his words, like "being hugged by the person who you know loves you the most on this planet while being buried in fuzzy puppies licking your face." The power of the treatment was in enabling him to safely access a memory that would otherwise be too painful. The work of identifying and addressing trauma doesn't necessarily involve work with psychedelic medicines or entheogens. But the key is to find a serious means of unraveling the origin of any debilitating internal noise.

Deep Play, Page 213

Bring childlike wonder to something you love. In her book *Deep Play*, Diane Ackerman writes of "play" as "a refuge from ordinary life, a sanctuary of the mind, where one is exempt from life's customs, methods, and decrees." And "deep play" is what she calls the ecstatic form of play. It's the kind of experience that brings us into a prayer-like state of beholding. While Ackerman says that "deep play" is classified more by mood than by activity, there are some kinds of activities that are especially likely to prompt it: "art, religion, risk-taking, and some sports—especially those that take place in relatively remote, silent, and floaty environments, such as scuba diving, parachuting, hang gliding, mountain climbing." As you seek to overcome the noise of the modern world, consider these questions: What brings you closest to a childlike way of perceiving? How can you carry these ways of beholding into everyday life?

EVERYDAY PRACTICES WITH CO-WORKERS AND COLLABORATORS

Get Experimental, Page 233

Consider what you really want or need with respect to silence in your workplace. Start a conversation. Envision an experiment. At some organizations, it's "no email Fridays" or "no meeting Wednes-days." At others, it's eliminating the expectation of being available and on electronic devices during weekends or after 5:00 p.m. For some workplaces, a redesign of the floor plan might help specific kinds of workers get the focus they need. *Launch your experiment. Harvest lessons learned. Refine your experiment. Iterate.* Make sure it's safe for the experiment to fail. Design to learn, not to get it right the first time. With a little creativity, you can transform seemingly intractable norms of noise.

Ma *on the Job, Page 235*

Enshrine the value of *Ma*—reverence for the empty spaces "in be-tween"—in the culture of your organization. *Start with group activities*: For example, build in sanctioned time for quiet reflection, even within large discussions. In group brainstorming, safeguard the option to "sleep on a question," revisiting an inquiry fresh the next day. Consider new possibilities, like nonverbal report-outs, or Post-it note galleries of ideas on the walls so people can silently peruse and vote on ideas anonymously. Make space in order to encourage quieter voices and more marginalized perspectives to reach the center. *You can bring the value of* Ma *into the structure of the workday, too.* Schedule time for preparation—before starting a new project or heading into a meeting. Block off time for transitions between meetings and events; avoid scheduling back-to-back. Even five minutes—even five breaths—can make a difference. And finally, remember to schedule time for reflection and integration, especially for important and difficult projects.

Deep Work, Together, *Page 239*

Find a partner and make a pact to support each other's pristine attention. This may be a fellow team member or, if you work independently, another freelancer in need of focused work time. Set SMART (specific, mea-surable, attainable, relevant, and time-based) goals together. Work in parallel. Be accountable to each other. Work together to avoid distraction, like how the members of the Curie family worked together to find "perfect concentration."

Sitting in the Fire, Page 342

Next time you and your team are in conflict, consider gently requesting a couple minutes of silence before continuing. If the matter is heated and needs more space, consider asking for a recess until the following day (or the following week). The idea is to create adequate space for people to shift from purely oppositional stances. The more a team *turns to silence* in these moments, the more effective this method will become and the more enduring your group decisions will be.

Slow Down, There Isn't Much Time, Page 245

When you find yourself grappling with a problem that is both urgent and important, go against the grain: *slow down*. Rather than amping up the sound and intensity, seek quiet. If it's possible, take a break. Or have a nap. Read some poetry. Play catch with your dog. Make art. Head out into nature. Take a bath. Rest. Engage in an activity (or non-activity) that helps you *feel and be expansive*. In this expanded state, open yourself to new information. Invite in divergent thinking. Let ideas marinate over one good night's sleep. Then gather again to focus on the issue. Notice what emerges.

EVERYDAY PRACTICES FOR FAMILIES AND FRIENDS

Pumpernickel!, Page 254

What do you do when the soundscape of life becomes too discordant and the volume gets too high? Rosin Coven, a talented and delightfully eccentric musical ensemble, has a protocol for that. When the sound gets too crowded and the musicality is lost, someone shouts "Pumpernickel!" A declaration of "Pumpernickel!" is like the pulling of a rip cord. "It means 'what we really need is a subtractive process right now' in order to create space and silence," their front woman, Midnight Rose, tells us. In your life at home or among friends, find a lighthearted way to signal when it's time for shared quiet.

Remember the Sabbath Day, Page 255

If you don't have the time or inclination to hold a traditional weekend Sabbath day, then pick a day of the week for *a meal that can be different from all others*—where everyone commits to sharing time. *Make it a ritual.* Firm up your agreements about use of technology. Have a few things you always do like going around the table with a highlight and/or a lowlight from the week. Invite guests, break bread together. Leave the day-to-day worries of the workweek behind.

Intention and Attention, Page 257

Quiet with young kids isn't always so quiet. It often comes through moving, doodling, or building with blocks. Rather than a state of auditory silence, it's a state of presence. Still, there are moments when it's possible and powerful to be with children in a more literal state of silence. When you ask a child a meaningful question—like "what are you grateful for?"—leave an empty space for reflection. Let kids have ample time to tune in to the "still, small voice" that lives within.

Small Is Beautiful, Page 259

We can't always engineer a beautiful moment of shared silence. The poignancy of such moments may be due, in part, to their spontaneity. Still, there's one recommendation that helps us cultivate these experiences: Keep the silence small. Snack-sized, in fact. When you go on a hike or walk with a friend or loved one for an hour, see if you can spend five minutes—perhaps at a comfortable bench or beautiful vista—to be quiet together. Minimize the worries that arise with lofty plans for lengthy silence. Focus on quality rather than quantity.

Collective Effervescence, Page 261

When have you experienced a flow state *in a group*? Was it at a concert or a ceremony or a sporting event? The next time you find the opportunity, see how deeply you can enter the internal silence among other people. These moments of shared transcendence are relatively rare, but—as Bob Jesse's experience with the dance-based church reveals—there are elements of a gathering that you might be able to intentionally co-design to facilitate flow. The next time you plan a group event, think about brainstorming some ground rules or principles to help participants relax into what the French sociologist Émile Durkheim called "collective effervescence."

Tuning In, Together, Page 265

The power of silence is magnified when it's shared. But the degree to which it's magnified can depend on the degree of preparation. The pioneering psychologist Ralph Metzner believed in the power of "preparing the vessel" to be in silence. In his medicine circles, participants joined together for preparatory workshops for learning, meditation, and exercises by day so they could jointly prepare themselves for the most rapturous shared silence at night. When you have the opportunity to be in silence with others in a ceremonial way, what can you do to come together and prepare?

Healing Presence, Page 268

Schedule a retreat with your friend or your partner. While you may not be totally wordless for the entire retreat, you can predetermine some periods of silence interspersed with bracketed time for verbal connection. Perhaps you have creative projects under way or you're both bird-watchers or meditators or writers or readers. If you can, avoid using phones, sending emails, or doing anything else that might distract from pure presence. As Sheila Kappeler-Finn explains, a simple practice like rearranging your furniture at home can create a container for the sacred—one of many ways that you can establish a "temple." In a shared retreat with a partner or friend, the silence itself can be one of the pillars of the temple. When two people are together observing a commitment to silence, a rare ambience emerges. "Silence alters what the space feels like between two people," Sheila says. "It builds the tensile strength."

CHANGING PUBLIC POLICY AND CULTURE

Invest in Public Sanctuaries, Page 278

Think of a special public space—*like a forested reserve, a rose garden, a pocket park between skyscrapers, or an inviting library*—where you've been able to rest your nerves and recover your clarity. While quiet time is too often an exclusive luxury for people who can afford it, public sanctuaries democratize the power of silence. Consider what you can do to expand such sanctuaries. Maybe it's advocating for funding in the municipal budget; maybe it's envisioning a new public amenity and working with others in the community to create it.

Innovate Like the Amish, Page 281

Think carefully about what you value in life, and then work to ensure that any new technology you adopt really improves your well-being and honors your values. As part of his philosophy of "digital minimalism," Cal Newport suggests this way of relating to tech. His idea was inspired by the Amish, who, contrary to popular belief, aren't antitechnology. They simply subject new technologies to rigorous cost-benefit analysis before they adopt them as a community. As a society, we should consider the possibility of applying this ethos writ large. For example, just as the U.S. Food and Drug Administration assesses and reports on the side effects of drugs, governments could require clinical trials and independent cost-benefit analyses of certain new technologies that may have serious unintended consequences for our social, emotional, and cognitive health.

Measure What Matters, Page 284

How do you measure the success of your society? For the past century, our foremost indicator of collective success has been "growth"—factors like production, efficiency, and income. But "growth" often correlates with the roar of industrial machines, the number of hours that managers can keep employees glued to their computers, and the effectiveness of algorithms in steering us to buy products and services while diverting our attention away from what we intend to be doing. In order to transform a world of noise, we need to start measuring what matters—including preservation of nature and opportunities for rest, human connection, and quiet time. While we outline a variety of ways that governments can shift economic measurement, we can also start as individuals, families, and organizations by assessing our priorities with respect to the value of silence.

Enshrine the Right to Attention, Page 288

Most of us now spend a majority of our waking hours on computers, phones, TVs, and other electronic media on which advertisers compete for our attention. Yet—in contrast to other valuable and scarce resources—there are still few public rules that govern the manipulation of human attention. Consider how you can advocate for the defense of attention. It might be through political activism, demanding, for example, that governments "articulate what is off-limits" in terms of algorithms that seek to deliberately extract attention and send users, including children, down "rabbit holes" of endless watching or scrolling. As a worker, you can stand up for your "right to disconnect" from email, laptops, phones, and other "electronic leashes" after the workday has ended. Get creative in finding ways to manage the claims on our attention and reduce the burden of noise.

Deliberate Like the Quakers, Page 295

When you're grappling with a difficult question in public policy or the future of your community, let silence be an ally. In a Quaker business meeting, when it's clear that the participants aren't listening to each other, the clerk will typically ask for a period of silence. It's an opportunity to re-center, to take a few deep breaths, and to connect to the higher purpose of the meeting. The silence isn't forcing a resolution before the group is actually ready. It's simply helping people to get out of their own narrative, get present, and listen. What can you do to bring this ethos of *discernment* into public deliberation and the social discourse where you live?

OUR GRATITUDE

We'll start at the beginning. Profound thanks to Sarah Mitchell for following your intuition and introducing the two of us. You joked that we could be brother and sister. It turns out you were right.

To the person who first encouraged us to write on this topic, Katherine Bell, former editor at *Harvard Business Review* and now editor in chief at *Quartz*, thank you for your "yes" to the wild-card idea of writing about silence for a business audience. And gratitude to Laura Amico of *Harvard Business Review* for skillfully editing the piece.

Thank you to the people who helped demystify publishing and were so generous in offering us early guidance: Leslie Meredith, Simon Warwick-Smith, Felicia Eth, Steve Goldbart, Roman Mars, Rebecca Solnit, Andrea

Scher, Charlie Harding, and Marilyn Paul. To Marilyn, we also want to share our deepest thanks for your introduction to Jane von Mehren, who feels like an extension of our writing partnership and is the best agent we could have possibly imagined.

Thank you, Jane, for "getting" this project from the start, for your encyclopedic knowledge of the publishing world, and for your gentle and clear-eyed counsel every step of the way. Thank you also to the Aevitas Creative Management team, especially Erin Files, Arlie Johansen, and Chelsey Heller.

To Karen Rinaldi, our editor, our "Red Tara": Thank you for your mastery in orchestrating this process and for your full permission to allow this to evolve and manifest itself as it has. We are continually in awe of the synchronicities. And our gratitude to the HarperCollins/Harper Wave team, especially to Rebecca Raskin, Kirby Sandmeyer, Penny Makras, Amanda Pritzker, Yelena Nesbit, and Milan Božić.

Thank you to those who supported the mechanics and artistry of this book: Andy Couturier, Bridget Lyons, Cynthia Kingsbury, Monique Tavian, Rebecca Steinitz, Caryn Throop, Liz Boyd, Katherine Barner, Hanna Park, Jessica Lazar, Somsara Rielly, Dexter Wayne, Lizandra Vidal, Deb Durant, and Bob von Elgg.

And to the extraordinary people whose stories and insights fill this book:

To Aaron Maniam, for helping to crystallize the core message of this book; to Adam Gazzaley and Larry Rosen, for charting the course on noise; to Aimee Carrillo and Sheena Malhotra, for guidance on the moral dimensions of silence; to Arlene Blum, for trusting "slow down, there isn't much time"; to Arne Dietrich, for helping to illuminate the internal quiet of flow states; to Bob Jesse, for your wisdom and effervescence; to Brigitte van Baren, for the Zen of waiting in lines; to Carla Detchon, for honoring a beloved teacher; to Cherri Allison, for the silence needed to serve from the heart; to Clint Chisler, for sharing the kind of silence that lasts in the body; to Cyrus Habib, for being a connoisseur of creation; to David Jay and Randy Fernando, for defending pristine attention; to Dewa Berata, for sharing the beauty of Nyepi; to Don and Diane St. John, for the healing silence that keeps love flowing; to Estelle Frankel, for clarifying the higher octaves of consciousness; to Faith Fuller, for your sense of humor, your resilience, and your humility; to Gordon Hempton, for preserving the "think tank of the soul"; to Grace Boda, for being willing to enter the mystery with every cell of your being; to Janet Frood, for demonstrating that sabbaticals aren't just for academics; to Jarvis Jay Masters, for a thousand things, but most of all for the goodness of your heart and for showing what it means to "perceive and receive"; to Jay Newton-Small, for the art of simply listening; to Joan Blades, for the meditative power of deadheading; to Jon Lubecky, for doing the hard work and spreading the love; to Josh Schrei, for showing what it means to become a tuning fork for the primordial vibration; to Joshua Smyth, for teaching us "quiet is what people *think* quiet is"; to Joyce DiDonato, for being the gracious diva who leaves rapturous silence in her wake; to Jud Brewer, for your brilliant expansiveness; to Majid Zahid, for knowing your flow; to Marilyn Paul, for tending the oasis in time; to Matt Heafy, for putting the *Ma* in metal; to Michelle Millben, for bringing the spirit of silence into the halls of power; to Michael Barton, for your hilarity and your experimental prowess; to Michael Taft, for your sensory clarity, wise counsel, and generous introductions; to Midnight Rose and Rosin Coven, for calling "Pumpernickel!" when it's needed; to Nicole Wong, for imagining the legal and regulatory frameworks for a society that honors silence; to Pádraig Ó Tuama, for asking the strange questions; to Phillip Moffitt, for the compassionate kick in the tuchus; to Pir Shabda Kahn, for your trickster ways; to Renata Cassis Law, for helping to inspire this book with your insight that "silence can reset the nervous system"; to Rob Lippincott, for your discernment; to Roshi Joan Halifax, for normalizing the crumbling of ego "like old leaves or worn rock"; to Rupa Marya, for your courageous unlearning and exemplary listening; to Sheila Kappeler-Finn, for democratizing retreats; to Skylar Bixby, for cultivating the skill to do nothing; to Stephen DeBerry, for those three breaths; to Susan Griffin-Black, for your golden rule; to Congressman Tim Ryan, for bringing silence where it's most needed; to Tyson Yunkaporta, for remembering what it means to hear the true signal; to Yuri Morikawa, for your guidance on *Ma*; to Zach Taylor, for empowering the littlest among us to hear the "still, small voice"; and to Zana Ikels, for reaffirming the need for a non-meditator's guide for getting beyond the noise.

And to all those who helped to shape and nurture the thinking in this book:

Alan Byrum, Amira De La Garza, Anke Thiele, Anna Goldstein, Anne L. Fifield, Antona Briley, Barbara McBane, Brendan Bashin-Sullivan, Carlen Rader, Casey Emmerling, Cathy Coleman, Cécile Randoing Francois, Charlotte Toothman, Chris Radcliff, Chuck Roppel, Claude Whitmyer, Dallas Taylor, Dave Huffman, David Alvord, David Presti, Deborah Fleig, Diane Mintz, Dominique Lando, Duke Klauck, Erin Selover, Heidi Kasevich, Helen Austwick Zaltzman, Jamy and Peter Faust, Lieutenant Colonel Jannell MacAulay, Jessica Abbott Williams, Jill Hackett, Laura Tohe, Laurie Nelson Randlett, Leah Lamb, Leslie Sharpe, Linda Chang, Lisa Fischer, Lizandra Vidal, Lori A. Shook, Made Putrayasa, Mae Mars, Maggie Silverman, Michael A. Gardner, Rebecca Levenson, Regina Camargo, Rick Doblin, Rick Kot, Sam Greenspan, Sean Feit Oakes, Shaun Farley, Shauna Janz, Sheldon Norberg, Shelley Reid, Shoshana Berger, Silence Genti, Sridhar Kota, Stephen Badger, Stephanie Ramos, Susanne Parker, Tanis Day, Tim Gallati, Tim Salz, Todd and Susan Alexander, USef Barnes, Valerie Creane, Vanessa Lowe, Wes Look, and Zesho Susan O'Connell.

From Justin:

To our community of friends in Santa Fe, who cultivate and tend a garden that's brimming with laughter and life and nonetheless full of reverence for the silent presence. While I'm not able to name every one of you here, *I'm grateful to all of you.* Special thanks to dear friends who made it possible to write a book about pristine attention with three little ones crawling and running around the house: Brandon and Abi Lundberg, Shawn Parell and Russell Brott, Josh Schrei and Cigall Eacott, and Rafaela Cassis, among many others. To dear friends who—through specific conversations or feedback on manuscript drafts—have directly shaped this book in whole or in part: Solar and Renata Law, Maria Motsinger, John Baxter, Josh Schrei, Shawn Parell, Gary and Tama Lombardo, Elmano Carvalho, Jeffrey Bronfman, Tai and Satara Bixby, Pete Jackson, Julie Kove, Matt Bieber, and Daniel Tucker. To the one who guides me toward the most profound internal silence: José Gabriel da Costa.

To some of the dear friends with whom I've incubated the ideas in this book over many years: Ben Beachy, Wes Look, Neil Padukone, Zach Hindin, Evan Faber, Keane Bhatt, Mike Darner, Michael Shank, Mathias Alencastro, David John Hall, Lorin Fries, Jaime Louky, Laine Middaugh, Lauren Lyons, Sangeeta Tripathi, Jove Oliver, Paul Jensen and Carolyn Barnwell, Kim Samuel, Bettina Warburg, Travis Sheehan, Nathaniel Talbot and Annie Jesperson, Mark Weisbrot, Ben-Zion Ptashnik, Dan Hervig, Erik Sperling, Sebastian Ehreiser, Stephen Badger, Javier Gonzales, Hansen Clarke, and Mena Mark Hanna. To my oldest friends, including Kristin Lewter, Josh Weiss, Rajiv Bahl, Kyle Foreman, and, finally, Rob Eriov, whom I miss every single day of my life and who taught me an immense amount about the message of this book.

To three teachers who shaped my thinking most—at the beginning of my formal schooling and at the conclusion: Susan Altenburg, Leon Fuerth, and Richard Parker.

To my dear ma and pa, Susan and Steven, who have provided a container of unconditional love that has made so much goodness possible in my life. To my brother, Jeremy, who always tells me the truth with love and care and then proceeds to pick up his guitar and serenade me with a gorgeous and gritty rendition of a Dylan song. To my in-laws, Tom and Caryn—whom I count among my closest friends alive.

To my companion, Meredy, my beloved partner in navigating this world and learning and dancing and evolving through this life. Thank you for your patience. Thank you for your insights. Thank you for making this book possible. Thank you for filling my life with meaning and joy.

To my son, Jai, whose 5:00 a.m. wake-up calls enabled me to get essential writing done and whose hugs now sustain me with energy throughout the day. To my daughter Saraya, whose bright and mysterious smile opens my heart like a flower. To my daughter Tierra, who, at five years old, teaches me as much as I teach her—including why and how to be quiet around fairy houses in the forest.

From Leigh:

To my Women's Circle, who shall remain unnamed, you know exactly who you are and how indebted I am to each of your souls—this book would never *be* without you; to Ralph Metzner's circles—those of the past and those who continue today in his memory; to the infinite wisdom of my Rising Fools circle and the great bounty of my Deep Harvest circle; to the open arms of the Amethyst Opening circle; to my infinitely entertaining Memorial Day family; and to all my cosmic co-conspirators—*may we keep the fringe alive.*

To my dance communities—where I find my everyday quiet and my everyday joy—El Cerrito Dance Fitness and Rhythm & Motion. Thank you for cheering me on and celebrating each milestone along the way. I cherish you.

Thank you for all the physical, emotional, and spiritual tending provided by my nearest and dearest—especially Sheila Kappeler-Finn, Eilish Nagle, Anne L. Fifield, Grace Boda, Dominique Lando, Carla Detchon, Mayra Rivas, Rachel Berinsky, John Nelson, Fran Kersh, Kristina Forester-Thorp, Nuria Latifa Bowart, Sui-mi Cheung, Julie Brown, and Paul Catasus. Thank you to Andy Couturier for your genius in coaching writers and to Carrie "Rose" Katz for our weekly check-ins to stir the creativity cauldrons.

To my father, Richard L. Marecek—I thank you for this thread of life. *May you be free from all suffering.*

To my mom, Rickie C. Marecek—I thank you for this thread of life. Thank you, too, for demonstrating loving kindness—not solely with words, but also by example. *You are nothing shy of a miracle.* And to "My Betty," Betty Herbst, thank you for joining our family, for loving us up, and for bringing such laughter. Thank you, also, to my vibrant and warm mother-in-love, Nina Aoni, for your late-night texts of encouragement.

To my brother, Roman Mars—you've blown my mind and softened my heart since childhood. Thank you for joining me here and for always having faith in my inherent goodness. You make *everything* better.

To my passion-filled and radiant daughter, Ava Zahara: thank you for choosing us as your parents. Thank you for the idea of taking a "Wordless Wednesday" amidst the glaciers and for *joining me* on that glorious day. Thank you, too, for all the kitchen floor shnuggles. Our shared silence *feeds my soul.*

And, finally, to my delightfully unruly and adventurous husband, Michael Ziegler: thank you for teaching me so much about silence and for being my biggest fan. Thank you for sharing your panoramic inner and outer world with me. I couldn't ask for a more perfect partner; every ounce of this book is *for* you and *because of* you. *I am yours.*

And a final note from both of us: Writing a book about silence may seem like a solitary and somber undertaking. Yet this was anything but. We're thankful to each other for keeping the whole process harmonious, creative, full of momentum, and preposterously fun.

NOTES

Chapter 1: An Invitation

5   "*Sprechen ist silbern*": Thomas Carlyle, "Circumspective," in *Sartor Resartus: The Life and Opinions of Herr Teufels-dröckh in Three Books*, ed. Mark Engel (Berkeley: University of California Press, 2000), 198.

5   variants stretch back millennia: Albert Arazi, Joseph Sadan, and David J. Wasserstein, eds., *Compilation and Creation in Adab and Luġa: Studies in Memory of Naphtali Kinberg (1948–1997)* (Winona Lake, Ind.: Eisenbrauns, 1999).

7   "The Busier You Are": Justin Talbot Zorn and Leigh Marz, "The Busier You Are, the More You Need Quiet Time," *Harvard Business Review*, March 17, 2017, hbr. org/2017/03/the-busier-you-are-the-more-you-need-quiet-time.

8   mindfulness meditation has taken a remarkable journey: Kimberly Schaufenbuel, "Why Google, Target, and General Mills Are Investing in Mindfulness," *Harvard Business Review*, Dec. 28, 2015, hbr.org/2015/12/why-google-target-and-general-mills-are-investing-in-mindfulness. See also Marianne Garvey, "Meditation Rooms Are the Hottest New Work Perk," *MarketWatch*, Oct. 26, 2018, www.marketwatch.com/story/meditation-rooms-are-the-hottest-new-work-perk-2018-10-26; "Why GE Is Adding Mindfulness to the Mix," GE, Sept. 19, 2016, www.ge.com/news/reports/ge-putting-mindfulness-digital-industrial-business; Bryan Schatz, "Vets Are Using Transcendental Meditation to Treat PTSD—with the Pentagon's Support," *Mother Jones*, July 22, 2017, www.motherjones.com/politics/2017/07/vets-are-using-transcendental-meditation-to-treat-ptsd-with-the-pentagons-support.

10   weight-loss studies: Dishay Jiandani et al., "Predictors of Early Attrition and Successful Weight Loss in Patients Attending an Obesity Management Program," *BMC Obesity* 3, no. 1 (2016), doi:10.1186/s40608-016-0098-0.

Chapter 2: The Altar of Noise

14   "A Politician Takes a Sledgehammer": Frank Bruni, "A Politician Takes a Sledgehammer to His Own Ego," *New York Times*, April 11, 2020, www.nytimes.com/2020/04/11/opinion/sunday/cyrus-habib-jesuit.html.

16   "elephants, horses, chariots": Emily Ann Thompson, "Noise and Modern Culture, 1900–1933," in *The Soundscape of Modernity: Architectural Acoustics and the Culture of Listening in America, 1900–1933* (Cambridge, Mass.: MIT Press, 2004), 115.

16   These days, it's not just loud: For a wide-ranging overview of the research demonstrating the rise of auditory noise in the modern world, see John Stewart, *Why Noise Matters: A Worldwide Perspective on the Problems, Policies, and Solutions*, with Arline L. Bronzaft et al. (Abingdon, Eng.: Routledge, 2011).

17   The journalist Bianca Bosker reported: Bianca Bosker, "Why Everything Is Getting Louder," *The Atlantic*, Nov. 2019, www.theatlantic.com/magazine/archive/2019/11/the-end-of-silence/598366.

17 128 billion business emails: "Email Statistics Report, 2015–2019," Radicati Group, accessed Sept. 4, 2021, www.radicati.com/wp/wp-content/uploads/2015/02/Email-Statistics-Report-2015–2019-Executive-Summary.pdf.

17 five times as much information: Daniel J. Levitin, "Hit the Reset Button in Your Brain," *New York Times*, Aug. 9, 2014, www.nytimes.com/2014/08/10/opinion/sunday/hit-the-reset-button-in-your-brain.html.

18 shortcomings of our everyday attentional capacities: Guy Raz, "What Makes a Life Worth Living?," NPR, April 17, 2015, www.npr.org/transcripts/399806632.

18 "What information consumes": Hal R. Varian, "The Information Economy: How Much Will Two Bits Be Worth in the Digital Marketplace?," UC Berkeley School of Information, Sept. 1995, people.ischool.berkeley.edu/~hal/pages/sciam.html.

19 three-quarters of the population: Judson Brewer, *Unwinding Anxiety: New Science Shows How to Break the Cycles of Worry and Fear to Heal Your Mind* (New York: Avery, 2021).

19 320 State of the Union addresses': Ethan Kross, "When Talking to Ourselves Backfires," in *Chatter: The Voice in Our Head, Why It Matters, and How to Harness It* (New York: Crown, 2021), 22.

20 They call it "goal interference": Adam Gazzaley and Larry D. Rosen, "Interference," in *The Distracted Mind: Ancient Brains in a High-Tech World* (Cambridge, Mass.: MIT Press, 2016), 5–12.

22 "convenience addiction": Jocelyn K. Glei, ed., *Manage Your Day-to-Day: Build Your Routine, Find Your Focus, and Sharpen Your Creative Mind* (Seattle: Amazon, 2013).

23 In her 2019 feature in *The Atlantic*: Bosker, "Why Everything Is Getting Louder."

25 GDP wasn't supposed to be used: Ben Beachy and Justin Zorn, "Counting What Counts: GDP Redefined," *Kennedy School Review*, April 1, 2012, ksr.hkspublications.org/2012/04/01counting-what-counts-gdp-redefined.

26 "[It] counts air pollution": Robert F. Kennedy, "Remarks at the University of Kansas, March 18, 1968," John F. Kennedy Presidential

Library and Museum, www.jfklibrary.org/learn/about-jfk/the-ken
nedy-family/robert-f-kennedy/robert-f-kennedy-speeches/remarks
-at-the-university-of-kansas-march-18–1968.

29   "continuous partial attention": James Fallows, "Linda Stone on
Maintaining Focus in a Maddeningly Distractive World," *The Atlantic*, May 23, 2013, www.theatlantic.com/national/archive/2013/05
/linda-stone-on-maintaining-focus-in-a-maddeningly-distractive
-world/276201.

29   why a reported 69 percent of millennials: Mike Brown, "70% of Millennials Report Anxiety from Not Having Their Cell Phone," LendEDU,
May 28, 2020, lendedu.com/blogmillennials-anxiety-not-having-cell
-phone.

Chapter 3: Silence Is Presence

32   "All things in our universe": Tam Hunt, "The Hippies Were Right: It's
All About Vibrations, Man!," *Scientific American*, Dec. 5, 2018, blogs
.scientificamerican.com/observations/the-hippies-were-right-its-all
-about-vibrations-man.

33   "He heard "two sounds": Some experts now believe the high-pitched
sound was likely to be tinnitus, a ringing of the ears.

36   "I don't give them all that much credit": Carl McColman, "Barbara A.
Holmes: Silence as Unspeakable Joy (Episode 26)," *Encountering Silence*,
May 24, 2018, encounteringsilence.com/barbara-a-holmes-silence-as
-unspeakable-joy-episode-26.

41   "a vital virtue at the foundation": Jennifer E. Stellar et al., "Awe and
Humility," *Journal of Personality and Social Psychology* 114, no. 2 (2017):
258–69, doi:10.1037/pspi0000109.

42   "Be silent in your mind": Quoted in Robert Sardello, *Silence:
The Mystery of Wholeness* (Berkeley, Calif.: North Atlantic Books,
2008).

45   Silence was her companion: For more information on perinatal mood
and anxiety disorders, visit "Postpartum Support International—PSI,"
Postpartum Support International (PSI), accessed Sept. 5, 2021, www
.postpartum.net.

Chapter 4: The Moral Dimensions of Silence

52   "The only responsible choice": Carl McColman, "Barbara A. Holmes: Silence as Unspeakable Joy (Episode 26)," *Encountering Silence*, May 24, 2018, encounteringsilence.com/barbara-a-holmes-silence-as-unspeakable-joy-episode-26.

54   "One cannot help feeling": M. K. Gandhi, *Pathway to God* (New Delhi: Prabhat Prakashan, 1971).

56   edited an anthology: Sheena Malhotra and Aimee Carrillo Rowe, eds., *Silence, Feminism, Power: Reflections at the Edges of Sound* (New York: Palgrave Macmillan, 2013).

62   In her breakthrough book: Jenny Odell, *How to Do Nothing: Resisting the Attention Economy* (New York: Melville House, 2020).

63   "Silence is the work of justice": George Prochnik, "Listening for the Unknown," in *In Pursuit of Silence: Listening for Meaning in a World of Noise* (New York: Anchor Books, 2011), 43.

64   In 2021, they announced: Rachel L. Swarns, "Catholic Order Pledges $100 Million to Atone for Slave Labor and Sales," *New York Times*, March 15, 2021, www.nytimes.com/2021/03/15/us/jesuits-georgetown-reparations-slavery.html.

65   "In silence, essence speaks to us": David Whyte, *Consolations: The Solace, Nourishment, and Underlying Meaning of Everyday Words* (Langley, Wash.: Many Rivers Press, 2014).

Chapter 5: Florence Nightingale Would Be Pissed

74   silence was a more potent contributor: L. Bernardi, C. Porta, and P. Sleight, "Cardiovascular, Cerebrovascular, and Respiratory Changes Induced by Different Types of Music in Musicians and Non-musicians: The Importance of Silence," *Heart* 92, no. 4 (April 2006): 445–52, doi:10.1136/hrt.2005.064600.

75   Florence Nightingale, the gifted daughter: For a detailed account of Florence Nightingale's views on the importance of silence for human health, see Hillel Schwartz, *Making Noise: From Babel to the Big Bang & Beyond* (New York: Zone Books, 2011).

75 Ten times more soldiers died of diseases: Elizabeth Fee and Mary E. Garofalo, "Florence Nightingale and the Crimean War," *American Journal of Public Health* 100, no. 9 (Sept. 2010): 1591, doi:10.2105/AJPH.2009.188607.

76 reflecting on her experience: Florence Nightingale, "Notes on Nursing," A Celebration of Women Writers, accessed Sept. 6, 2021, digital.library.upenn.edu/women/nightingale/nursing/nursing.html.

77 samples of whale poop: Rosalind M. Rolland et al., "Evidence That Ship Noise Increases Stress in Right Whales," *Proceedings of the Royal Society B: Biological Sciences* 279, no. 1737 (2012): 2363–68, doi:10.1098/rspb.2011.2429.

77 When sound waves hit our eardrums: "How the Ear Works," Johns Hopkins Medicine, accessed Sept. 6, 2021, www.hopkinsmedicine.org/health/conditions-and-diseases/how-the-ear-works.

78 "safe and social conditions": Stephen W. Porges and Gregory F. Lewis, "The Polyvagal Hypothesis: Common Mechanisms Mediating Autonomic Regulation, Vocalizations, and Listening," *Handbook of Behavioral Neuroscience* 19 (2010): 255–64, doi:10.1016/B978–0–12–374593–4.00025–5.

78 But a broad set of peer-reviewed papers: Thomas Münzel et al., "Environmental Noise and the Cardiovascular System," *Journal of the American College of Cardiology* 71, no. 6 (Feb. 2018): 688–97, doi:10.1016/j.jacc.2017.12.015; Maria Klatte, Kirstin Bergström, and Thomas Lachmann, "Does Noise Affect Learning? A Short Review on Noise Effects on Cognitive Performance in Children," *Frontiers in Psychology* 4 (2013): 578, doi:10.3389/fpsyg.2013.00578; Ester Orban et al., "Residential Road Traffic Noise and High Depressive Symptoms After Five Years of Follow-Up: Results from the Heinz Nixdorf Recall Study," *Environmental Health Perspectives* 124, no. 5 (2016): 578–85, doi:10.1289/ehp.1409400; Soo Jeong Kim et al., "Exposure-Response Relationship Between Aircraft Noise and Sleep Quality: A Community-Based Cross-Sectional Study," *Osong Public Health and Research Perspectives* 5, no. 2 (April 2014): 108–14, doi:10.1016/j.phrp.2014.03.004.

79 WHO calculates a loss: "New Evidence from WHO on Health Effects of Traffic-Related Noise in Europe," World Health Organization, March 30, 2011, www.euro.who.int/en/media-centre/sections

/press-releases/2011/03/new-evidence-from-who-on-health
-effects-of-traffic-related-noise-in-europe. See also World Health
Organization Regional Office for Europe, "Burden of Disease from
Environmental Noise," ed. Frank Theakston, Joint Research Cen-
tre (2011), 1–126, www.euro.who.int/__data/assets/pdf_file/0008
/136466/e94888.pdf.

79   Paris ranks ninth in a recent index: Alex Gray, "These Are the Cities
with the Worst Noise Pollution," World Economic Forum, March 27,
2017, www.weforum.org/agenda/2017/03/these-are-the-cities-with
-the-worst-noise-pollution.

79   "Noise is never just about sound": Bianca Bosker, "Why Everything
Is Getting Louder," *The Atlantic*, Nov. 2019, www.theatlantic.com
/magazine/archive/2019/11/the-end-of-silence/598366.

80   "The best bridge between despair and hope": Matthew Walker, *Why
We Sleep: Unlocking the Power of Sleep and Dreams* (New York: Scribner,
2018).

80   peaks above 85 dBA": Julie L. Darbyshire and J. Duncan Young, "An
Investigation of Sound Levels on Intensive Care Units with Reference to the WHO Guidelines," *Critical Care* 17, no. 5 (2013): 187,
doi:10.1186/cc12870.

80   decibel levels of its hospitals: Ilene J. Busch-Vishniac et al., "Noise
Levels in Johns Hopkins Hospital," *Journal of the Acoustical Society of
America* 118, no. 6 (2005): 3629–45, doi:10.1121/1.2118327.

80   72 to 99 percent of clinical alarms: Sue Sendelbach and Marjo-
rie Funk, "Alarm Fatigue: A Patient Safety Concern," *AACN Advanced Critical Care* 24, no. 4 (Oct. 2013): 378–86, doi:10.1097/
NCI.0b013e3182a903f9.

80   a condition of alarm fatigue: Patricia Robin McCartney, "Clinical Alarm Management," *MCN: The American Journal of Ma-
ternal/Child Nursing* 37, no. 3 (May 2012): 202, doi:10.1097/
nmc.0b013e31824c5b4a.

81   the neuroscientist-psychologist duo: Adam Gazzaley and Larry D.
Rosen, *The Distracted Mind: Ancient Brains in a High-Tech World* (Cambridge, Mass.: MIT Press, 2017).

83 the reading test scores: Ari Goldman, "Student Scores Rise After Nearby Subway Is Quieted," *New York Times*, April 26, 1982.

84 A recent study of several hundred teenagers: Maartje Boer et al., "Attention Deficit Hyperactivity Disorder–Symptoms, Social Media Use Intensity, and Social Media Use Problems in Adolescents: Investigating Directionality," *Child Development* 91, no. 4 (July 2020): 853–65, doi:10.1111/cdev.13334.

84 a one-month break from Facebook: Hunt Allcott et al., "The Welfare Effects of Social Media," *American Economic Review* 110, no. 3 (March 2020): 629–76, doi:10.1257/aer.20190658.

85 "Verbal rumination concentrates our attention": Ethan Kross, *Chatter: The Voice in Our Head, Why It Matters, and How to Harness It* (New York: Crown, 2021).

87 *Listening to silence* demonstrably accelerated: Imke Kirste et al., "Is Silence Golden? Effects of Auditory Stimuli and Their Absence on Adult Hippocampal Neurogenesis," *Brain Structure and Function* 220, no. 2 (2013): 1221–28, doi:10.1007/s00429–013–0679–3.

Chapter 6: A Mute Button for the Mind

91 a large-scale study of perceptions of flow: Mihaly Csikszentmihalyi, *Flow: The Psychology of Optimal Experience* (New York: HarperCollins, 2008).

92 the "sweet spot" between distress and boredom: Shane J. Lopez and C. R. Snyder, eds., *Handbook of Positive Psychology* (Oxford: Oxford University Press, 2011).

93 99.999 percent of gathered bits of information: *Encyclopaedia Britannica*, s.v. "Physiology," accessed Sept. 6, 2021, www.britannica.com /science/information-theory/Physiology.

93 to screen the roughly 0.001 percent of relevant stimuli: Csikszentmihalyi, *Flow*, 28–29.

95 "Had the human self been installed": Mark R. Leary, *The Curse of the Self: Self-Awareness, Egotism, and the Quality of Human Life* (Oxford: Oxford University Press, 2007).

95 He coined the term "transient hypofrontality": Arne Dietrich, "Functional Neuroanatomy of Altered States of Consciousness: The Transient Hypofrontality Hypothesis," *Consciousness and Cognition* 12, no. 2 (June 2003): 231–56, doi:10.1016/s1053-8100(02)00046-6.

96 "synchronization" theory: René Weber et al., "Theorizing Flow and Media Enjoyment as Cognitive Synchronization of Attentional and Reward Networks," *Communication Theory* 19, no. 4 (Oct. 2009): 397–422, doi:10.1111/j.1468-2885.2009.01352.x.

97 "The default mode network appears": Michael Pollan, "The Neuroscience: Your Brain on Psychedelics," in *How to Change Your Mind: What the New Science of Psychedelics Teaches Us About Consciousness, Dying, Addiction, Depression, and Transcendence* (New York: Penguin Press, 2018), 303–4.

98 several of the novice meditators: Michael W. Taft, "Effortlessness in Meditation, with Jud Brewer," *Deconstructing Yourself*, June 7, 2020, deconstructingyourself.com/effortlessness-in-meditation-with-jud-brewer.html.

99 meditators showed less DMN activity: Kathryn J. Devaney et al., "Attention and Default Mode Network Assessments of Meditation Experience During Active Cognition and Rest," *Brain Sciences* 11, no. 5 (2021): 566, doi:10.3390/brainsci11050566.

99 practitioners are able to rewire their brains: Judson A. Brewer et al., "Meditation Experience Is Associated with Differences in Default Mode Network Activity and Connectivity," *Proceedings of the National Academy of Sciences of the United States of America* 108, no. 50 (2011): 20254–59, doi:10.1073/pnas.1112029108.

101 self-transcendent experiences: Piers Worth and Matthew D. Smith, "Clearing the Pathways to Self-Transcendence," *Frontiers in Psychology*, April 30, 2021, doi:10.3389/fpsyg.2021.648381.

101 "transient mental states": David Bryce Yaden et al., "The Varieties of Self-Transcendent Experience," *Review of General Psychology* 21, no. 2 (2017): 143–60, doi:10.1037/gpr0000102.

102 define awe as a combination of two factors: Dacher Keltner and Jonathan Haidt: "Approaching Awe, a Moral, Spiritual, and Aesthetic

Emotion," *Cognition and Emotion* 17, no. 2 (March 2003): 297–314, doi:10.1080/02699930302297.

102 "Whereof one cannot speak": Anat Biletzki and Anat Matar, "Ludwig Wittgenstein," in *Stanford Encyclopedia of Philosophy*, Nov. 8, 2002, plato.stanford.edu/entries/wittgenstein.

102 development in children occurs: Fatima Malik and Raman Marwaha, "CognitiveDevelopment,"StatPearls,July31,2021,www.ncbi.nlm.nih .gov/books/NBK537095.

103 a new wave of theorists and psychologists: "Rethinking Adult Development," American Psychological Association, June 9, 2020, www.apa.org /pubs/highlights/spotlight/issue-186.

103 benefits of self-transcendence: Summer Allen, "The Science of Awe," Greater Good Science Center, Sept. 2018, ggsc.berkeley.edu/images /uploads/GGSC-JTF_White_Paper-Awe_FINAL.pdf.

104 the unifying characteristics of the mystical experience: William James, "Lectures XVI and XVII: Mysticism," in *The Varieties of Religious Experience: A Study in Human Nature*, ed. Martin E. Marty (New York: Penguin Classics, 1982), 287.

107 "like the dreaming brain": Pollan, "Neuroscience," 301.

107 a relative deactivation of "the me network": Robin L. Carhart-Harris et al., "Neural Correlates of the Psychedelic State as Determined by fMRI Studies with Psilocybin," *Proceedings of the National Academy of Sciences of the United States of America* 109, no. 6 (2012): 2138–43, doi:10.1073/pnas.1119598109.

107 diminishment of the sense of a separate self: "How LSD Can Make Us Lose Our Sense of Self," ScienceDaily, April 13, 2016, www.sciencedaily .com/releases/2016/04/160413135656.htm.

Chapter 7: Why Silence Is Scary

115 "understanding of the source": Manly P. Hall, "The Life and Philosophy of Pythagoras," in *The Secret Teachings of All Ages* (New York: Jeremy P. Tarcher/Penguin, 2003).

117   In a 2014 study: Timothy D. Wilson et al., "Just Think: The Challenges of the Disengaged Mind," *Science* 345, no. 6192 (2014): 75–77, doi:10.1126/science.1250830.

117   "primary, objective reality": Max Picard, *The World of Silence* (Wichita, Kans.: Eighth Day Press, 2002).

120   "encounter anxiety, fear, fantasy": Robert Sardello, *Silence: The Mystery of Wholeness* (Berkeley, Calif.: North Atlantic Books, 2008).

120   "When we stop our habitual": Joan Halifax, *Being with Dying* (Boulder, Colo.: Shambhala, 2009).

120   "If we have courage": Joan Halifax, *The Fruitful Darkness: A Journey Through Buddhist Practice and Tribal Wisdom* (New York: Grove Press, 2004).

122   "In Jewish law, one who visits": Estelle Frankel, *The Wisdom of Not Knowing: Discovering a Life of Wonder by Embracing Uncertainty* (Boulder, Colo.: Shambhala, 2017).

124   "If we were not so single-minded": Pablo Neruda, *Extravagaria*, trans. Alastair Reid (New York: Farrar, Straus and Giroux, 2001).

126   "decreased self-salience": David Bryce Yaden et al., "The Varieties of Self-Transcendent Experience," *Review of General Psychology* 21, no. 2 (2017): 143–60, doi:10.1037/gpr0000102.

127   the lesser-recognized aspects of awe: Wisdom 2.0, March 23, 2019, www.youtube.com/watch?v=l8NaWq-xSbM&t=1243s.

Chapter 8: Lotuses and Lilies

131   "not to get attached to words": Red Pine, trans., *The Lankavatara Sutra: A Zen Text* (Berkeley, Calif.: Counterpoint, 2013).

132   "A finger pointing at the moon": Thích Nhất Hạnh, *Old Path White Clouds: The Life Story of the Buddha* (London: Rider, 1992).

135   he sought to identify the mystical core: Aldous Huxley, *The Perennial Philosophy: An Interpretation of the Great Mystics, East and West* (New York: Franklin Classics, 2009).

135 "The first time you practice": Unknown Monk, *The Cloud of Unknowing*, ed. Dragan Nikolic and Jelena Milić (Scotts Valley, Calif.: Create Space, 2015).

137 both the *kataphatic* and the *apophatic* ways: Harvey D. Egan, "Christian Apophatic and Kataphatic Mysticisms," *Theological Studies* 39, no. 3 (1978): 399–426, doi:10.1177/004056397803900301.

Chapter 9: A Field Guide to Finding Silence

148 the title of his recent biography: David Sheff, *The Buddhist on Death Row: How One Man Found Light in the Darkest Place* (New York: Simon & Schuster, 2021).

149 he wrote most of his book: Jarvis Jay Masters, *Finding Freedom: How Death Row Broke and Opened My Heart* (Boulder, Colo.: Shambhala, 2020).

152 "A number of older prisoners": Timothy Williams and Rebecca Griesbach, "San Quentin Prison Was Free of the Virus. One Decision Fueled an Outbreak," *New York Times*, June 30, 2020, www.nytimes.com/2020/06/30/us/san-quentin-prison-coronavirus.html.

154 *sphere of control*: Many leadership experts, including the business guru Stephen R. Covey, use variants of the sphere of control model to train leaders to take charge where they can and let go of what they can't. Such models popularized a notion that psychologists have long taken seriously: our sense of personal power.

Chapter 10: The Healthy Successor to the Smoke Break

163 why young people choose to use cigarettes: Hannah Delaney, Andrew MacGregor, and Amanda Amos, "'Tell Them You Smoke, You'll Get More Breaks': A Qualitative Study of Occupational and Social Contexts of Young Adult Smoking in Scotland," *BMJ Open* 8, no. 12 (2018), doi:10.1136/bmjopen-2018–023951.

166 "Turn your attention": Ajahn Amaro, "The Sound of Silence," *Lion's Roar*, Nov. 9, 2012, www.lionsroar.com/the-sound-of-silence.

170 "when things fall apart": Pema Chödrön, *When Things Fall Apart: Heart Advice for Difficult Times* (Boulder, Colo.: Shambhala, 2005).

175 It's in his poetry: Aaron Maniam, "Standing Still," in *Morning at Memory's Border* (Singapore: Firstfruits, 2005).

179 In *The Shallows*: Nicholas Carr, *The Shallows: What the Internet Is Doing to Our Brains* (New York: W. W. Norton, 2010).

180 Nakamura and Csikszentmihalyi have suggested: Shane J. Lopez and C. R. Snyder, eds., *Handbook of Positive Psychology* (Oxford: Oxford University Press, 2011).

180 translated from Latin as "divine reading": M. Basil Pennington, *Lectio Divina: Renewing the Ancient Practice of Praying the Scriptures* (Chestnut Ridge, N.Y.: Crossroad, 1998).

180 "Poetry comes out of silence": Marilyn Nelson, "Communal Pondering in a Noisy World," *On Being*, Public Radio Exchange, Feb. 23, 2017.

181 "Poetry is the language": Ezra Klein, "Pulitzer Prize–Winning Poet Tracy K. Smith on the Purpose and Power of Poetry," *Vox Conversations* (audio blog), Feb. 27, 2020, www.vox.com/pod casts/2020/2/27/21154139/tracy-k-smith-poet-laureate-the-ezra -klein-show-wade-in-the-water.

181 "leaves silence in its wake": Susan Sontag, *Styles of Radical Will* (New York: Farrar, Straus and Giroux, 1969), 23.

183 spike in downloads of birding apps: Gillian Flaccus, "Bird-Watching Soars amid COVID-19 as Americans Head Outdoors," Associated Press, May 2, 2020, apnews.com/article/us-news-ap-top-news-ca-state-wire -or-state-wire-virus-outbreak-94a1ea5938943d8a70fe794e9f62 9b13.

184 Roger Ulrich's study demonstrated: Roger S. Ulrich, "View Through a Window May Influence Recovery from Surgery," *Science* 224, no. 4647 (1984): 420–21, doi:10.1126/science.6143402.

184 Studies in both the U.K. and the Netherlands: Mark S. Taylor et al., "Research Note: Urban Street Tree Density and Antidepressant Prescription Rates—a Cross-Sectional Study in London, UK," *Landscape*

and Urban Planning 136 (April 2015): 174–79, doi:10.1016/j.landurb-plan.2014.12.005; Marco Helbich et al., "More Green Space Is Related to Less Antidepressant Prescription Rates in the Netherlands: A Bayesian Geoadditive Quantile Regression Approach," *Environmental Research* 166 (2018): 290–97, doi:10.1016/j.envres.2018.06.010.

184 Scotland became one of the first governments: Evan Fleischer, "Doctors in Scotland Can Now Prescribe Nature," World Economic Forum, Oct. 15, 2018, www.weforum.org/agenda/2018/10/doctors-in -scotland-can-now-prescribe-nature.

185 "Just playing with soil for five minutes": Jeanette Marantos, "Why Plant Sales Are Soaring, Even at Nurseries Closed due to Coronavirus," *Los Angeles Times*, May 30, 2020, www.latimes.com/lifestyle/story /2020–05–30/why-plant-sales-are-soaring-even-at-nurseries-closed -due-to-coronavirus.

185 "body contact with the ground": James Oschman, Gaetan Chevalier, and Richard Brown, "The Effects of Grounding (Earthing) on Inflammation, the Immune Response, Wound Healing, and Prevention and Treatment of Chronic Inflammatory and Autoimmune Diseases," *Journal of Inflammation Research*, March 24, 2015, 83–96, doi:10.2147/jir. s69656.

189 "So, say hello to old wounds": Pádraig Ó Tuama, *In the Shelter: Finding a Home in the World* (London: Hodder & Stoughton, 2015).

Chapter 11: Rapturous Silence

195 "not altered states but altered traits": Huston Smith, "Encountering God," in *The Way Things Are: Conversations with Huston Smith on the Spiritual Life*, ed. Phil Cousineau (Berkeley, Calif.: University of California Press, 2003), 95–102.

197 "the quietest place in the United States": "What Is One Square Inch?," One Square Inch: A Sanctuary for Silence at Olympic National Park, accessed Sept. 6, 2021, onesquareinch.org/about.

200 the largest block of protected park land: "Tatshenshini-Alsek Provincial Park," BC Parks, accessed Sept. 6, 2021, bcparks.ca/explore /parkpgs/tatshens.

203 "When an observer doesn't immediately turn": Barry Lopez, "The Invitation," *Granta*, Nov. 18, 2015, granta.com/invitation.

203 the more than five-hundred-year-old spiritual book: Unknown Monk, *The Cloud of Unknowing*, ed. Dragan Nikolic and Jelena Milić (Scotts Valley, Calif.: CreateSpace, 2015).

209 In her book *Wintering*: Katherine May, *Wintering: The Power of Rest and Retreat in Difficult Times* (New York: Riverhead Books, 2020).

212 a legally authorized study of MDMA-assisted psychotherapy: "MDMA-Assisted Therapy Study Protocols," MAPS: Multidisciplinary Association for Psychedelic Studies, accessed Sept. 6, 2021, maps.org/research /mdma.

213 "There is a way of beholding": Diane Ackerman, *Deep Play* (New York: Vintage Books, 2000).

214 Peachoid, the giant peach water tower: "The Peachoid," Discover: South Carolina, accessed Sept. 6, 2021, discoversouthcarolina.com /products/340.

Chapter 12: Working Quiet

223 a gigantic mound of dirt: George Prochnik, *In Pursuit of Silence: Listening for Meaning in a World of Noise* (New York: Anchor Books, 2011).

237 She recently teamed up: Rupa Marya and Raj Patel, *Inflamed: Deep Medicine and the Anatomy of Injustice* (New York: Farrar, Straus and Giroux, 2021).

239 "She had a passionate love": Eve Curie, *Madame Curie: A Biography* (Boston: Da Capo Press, 2001).

241 In his 2016 book: Cal Newport, *Deep Work: Rules for Focused Success in a Distracted World* (New York: Grand Central Publishing, 2016).

243 "as a way of indicating": Pádraig Ó Tuama, *Sorry for Your Troubles* (Norwich, Eng.: Canterbury Press, 2013).

247 now known as "the Six Classes": "The Six Classes Approach to Reducing Chemical Harm," SixClasses, June 18, 2019, www.sixclasses.org.

Chapter 13: Living Quiet

257 she wrote a second book: Marilyn Paul, *An Oasis in Time: How a Day of Rest Can Save Your Life* (Emmaus, Pa.: Rodale, 2017).

267 In the film *Entheogen*: *Entheogen: Awakening the Divine Within*, directed by Rod Mann, Nikos Katsaounis, and Kevin Kohley (Critical Mass Productions, 2007).

269 The relationship gurus Drs. John and Julie Gottman: "Find the Passion Again: All About Love Bundle," A Research-Based Approach to Relationships, accessed Sept. 6, 2021, www.gottman.com.

Chapter 14: Ma Goes to Washington

276 Noise Control Act of 1972: Environmental Protection Agency, *Summary of the Noise Control Act*, July 31, 2020, www.epa.gov/laws-regulations/summary-noise-control-act.

276 Office of Noise Abatement and Control: Administrative Conference of the United States, *Implementation of the Noise Control Act*, June 19, 1992, www.acus.gov/recommendation/implementation-noise-control-act.

276 Reagan's administration defunded and dismantled: "A Voice to End the Government's Silence on Noise," International Noise Awareness Day, accessed Sept. 6, 2021, noiseawareness.org/info-center/government-noise-bronzaft.

278 In his 2010 book: George Prochnik, *In Pursuit of Silence: Listening for Meaning in a World of Noise* (New York: Doubleday, 2010).

279 ensuring that 80 percent of households: Singapore, Ministry of Foreign Affairs, *Sustainable Development Goals: Towards a Sustainable and Resilient Singapore* (2018), sustainabledevelopment.un.org/content/documents/19439Singapores_Voluntary_National_Review_Report_v2.pdf.

279 its "garden city" vision: Singapore, Ministry of Communications and Information, HistorySG, *"Garden City" Vision Is Introduced*, accessed Sept. 6, 2021, eresources.nlb.gov.sg/history/events/a7fac49f-9c96-4030-8709-ce160c58d15c.

279 For comparison, green cover: Vicky Gan, "The Link Between Green Space and Well-Being Isn't as Simple as We Thought," *Bloomberg City Lab*, Aug. 14, 2015, www.bloomberg.com/news/articles/2015–08–14 /singapore-study-finds-no-significant-relationship-between-access -to-green-space-and-well-being.

279 During a trip to Singapore: Florence Williams, *The Nature Fix: Why Nature Makes Us Happier, Healthier, and More Creative* (New York: W. W. Norton, 2018).

281 In his 2010 book: Kevin Kelly, *What Technology Wants* (London: Penguin Books, 2010).

282 philosophy of "digital minimalism": Cal Newport, *Digital Minimalism: On Living Better with Less Technology* (New York: Portfolio, 2019).

283 Office of Technology Assessment: U.S. Congress, CRS Report, *The Office of Technology Assessment: History, Authorities, Issues, and Options*, April 14, 2020, www.everycrsreport.com/reports/R46327.html.

283 As Justin and his colleague Sridhar Kota: Justin Talbot Zorn and Sridhar Kota, "Universities Must Help Educate Woefully Uninformed Lawmakers," *Wired*, Jan. 11, 2017, www.wired.com/2017/01/universities-must-help-edu cate-woefully-uninformed-lawmakers/?utm_source=WIR_REG_GATE.

284 In 1930, the legendary economist: John Maynard Keynes, *Economic Possibilities for Our Grandchildren* (Seattle, Wash.: Entropy Conservationists, 1987).

286 Justin and Ben published a piece: Justin Talbot Zorn and Ben Beachy, "A Better Way to Measure GDP," *Harvard Business Review*, Feb. 3, 2021, hbr.org/2021/02/a-better-way-to-measure-gdp.

296 In his 1983 book: Michael J. Sheeran, *Beyond Majority Rule: Voteless Decisions in the Religious Society of Friends* (Philadelphia: Philadelphia Yearly Meeting of the Religious Society of Friends, 1983).

296 In the 1951 book: Stuart Chase and Marian Tyler Chase, *Roads to Agreement: Successful Methods in the Science of Human Relations* (London: Phoenix House, 1952).

297 the oldest participatory democracy on Earth: Editors of Encyclopaedia Britannica, "Iroquois Confederacy: American Indian Confederation," *Encyclopaedia Britannica* (Chicago: Encyclopaedia Britannica, 2020).

302   *In War and Peace*: Francisco Salazar, "Teatro Digital to Stream Joyce Di-
Donato's 'In War and Peace,'" *OperaWire*, Nov. 6, 2019, operawire.com
/teatro-digital-to-stream-joyce-didonatos-in-war-and-peace.

305   Ngrupuk Parade: NOW Bali Editorial Team, "The Ogoh-Ogoh Monsters of Bali's Ngrupuk Parade," *NOW! Bali*, March 10, 2021, www
.nowbali.co.id/ngrupuk-monster-parade.

306   Nyepi—the Day of Silence: "Balinese New Year - NYEPI - Bali
.com: A Day for Self-Reflection," The Celebration for a New Beginning: The Biggest Annual Event on the Island, accessed Sept. 6, 2021,
bali.com/bali-travel-guide/culture-religion-traditions/nyepi-balinese
-new-year.

307   the book *Sand Talk*: Tyson Yunkaporta, *Sand Talk: How Indigenous
Thinking Can Save the World* (New York: HarperOne, 2021).

312   *eudaimonia*: "Virtue Ethics," *Stanford Encyclopedia of Philosophy*, July 18,
2003, plato.stanford.edu/entries/ethics-virtue.

INDEX

ABOUT THE AUTHORS

JUSTIN TALBOT ZORN has served as both a policymaker and a meditation teacher in the U.S. Congress. A Harvard-and-Oxford-trained specialist in the economics and psychology of well-being, Justin has written for the *Washington Post*, *The Atlantic*, *Harvard Business Review*, *Foreign Policy*, and other publications. He is co-founder of Astrea Strategies, a consultancy that bridges deep visioning with impactful communications and action. He lives in Santa Fe, New Mexico, with his wife and three children.

You can learn more about Justin's work at www.justinzorn .com and www.astreastrategies.com.

LEIGH MARZ is a leadership coach and collaboration consultant who has led diverse initiatives, including a training program to promote an experimental mindset among multi-generational teams at the NASA Goddard Space Flight Center and a decade-long cross-sector collaboration to reduce toxic chemicals, in partnership with the Green Science Policy Institute, Harvard University, IKEA, Google Green Team, and Kaiser Permanente. She is the co-founder of Astrea Strategies. Leigh lives in Berkeley, California, with her husband and daughter.

You can learn more about Leigh's work at leighmarz.com and www.astreastrategies.com.